S0-BXR-055

PART ONE

FAIRCHILD'S DESIGNER'S/STYLIST'S HANDBOOK

Debbie Ann Gioello

Adjunct Associate Professor: Fashion Design Department

Fashion Institute of Technology

Fairchild Publications • New York

Copyright © 1980 by Fairchild Publications

Division of Capital Cities Media, Inc.

All rights reserved. No part of this book may be reproduced in any form
without permission in writing from the publisher, except by a reviewer
who wishes to quote passages in connection with a review written for
inclusion in a magazine or newspaper.

Standard Book Number: 87005-332-9

Library of Congress Catalog Card Number: 79-55383

Printed in the United States of America

A ballet, classical, jazz or tap dancer learns the basic steps, the terminology and manner of action or movements. The same steps may then be presented alone or in a variety of combinations, in different arrangements, fast or slow movements, against different backgrounds. Similarly, so it is with music. The notes are known or learned, the notes are combined, the combinations played on selected instruments or groups of instruments, the arrangement includes forward and/or backward tempos.

As it is with dance or music designing a garment utilizes the limitless combinations and arrangements of what is known. Designing utilizes basic components and interprets them in harmony, balance and proper proportion for a particular presentation. The presentation of the design may be further dramatized, toned down, made pleasing or more appealing by the selected use of fabric, color, texture and patterns, alone or in any combination.
- What is it that proclaims each presentation lovely, pleasant, exciting or dramatic?
- Why is the presentation considered new, before its time, not acceptable when presented or exciting when rediscovered?

The manner of the arrangement and rearrangement is what will render the design new, acceptable, current and desirable. It is the individual interpretation of harmony, balance and proportion of all the integral parts working as a whole that makes the design acceptable for the time, place, type and end use of the garment. All the parts, each segment or component, complementing or playing upon or against each other completes the whole.

The unity of all the parts as selected by the arranger, the organizer, the coordinator, the stylist, or the designer produces a new design.

Fairchild's Designer's/Stylist's Handbook is presented as a reference portfolio and source of visual ideas. The vast selection of material of individual items, ideas and designs are presented for anyone. The individual may use these ideas in any form to pull together their own unique, individualized, creative design.

The aim of this handbook is to make available to the designer, stylist, coordinator, educator and student many examples of various styles and types of garment silhouettes, parts, sections and components of garments and design details. The sketches are offered as a guide for inspiration and development of original and unusual designs. All the designs are ready for use. The individual design elements may be used individually or in any combination.

I have used the concept of combining and varying all known aspects of designs and different garment components during my career as a designer, stylist and manufacturer and as an educator in the field of apparel design. The designs and various garment components in this handbook have been compiled from my collection of designs and references gathered and used over a period of years.

The examples and ideas in *Fairchild's Designer's/Stylist's Handbook* are arranged and classified with regard to:
- The upper torso and all related garment components and design details

PREFACE

- Design features, details and components of the middle section which may relate or be utilized for both upper and lower torso garments
- The lower torso and all related garment components and design details
- Silhouettes of vests, jackets, garments, coats and capes
- Other design features, details or theories which may be utilized for any silhouette, upper or lower garment section

The sketches have been executed with the assistance of David Davis, a student of design and illustration. I wish to also thank Barbara Scholey, book designer, and Olga Kontzias, editor.

1980

Debbie Ann Gioello
New York

CONTENTS

Figures 541, 154, 372

HOW TO USE THIS HANDBOOK & TRACING PAD

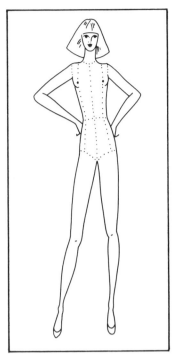

1. Remove a sheet of tracing paper with fashion figure from pad.

2. Select garment component or silhouette from Handbook.

3. Place fashion figure over sketch. Line up head and shoulders or waist area.

4. Trace all or part of garment as desired.

5. Continue procedure until desired design is complete.

6. Finished design.

ONE·BODICES

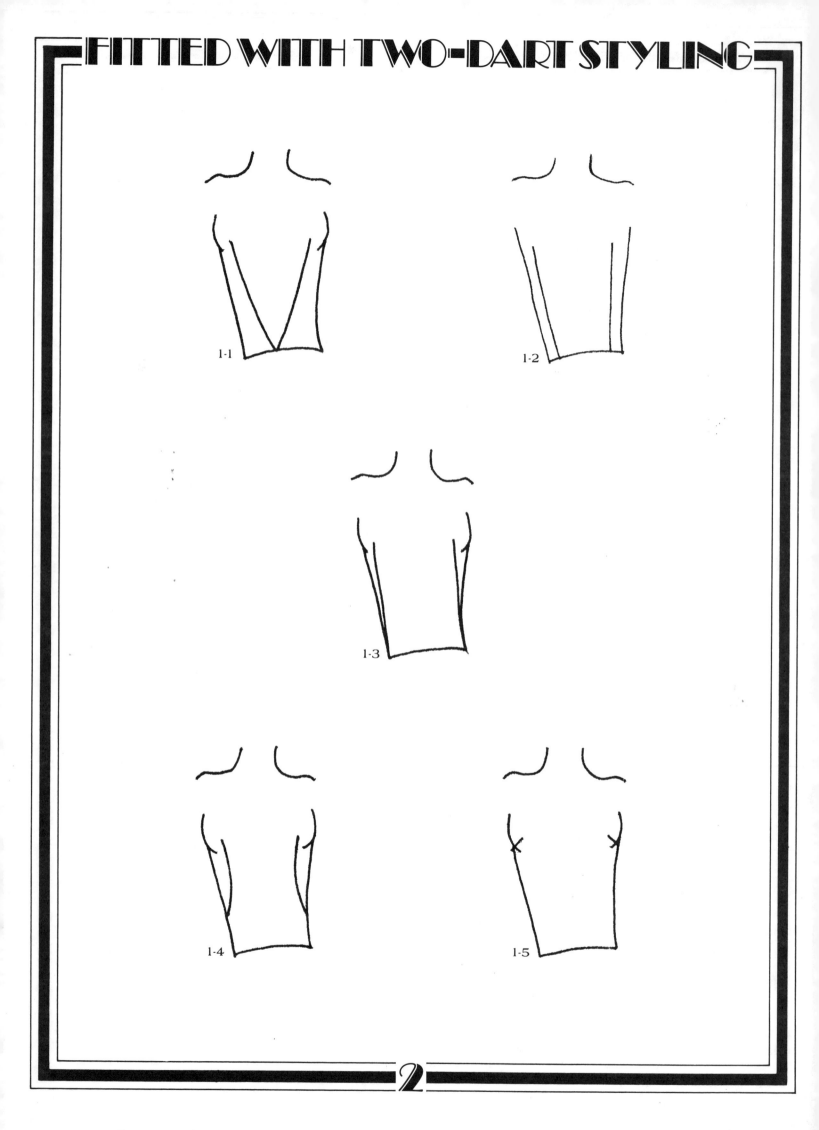

1-1

1-2

1-3

1-4

1-5

1-6

1-7

1-8

1-9

1-10

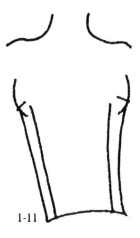

1-11

1-12

1-13

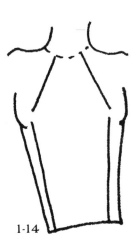

1-14

1-15

1-16

1-17

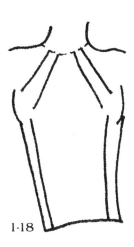

1-18

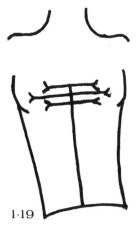

1-19

1-20

1-21

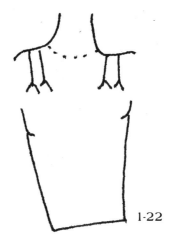

1-22

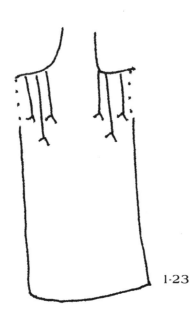

1-23

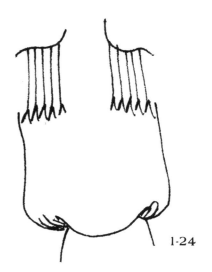

1-24

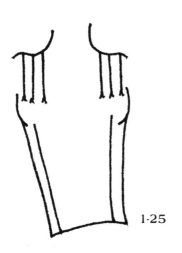

1-25

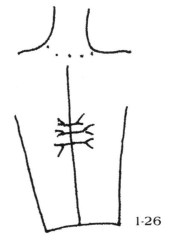

1-26

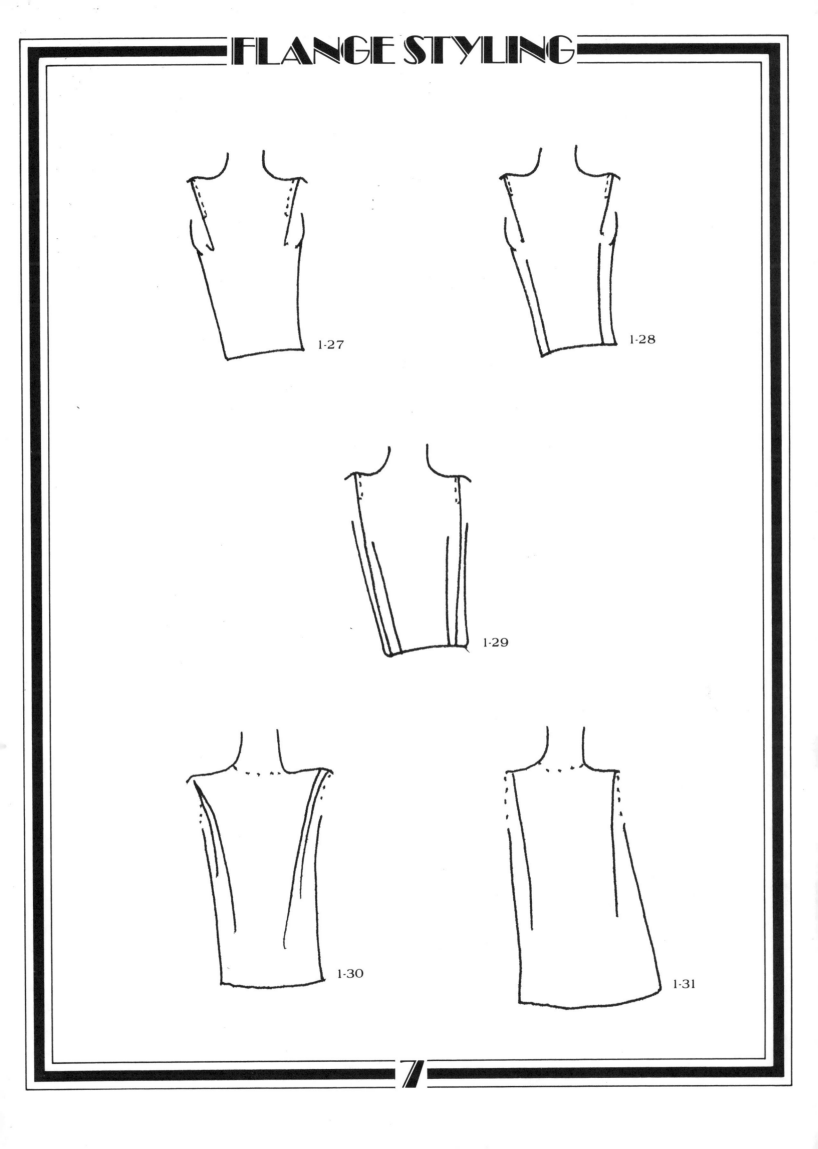

1·27

1·28

1·29

1·30

1·31

1-32

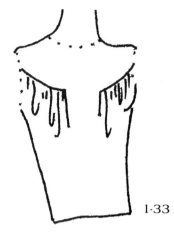

1-33

1-34

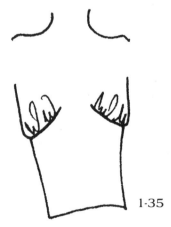

1-35

1-36

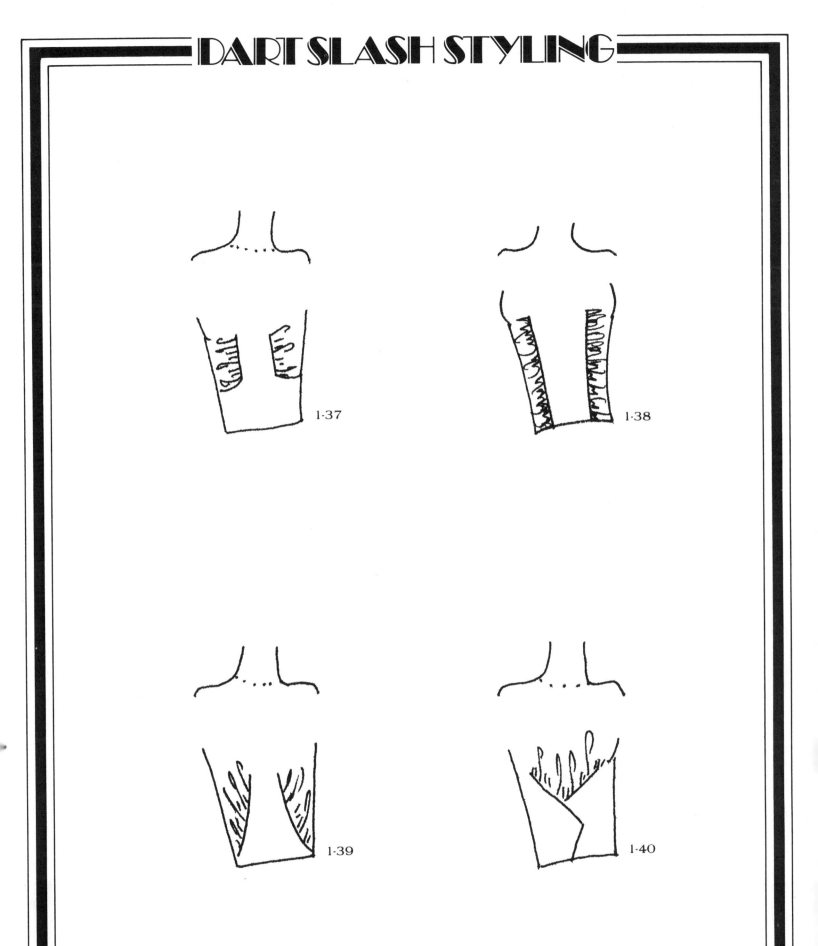

1-37

1-38

1-39

1-40

1-41

1-42

1-43

1-44

1-45

1-46

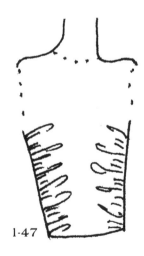

1-47

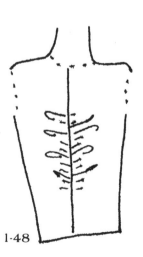

1-48

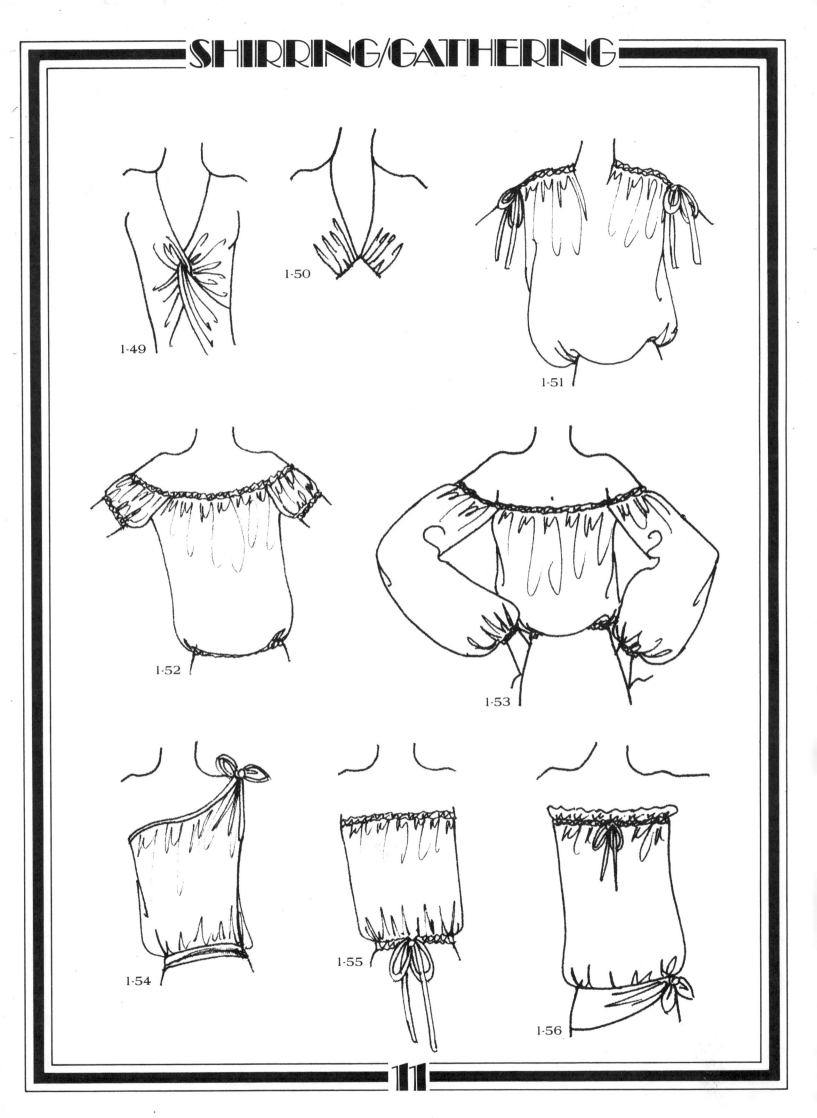

1-49

1-50

1-51

1-52

1-53

1-54

1-55

1-56

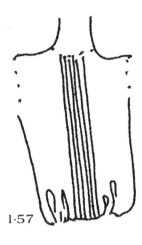

1-57

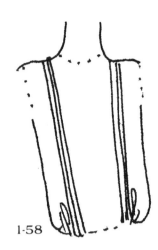

1-58

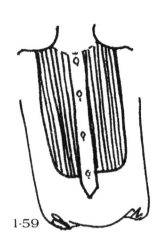

1-59

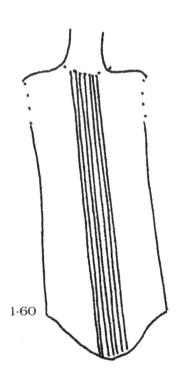

1-60

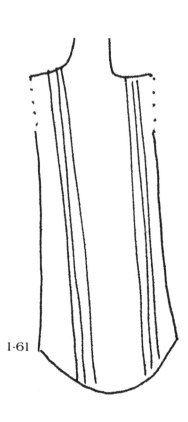

1-61

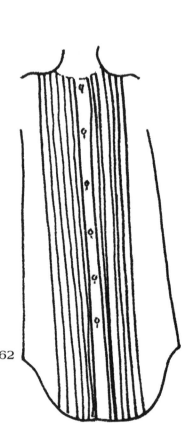

1-62

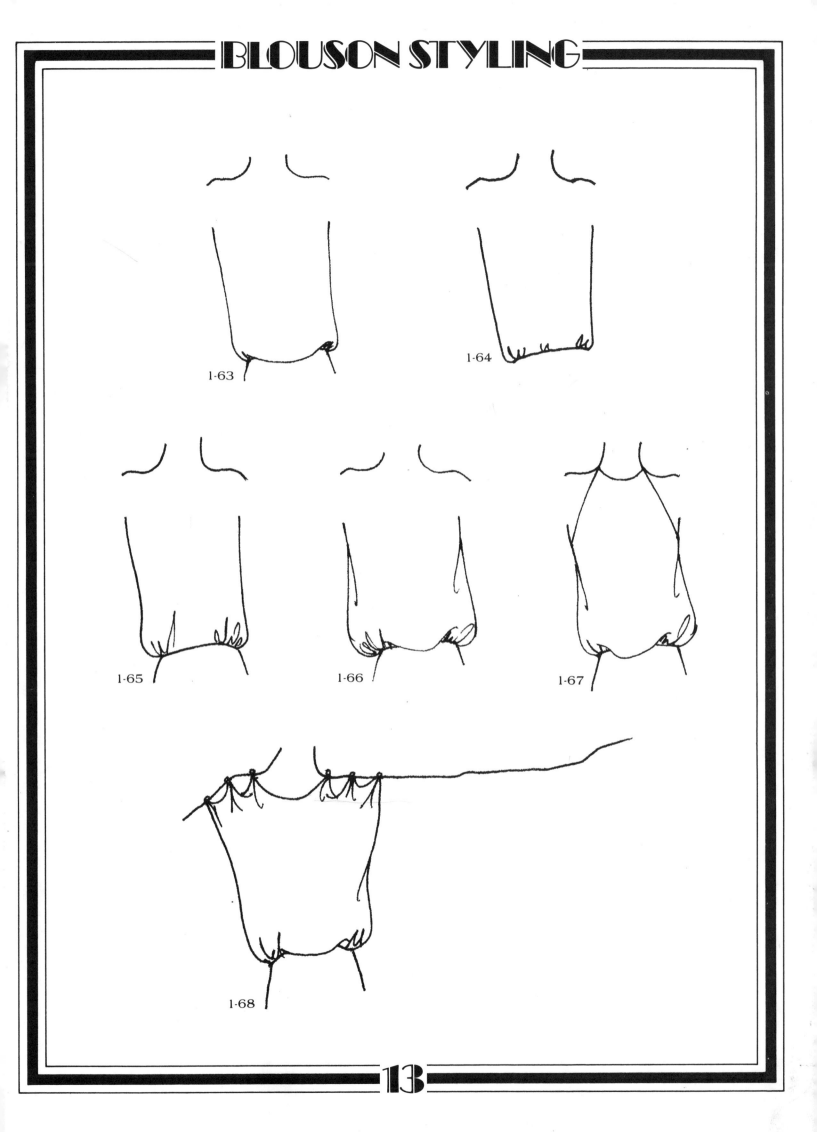

1-63

1-64

1-65

1-66

1-67

1-68

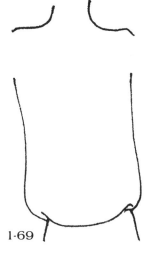

1-69

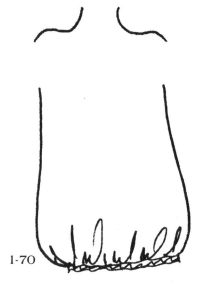

1-70

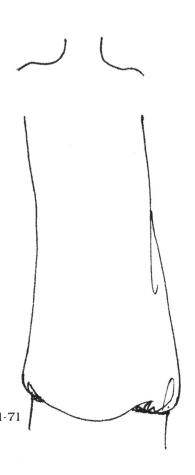

1-71

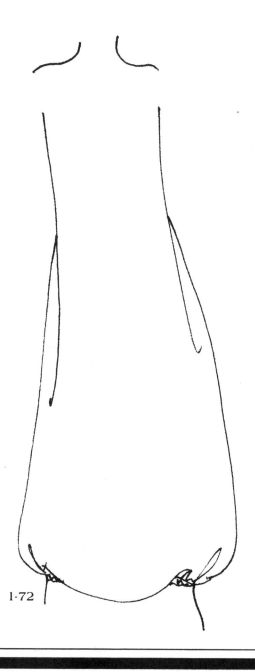

1-72

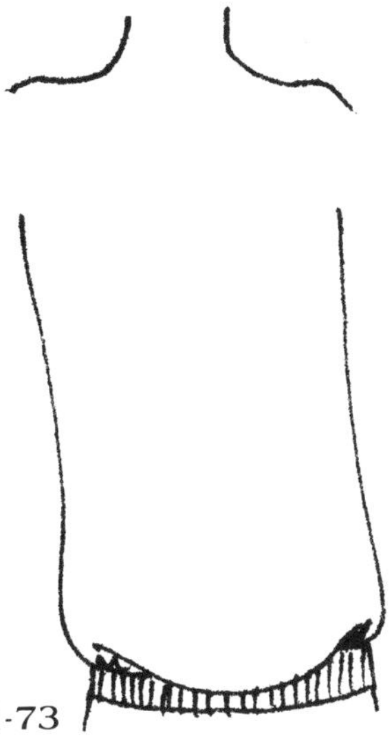

1-73

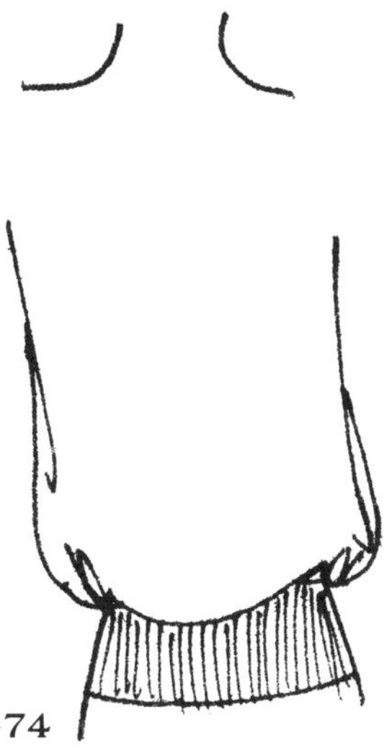

1-74

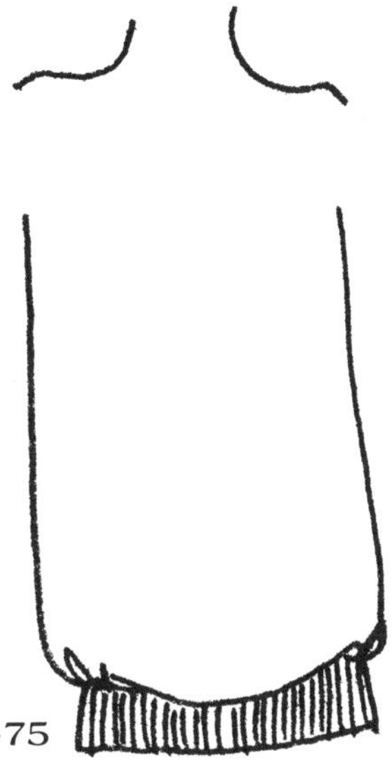

1-75

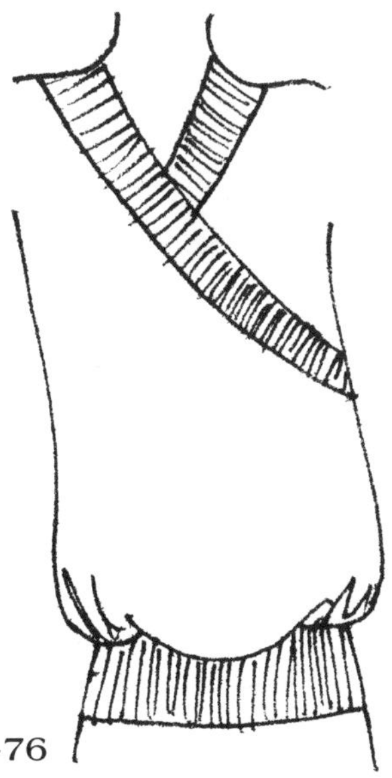

1-76

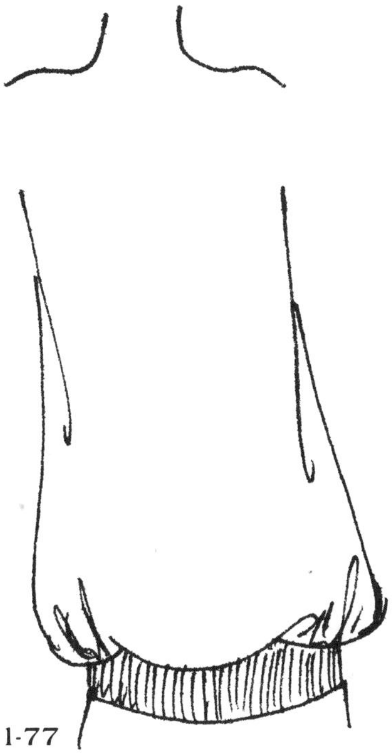

1-77

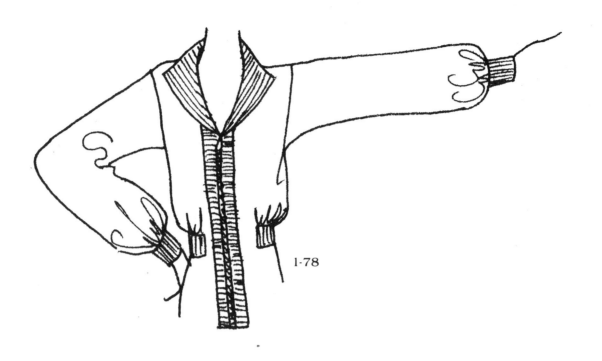

1-78

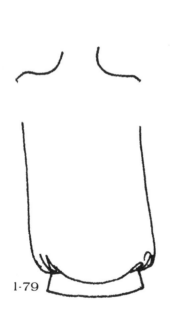

1-79

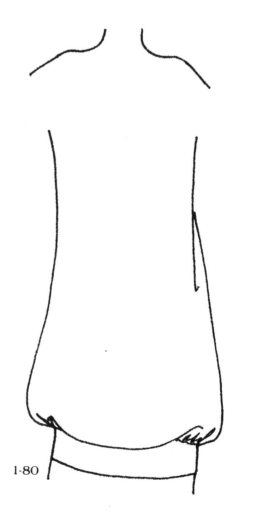

1-80

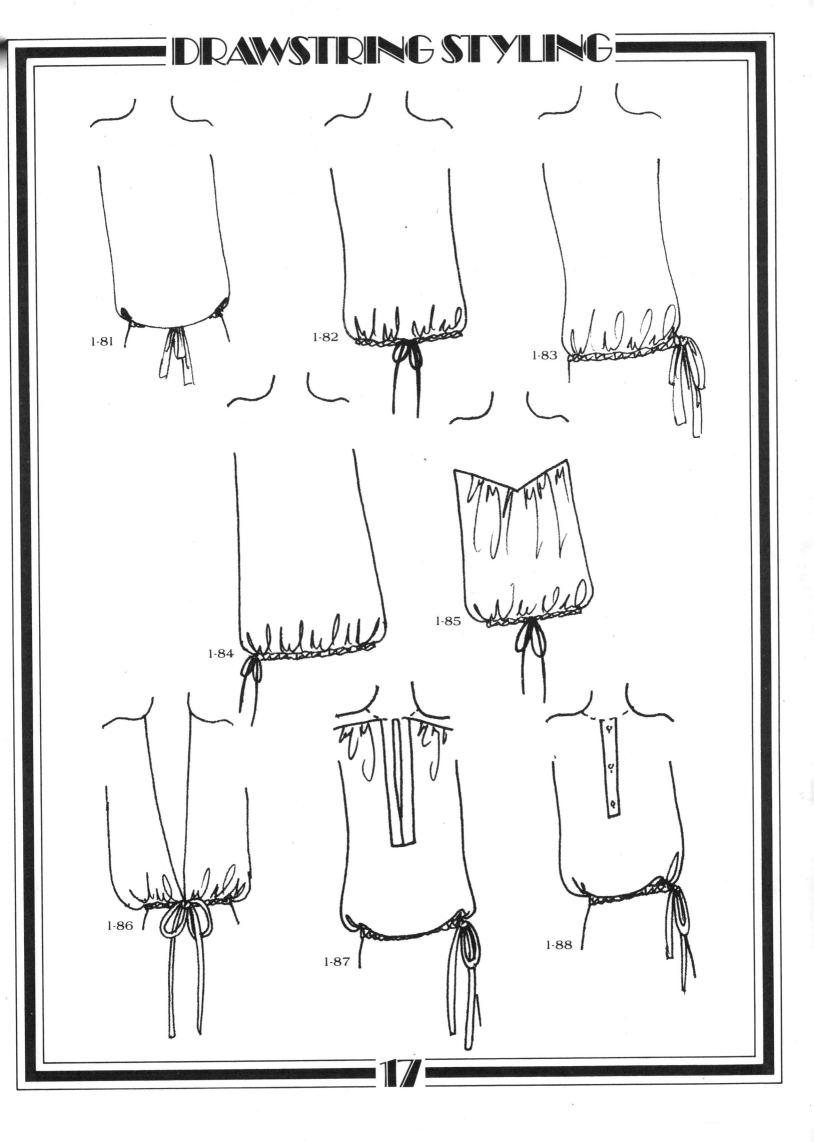

1-81

1-82

1-83

1-84

1-85

1-86

1-87

1-88

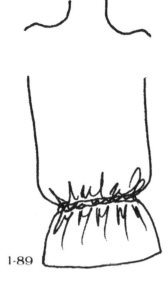

1-89

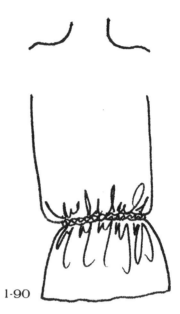

1-90

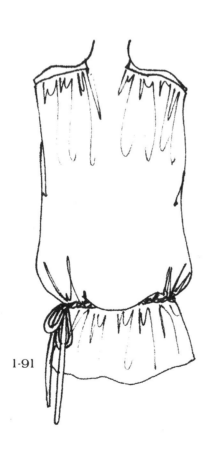

1-91

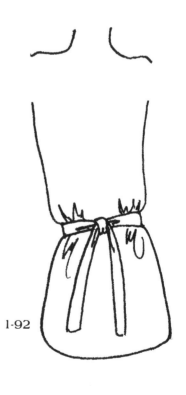

1-92

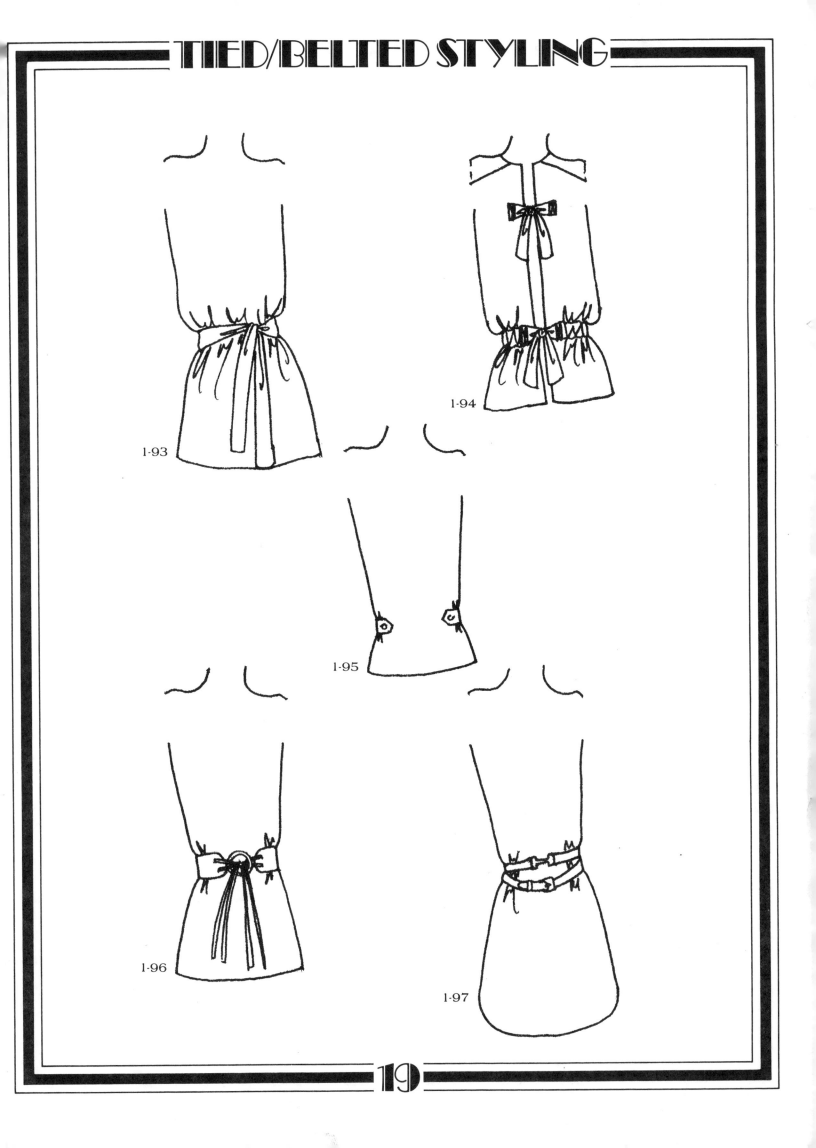

1-93

1-94

1-95

1-96

1-97

1-98

1-99

1-100

1-101

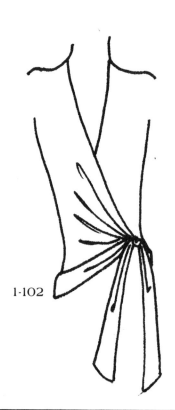

1-102

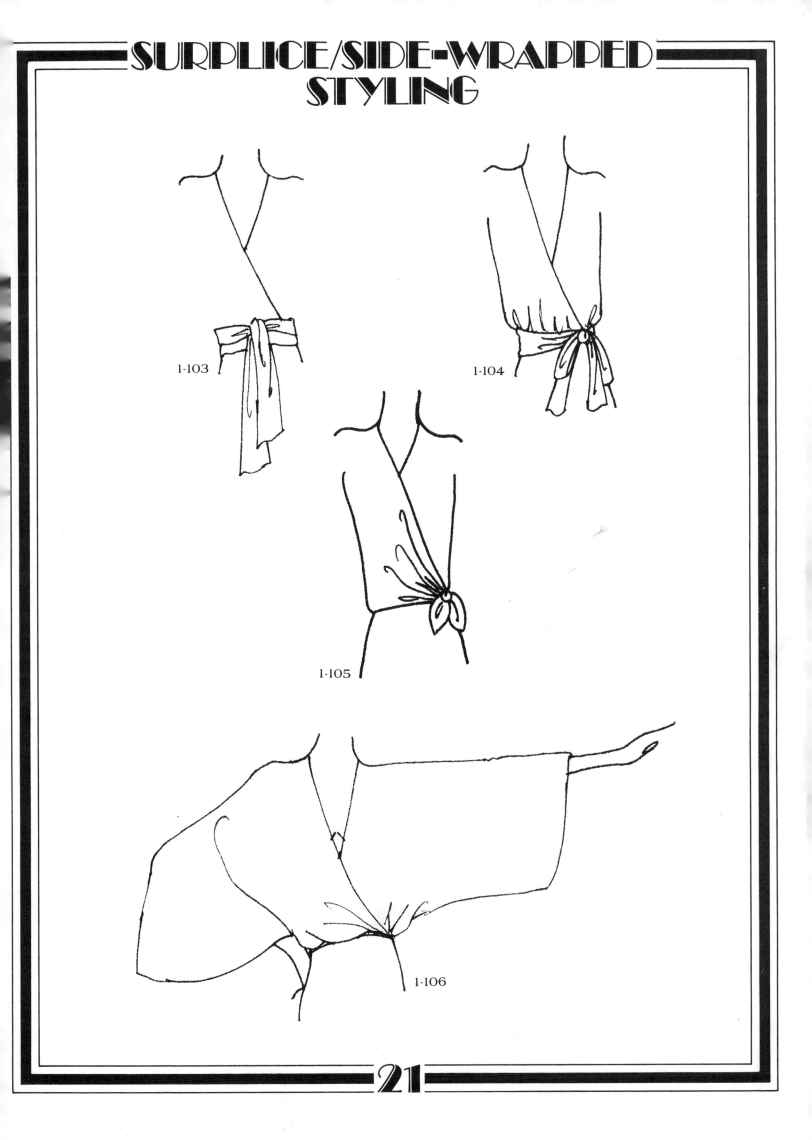

1-103

1-104

1-105

1-106

1-107

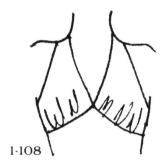

1-108

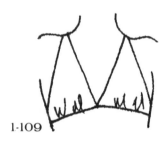

1-109

1-110

1-111

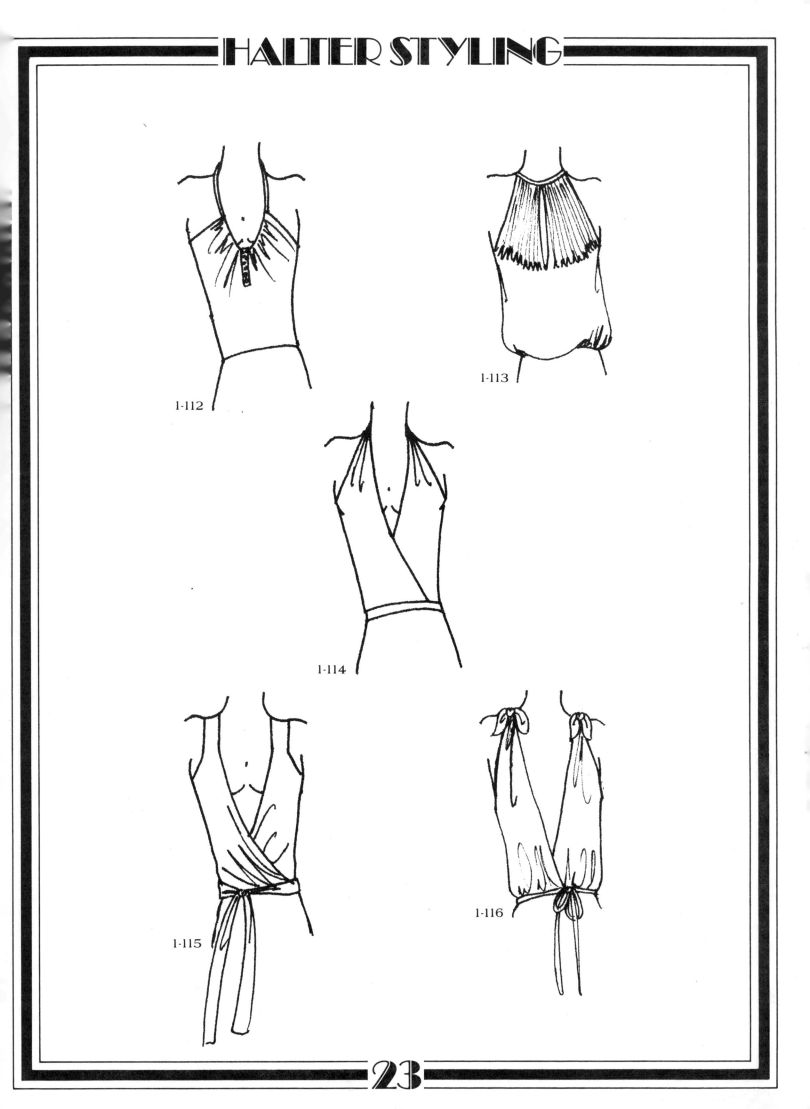

1-112

1-113

1-114

1-115

1-116

1-117

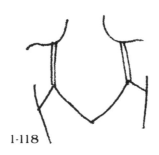

1-118

1-119

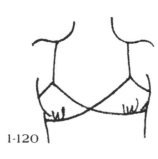

1-120

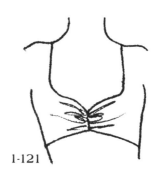

1-121

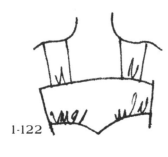

1-122

1-123

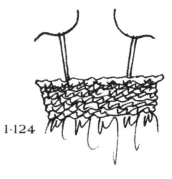

1-124

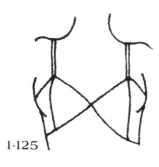

1-125

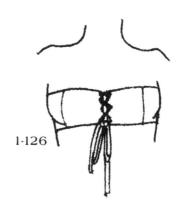

1-126

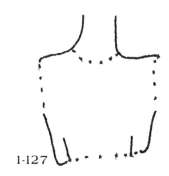

1-127

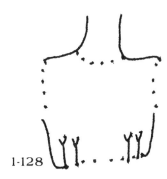

1-128

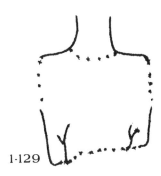

1-129

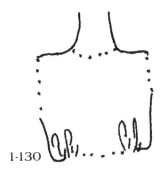

1-130

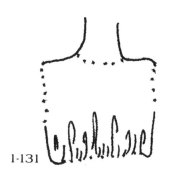

1-131

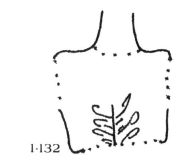

1-132

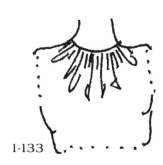

1-133

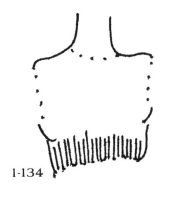

1-134

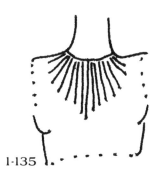

1-135

1-136

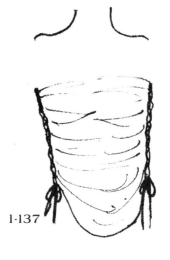

1-137

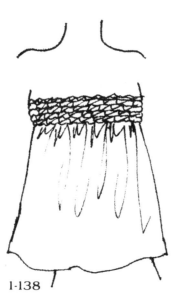

1-138

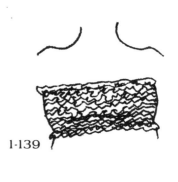

1-139

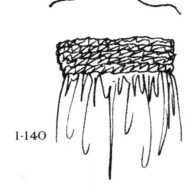

1-140

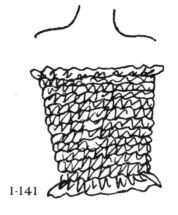

1-141

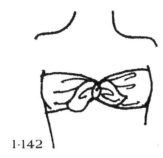

1-142

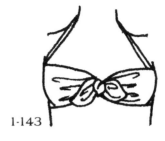

1-143

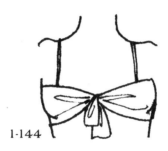

1-144

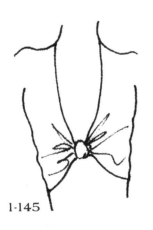

1-145

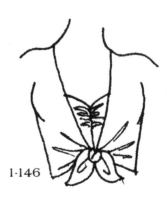

1-146

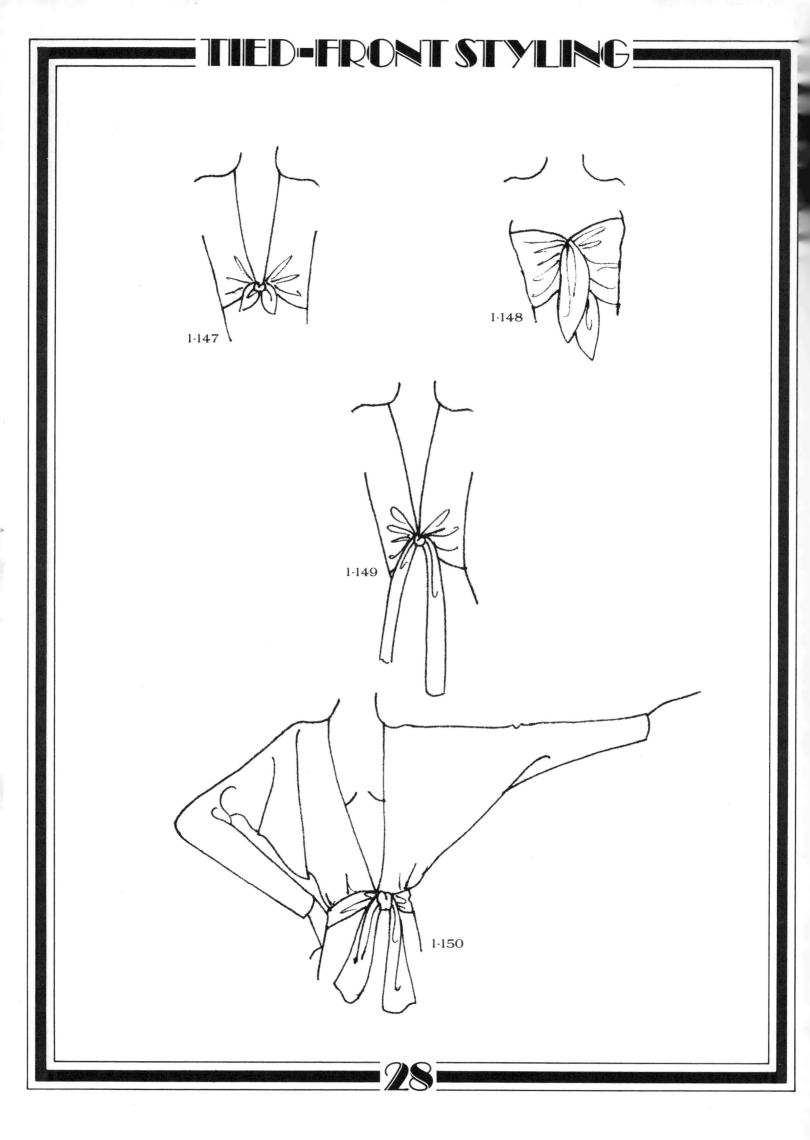

1-147

1-148

1-149

1-150

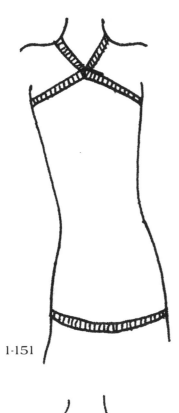

1-151

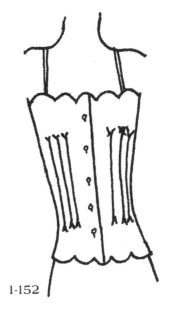

1-152

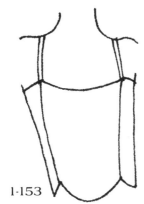

1-153

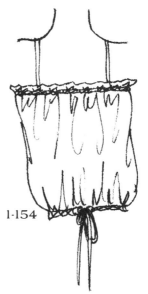

1-154

1-155

1-156

1-157

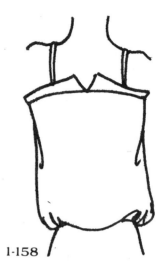

1-158

1-159

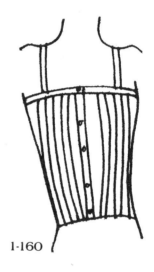

1-160

1-161

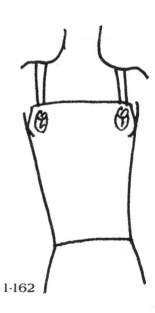

1-162

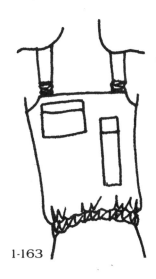

1-163

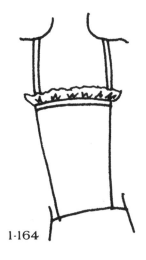

1-164

1-165

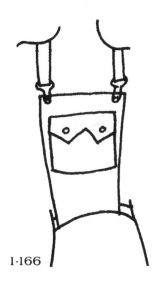

1-166

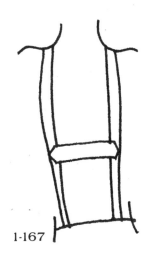

1-167

1-168

1-169

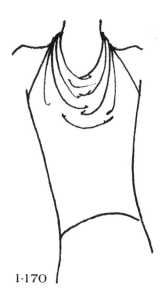

1-170

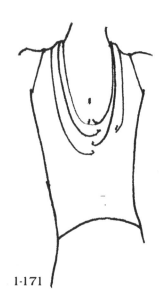

1-171

1-172

1-173

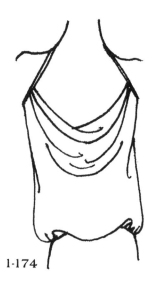

1-174

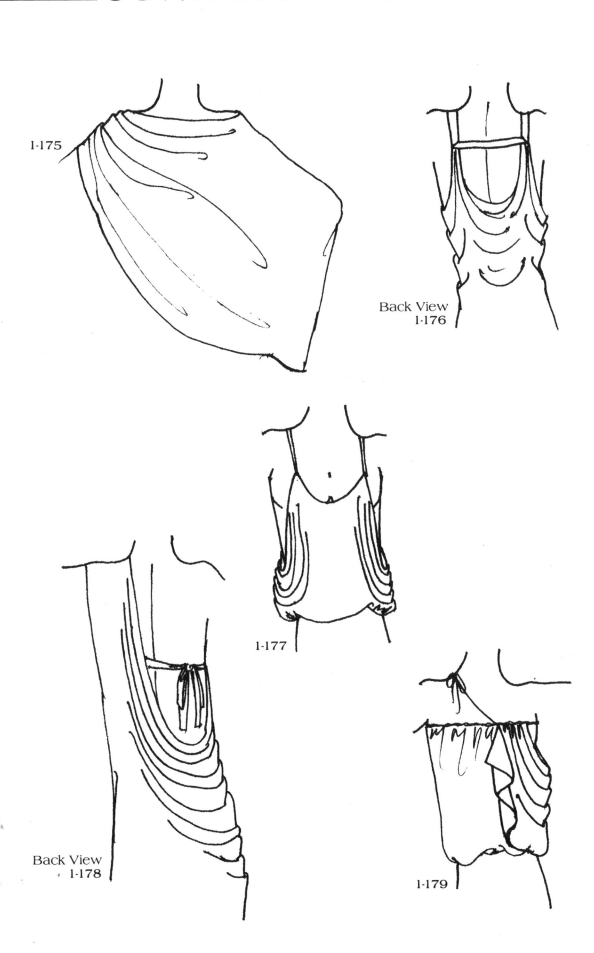

1-175

Back View
1-176

1-177

Back View
1-178

1-179

1-180

1-181

1-182

1-183

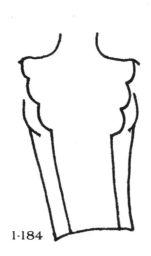

1-184

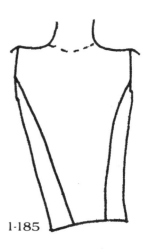

1-185

1-186

1-187

1-188

1-189

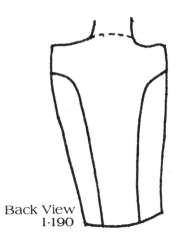

Back View
1-190

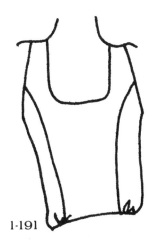

1-191

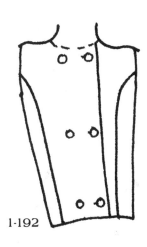

1-192

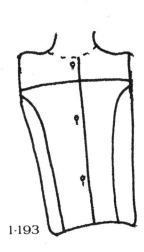

1-193

1-194

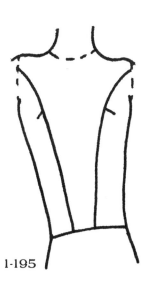

1-195

1-196

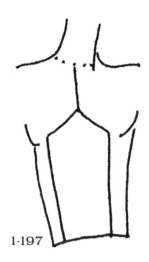

1-197

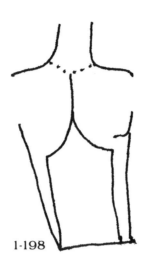

1-198

1-199

1-200

1-201

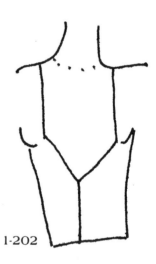

1-202

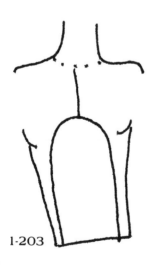

1-203

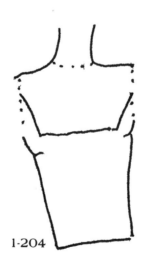

1-204

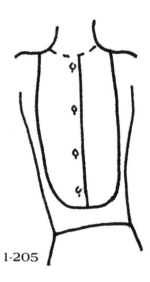

1-205

1-206

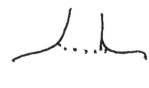

1-207

1-208

1-209

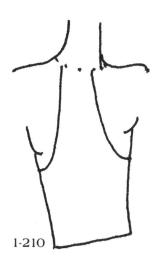

1-210

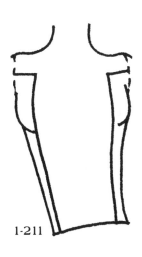

1-211

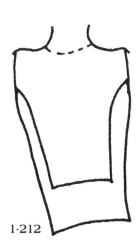

1-212

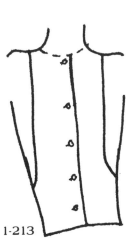

1-213

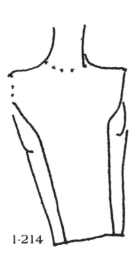

1-214

1-215

1-216

1-217

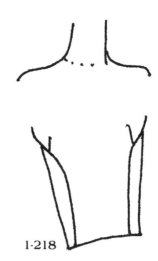

1-218

1-219

1-220

1-221

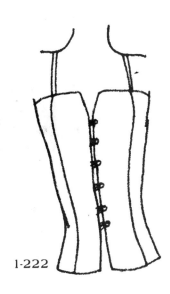

1-222

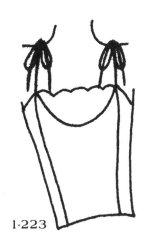

1-223

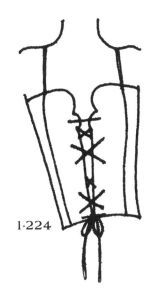

1-224

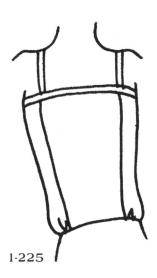

1-225

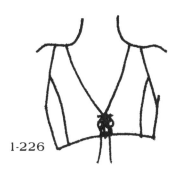

1-226

1-227

1-228

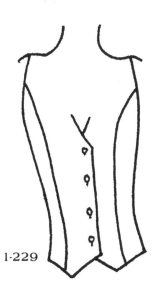

1-229

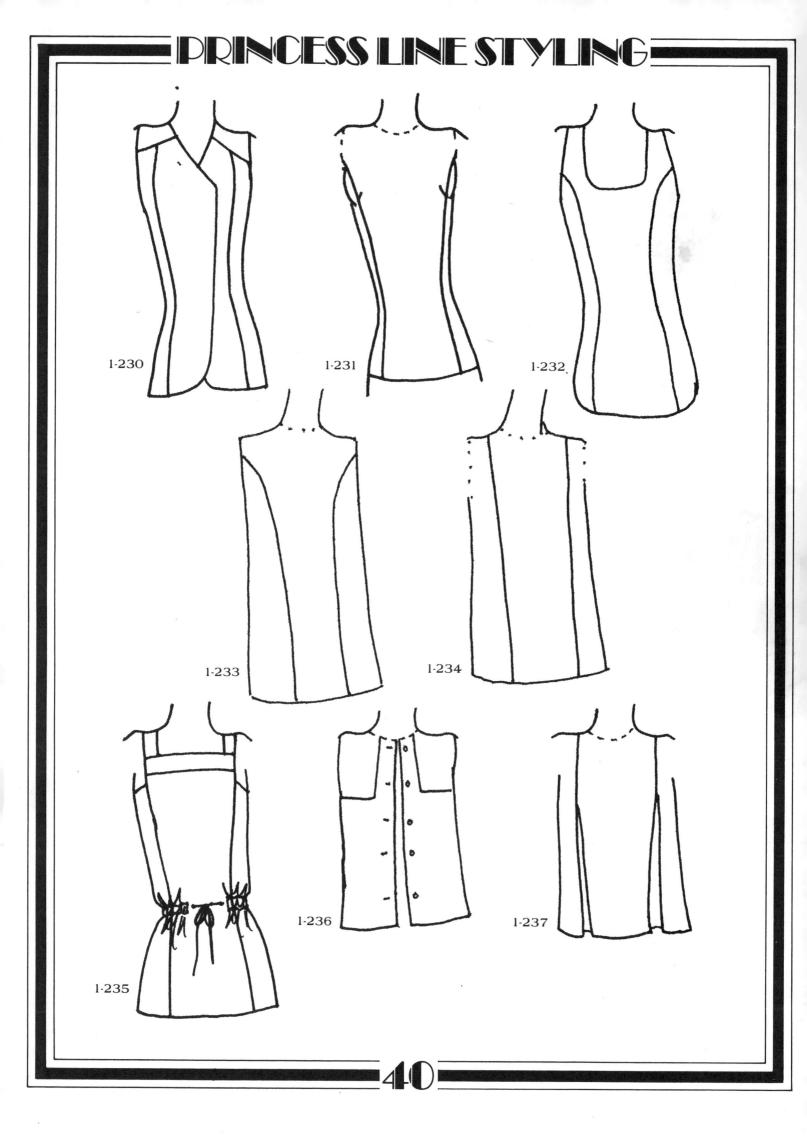

1-230

1-231

1-232

1-233

1-234

1-235

1-236

1-237

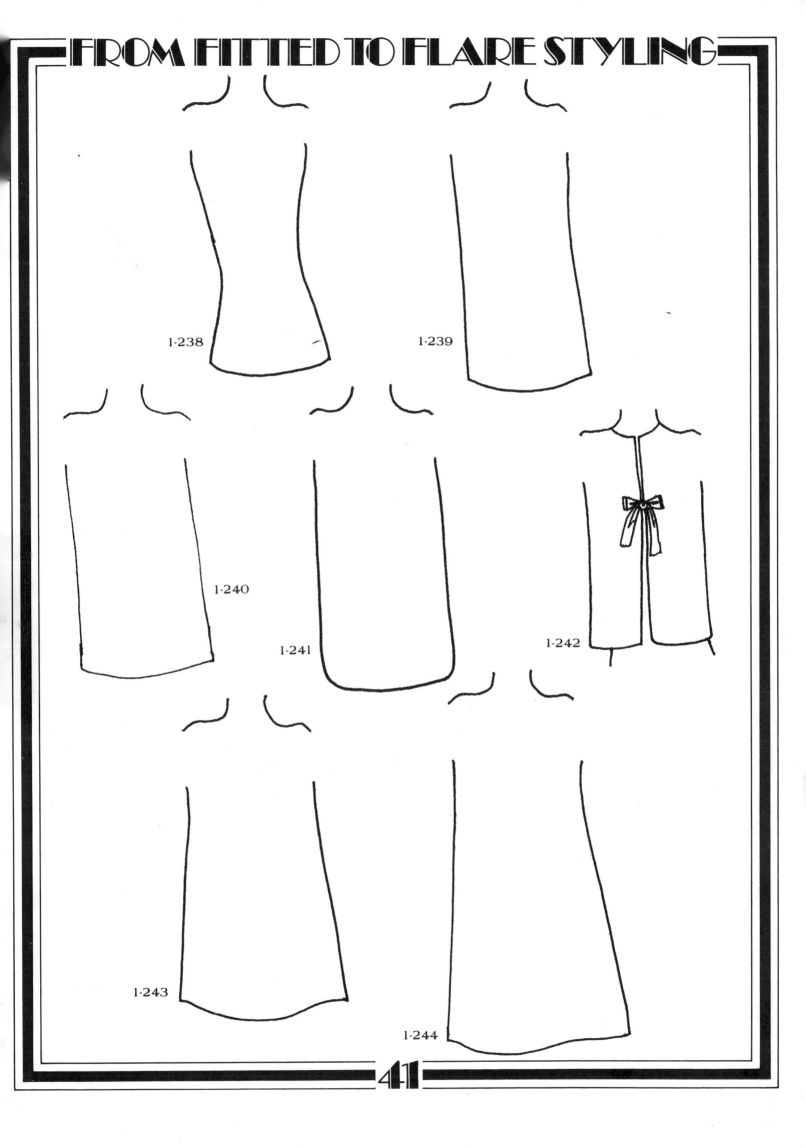

1-238

1-239

1-240

1-241

1-242

1-243

1-244

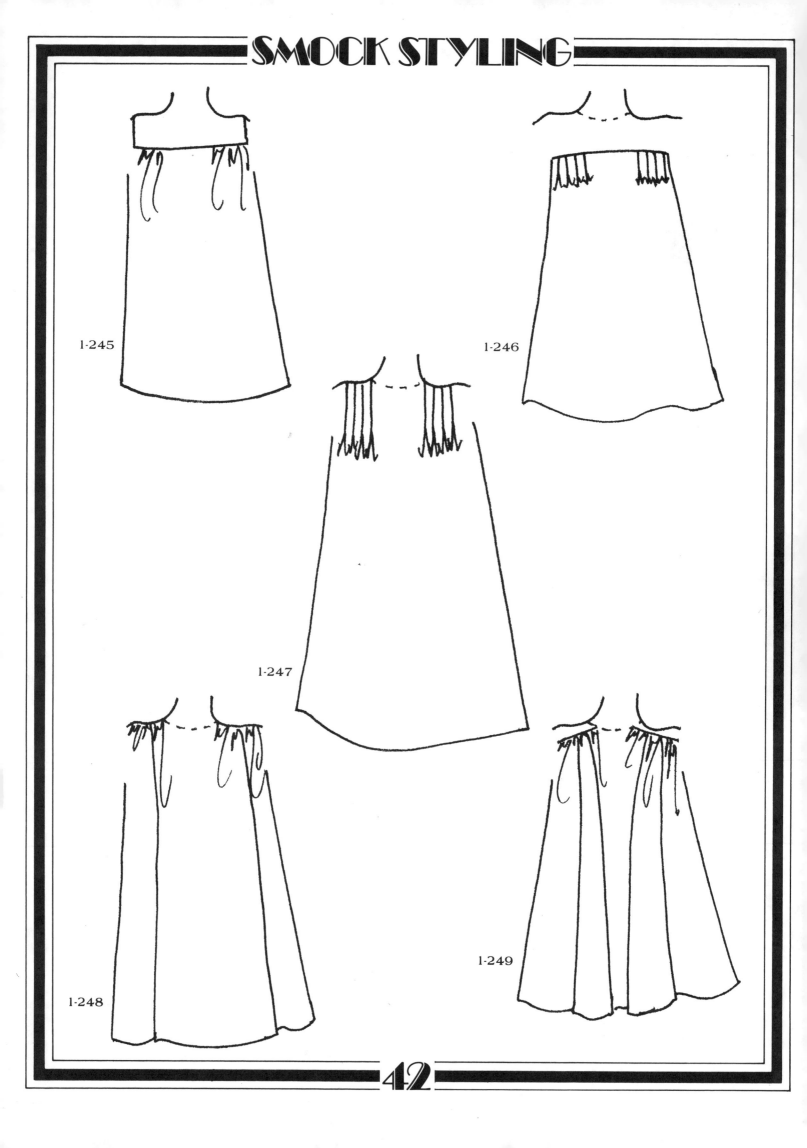

1·245

1·246

1·247

1·248

1·249

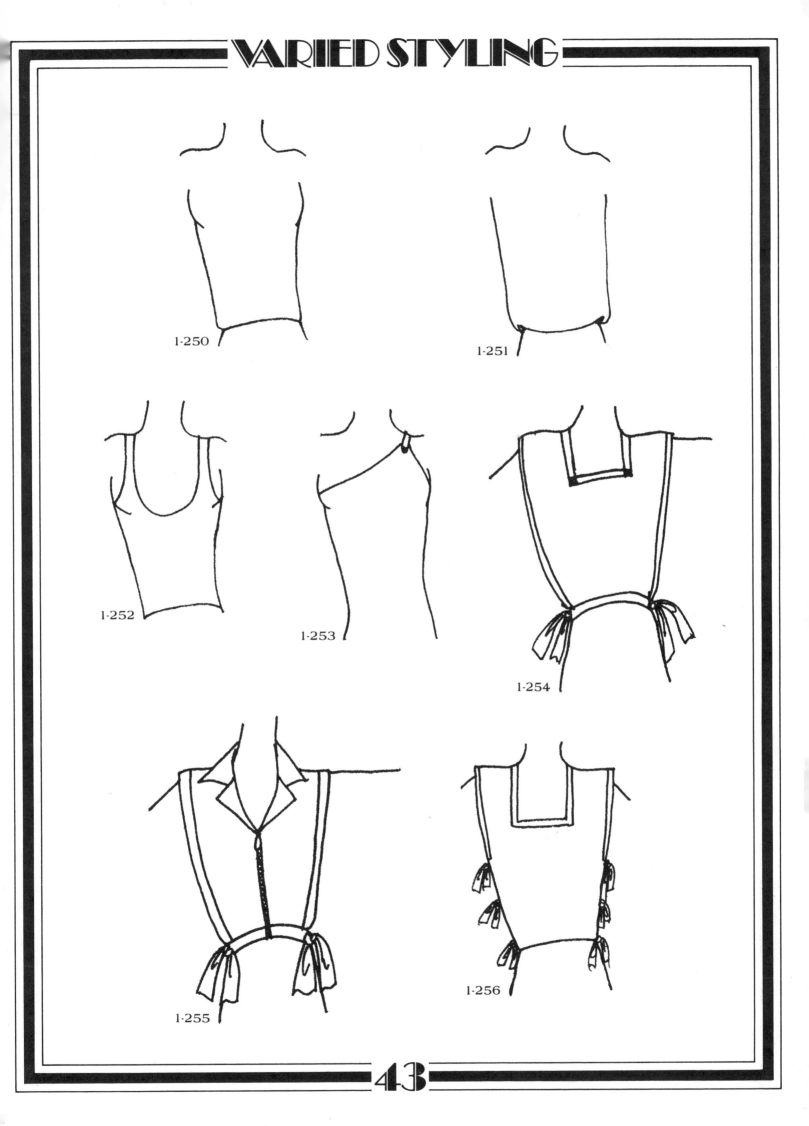

1-250

1-251

1-252

1-253

1-254

1-255

1-256

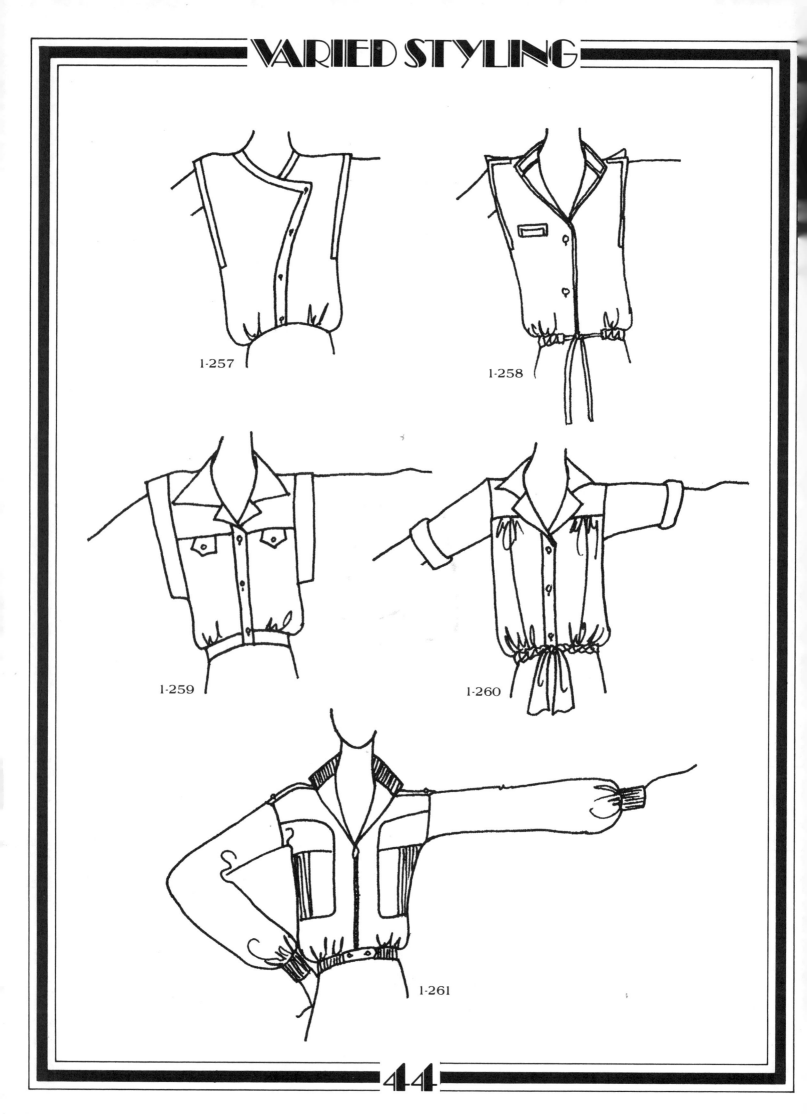

1-257

1-258

1-259

1-260

1-261

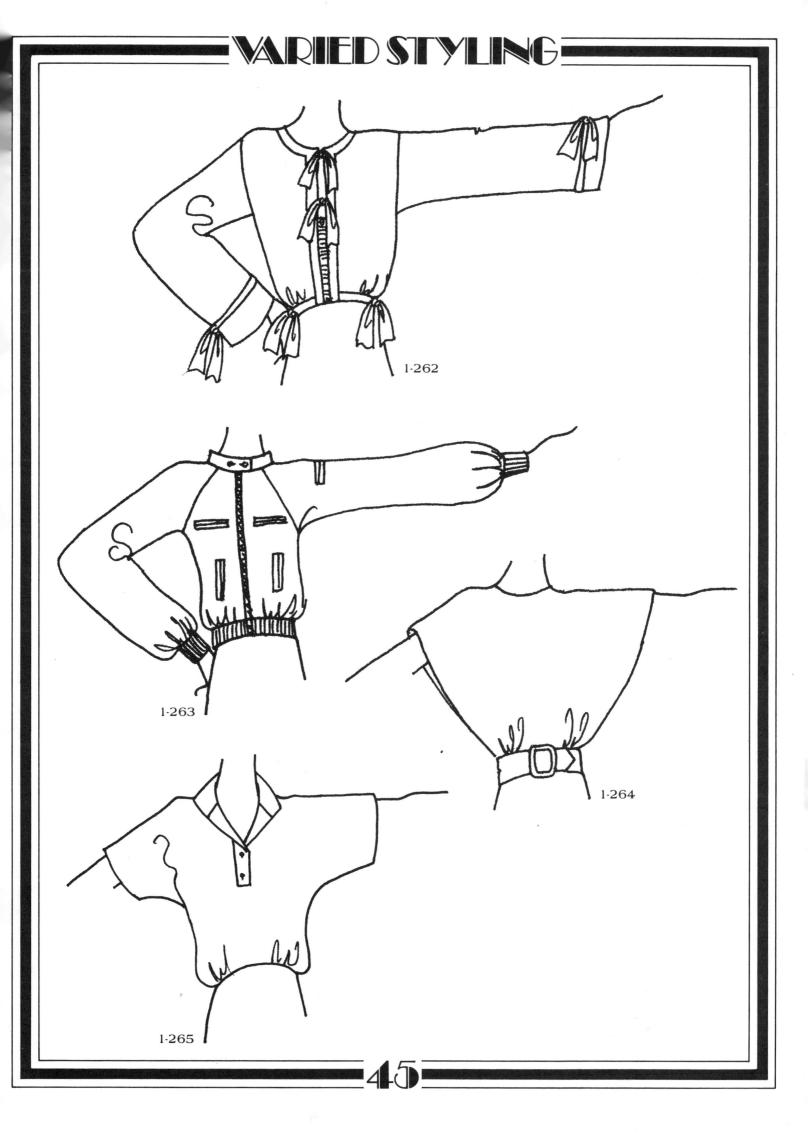

1-262

1-263

1-264

1-265

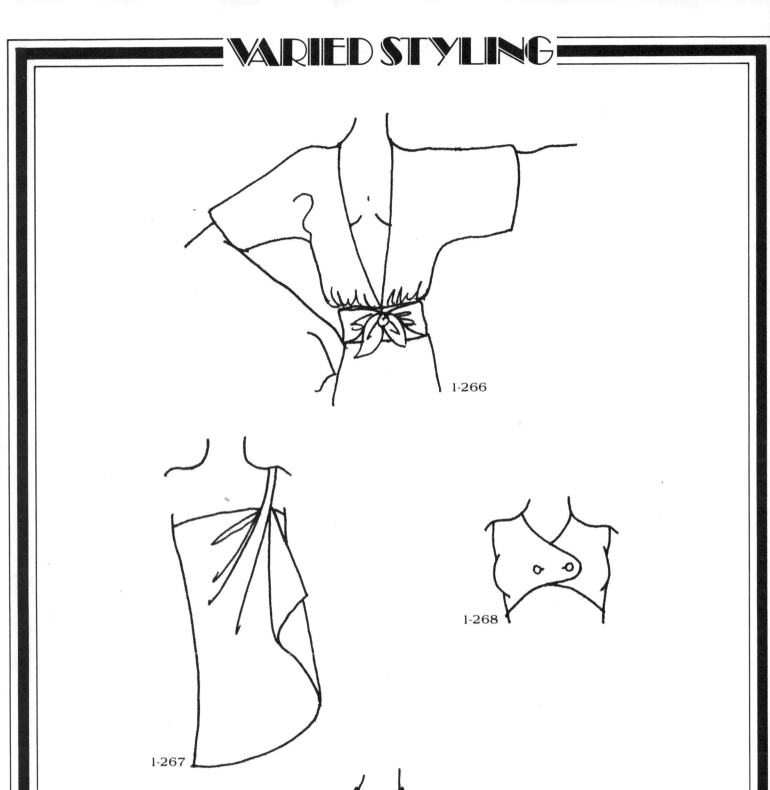

1-266

1-267

1-268

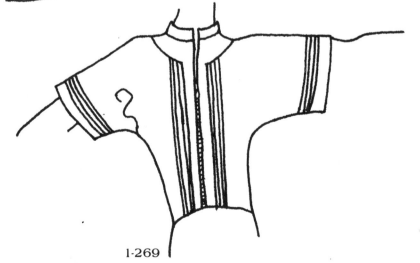

1-269

2-1

2-2
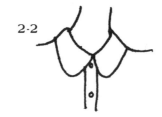

2-3
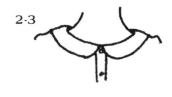

2-4
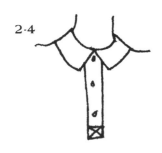

2-5

2-6

2-7

2-8
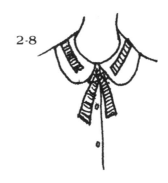

2-9
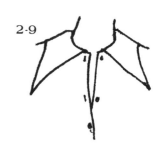

2-10

2-11

2-12
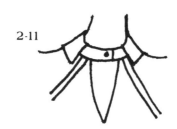

2-13

2-14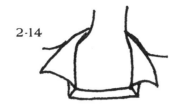

2-15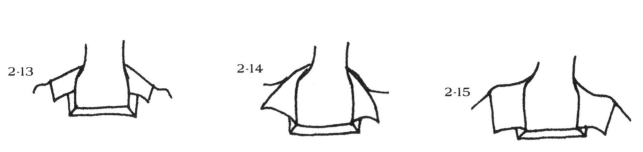

2-16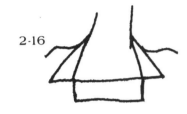

2-17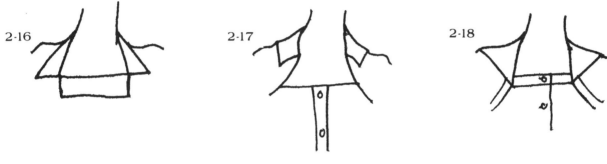

2-18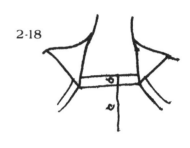

2-19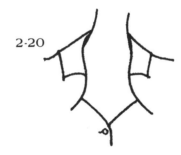

2-20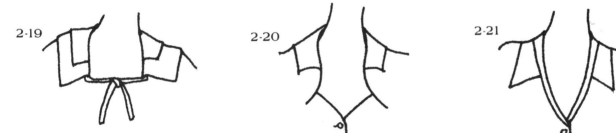

2-21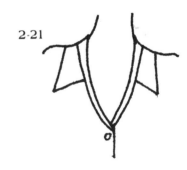

2-22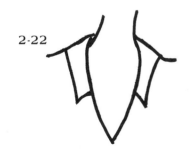

2-23

2-24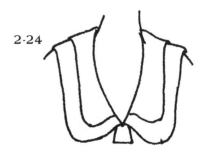

2-25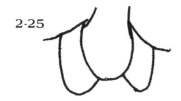

2-26

2-27

CHELSEA STYLING

2-28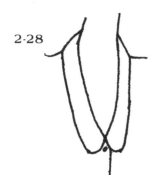

2-29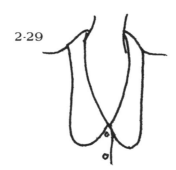

2-30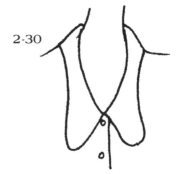

2-31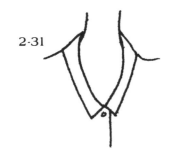

2-32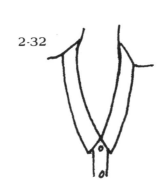

2-33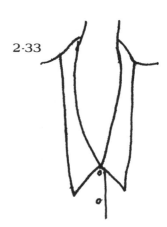

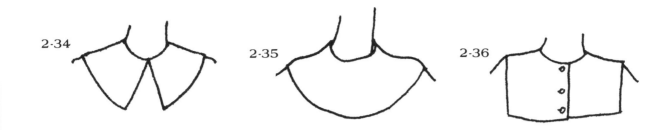

2-34
2-35
2-36

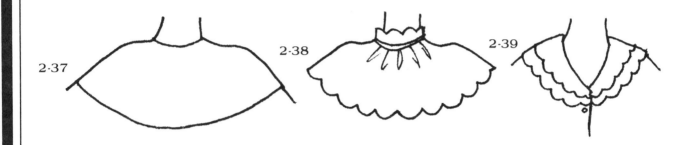

2-37
2-38
2-39

CAPE/CAPELET STYLING

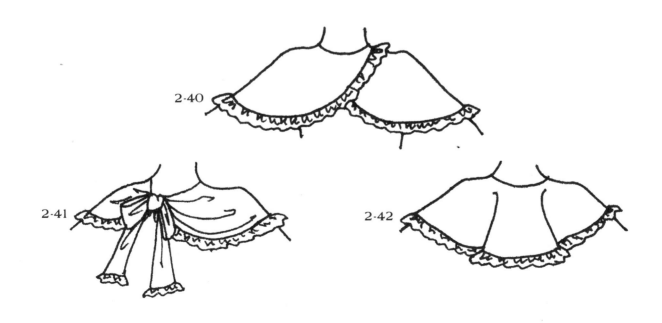

2-40

2-41
2-42

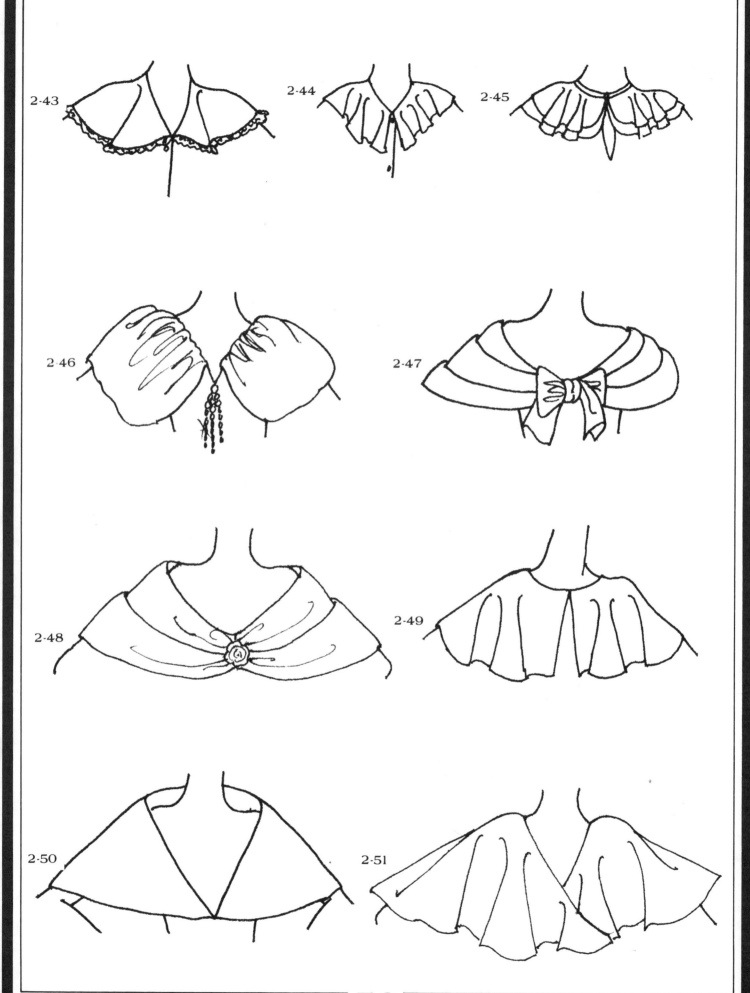

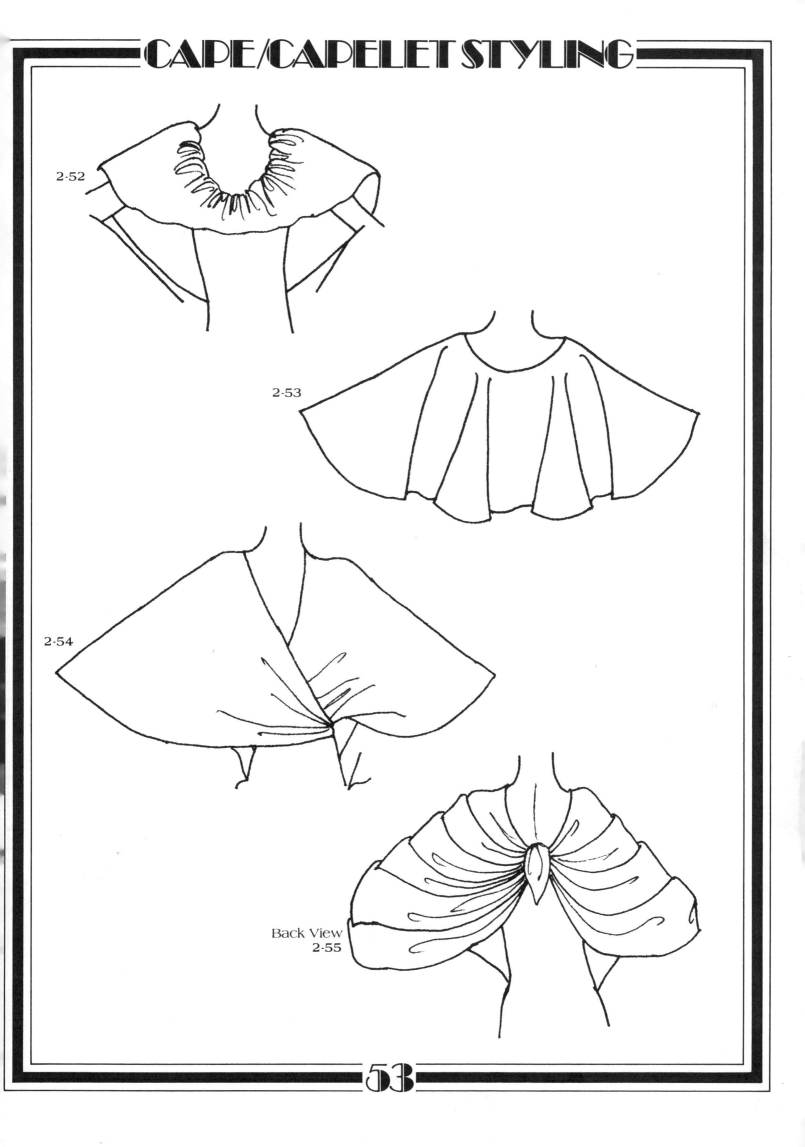

2-52

2-53

2-54

Back View
2-55

2·56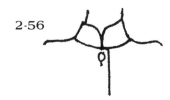

2·57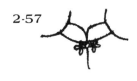

2·58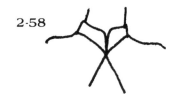

2·59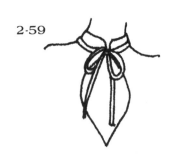

2·60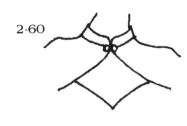

2·61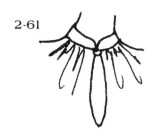

2·62

2·63

2·64

2·65

2·66

2·67

2-68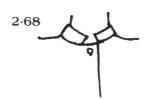

2-69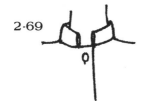

2-70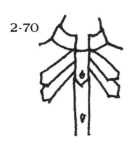

2-71

2-72

2-73

2-74

2-75

2-76

2-77

2-78

2-79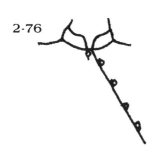

2-80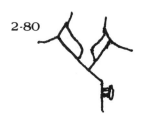

2-81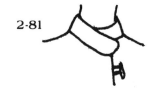

2-82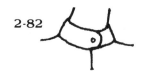

2-83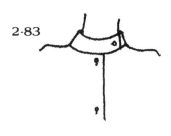

2-84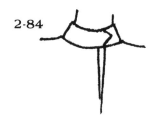

2-85

2-86

2-87

2-88

2-89

2-90

2-91

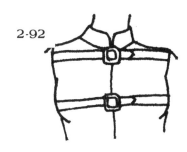

2-92

2-93

TURTLENECK STYLING

2-94

2-95

2-96

2-97

2-98

2-99

2-100

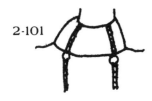 2-101

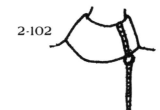 2-102

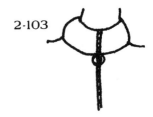 2-103

2-104

2-105

2-106

2-107

2-108

2-109

2-110

2-111

2-112

2-113

2-114

2-115

2-116

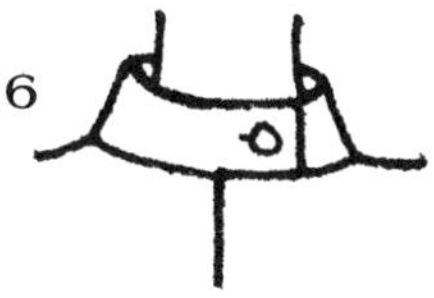

2-117

2-118

2-119

2-120

2-121

2-122

2-123

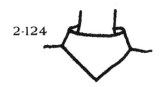

2-124

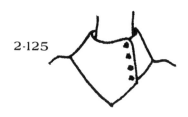 2-125

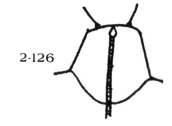 2-126

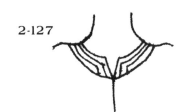 2-127

BIAS ROLL/BIAS DRAPE STYLING

2-128

2-129

2-130

2-131

2-132

2-133

2-134

2-135

2-136

2-137 2-138  2-139

2-140 2-141  2-142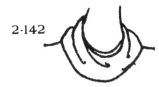

2-143 2-144  2-145

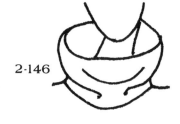

2-146

2-147

2-148

BIAS TUBE STYLING

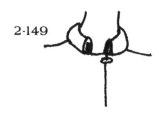

2-149

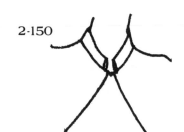

2-150

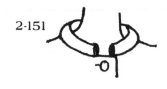

2-151

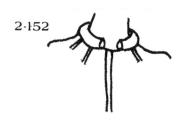

2-152

2-153

2-154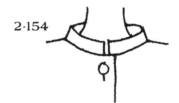

2-155

2-156

2-157

2-158

2-159

2-160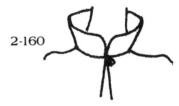

2-161

2-162

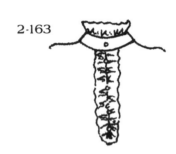

2-163

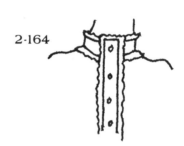

2-164

WING TIP/DANDY STYLING

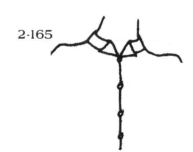

2-165

2-166

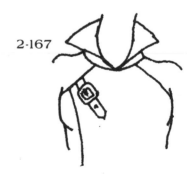

2-167

2-168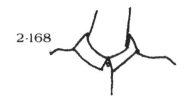

2-169

2-170

2-171

2-172

2-173

2-174

2-175

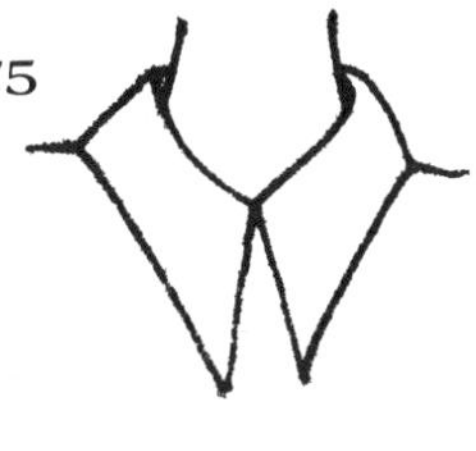

2-176

2-177

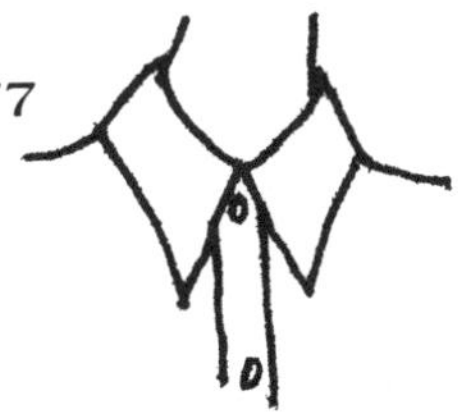

2-178

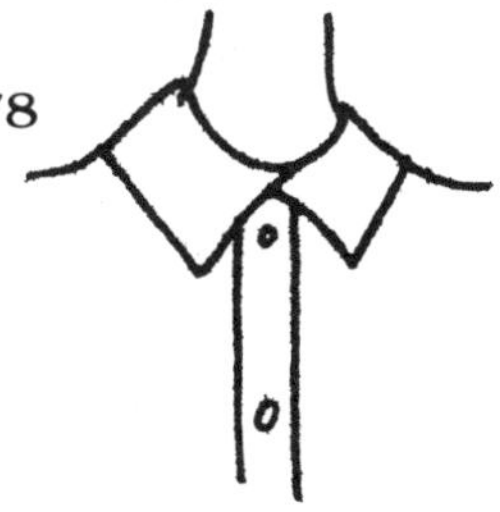

2-179

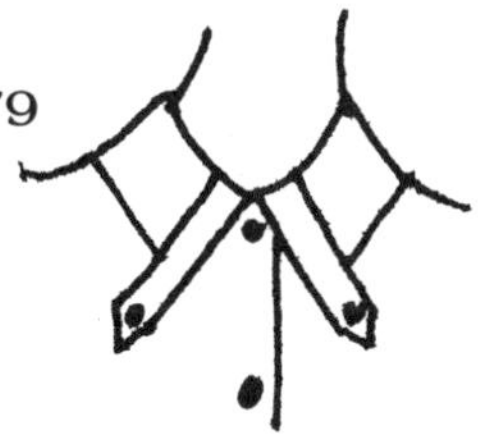

2-180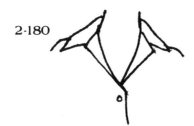

2-181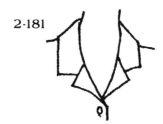

2-182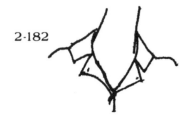

2-183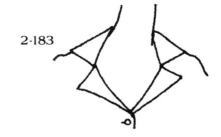

2-184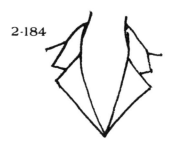

2-185

2-186

2-187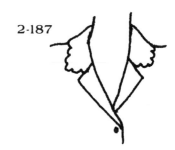

2-188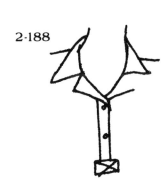

2-189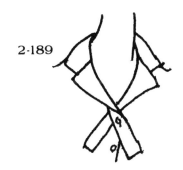

2-190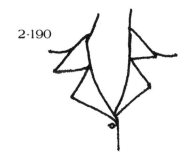

2-191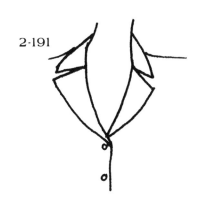

2-192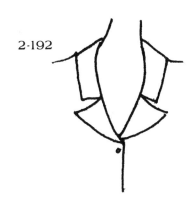

2-193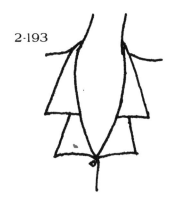

2-194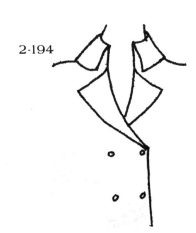

2-195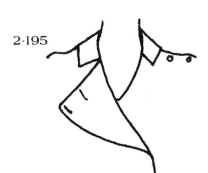

2-196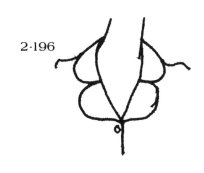

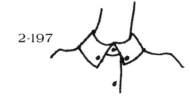

2-197

2-198

2-199

2-200

2-201

2-202

2-203

2-204

2-205

2-206

2-207

2-208

2-209

2-210

2-211

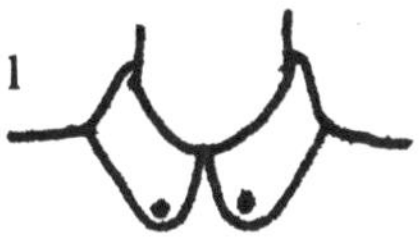

2-212

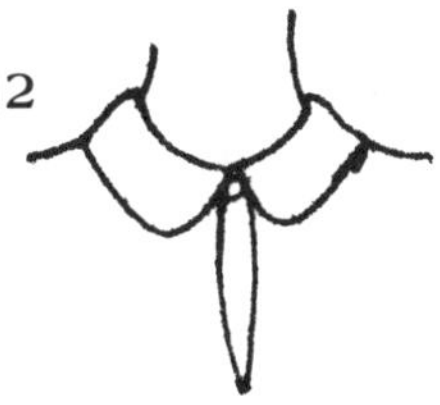

2-213

2-214

2-215

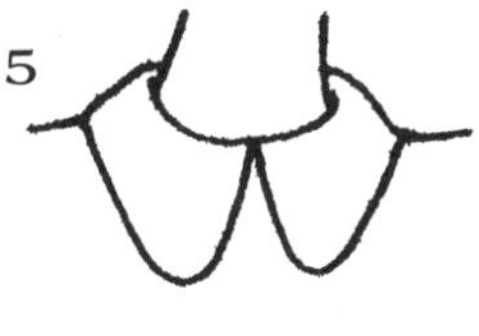

2-216

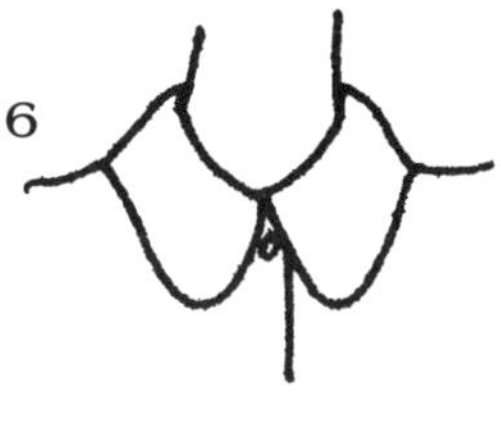

2-217

2-218

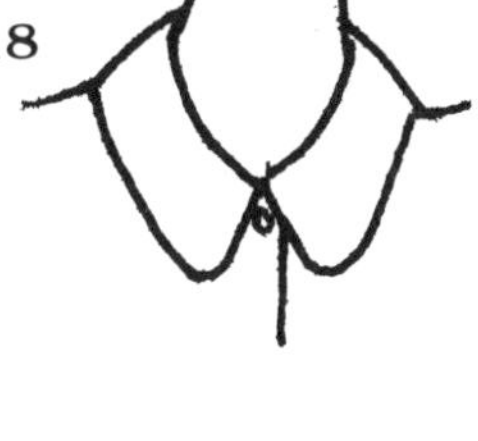

2-219

2-220

2-221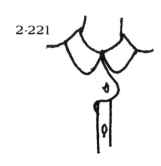

2-222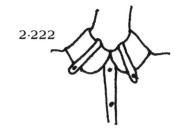

2-223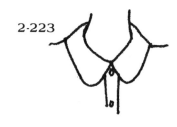

2-224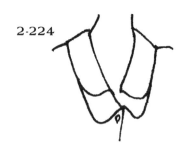

2-225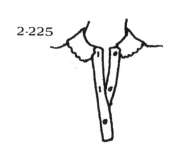

2-226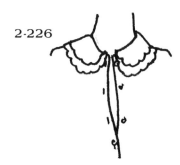

2-227

2-228

2-229

2-230

2-231

2-232

2-233

2-234

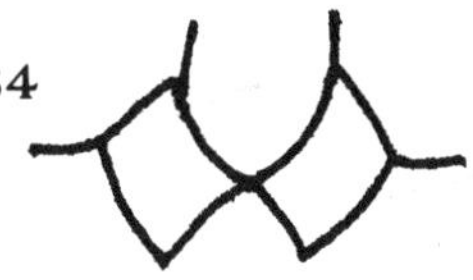

2-235

2-236

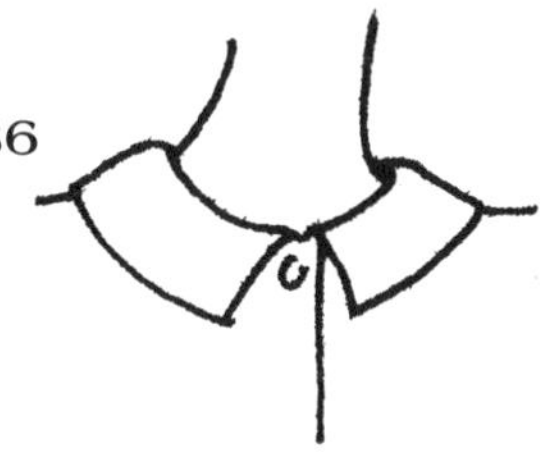

2-237

2-238

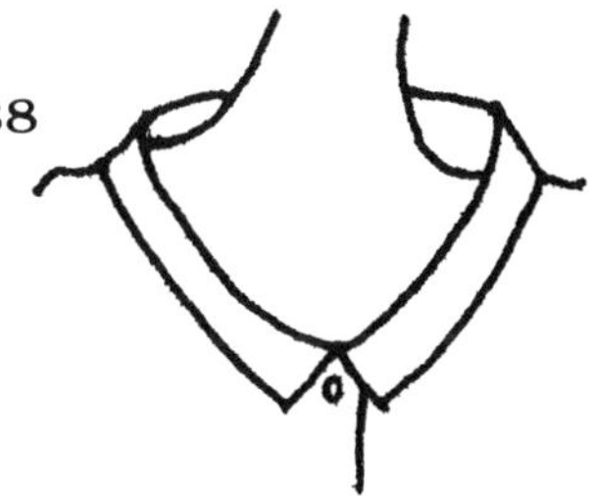

2-239

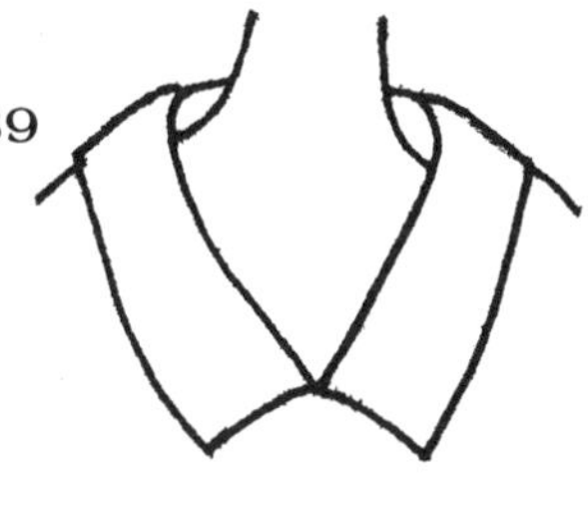

2-240

2-241

2-242

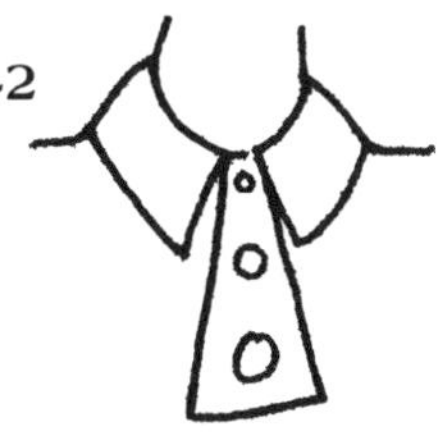

2-243

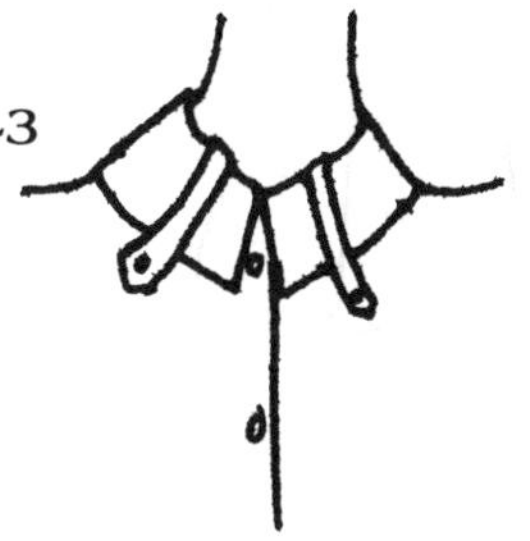

2-244

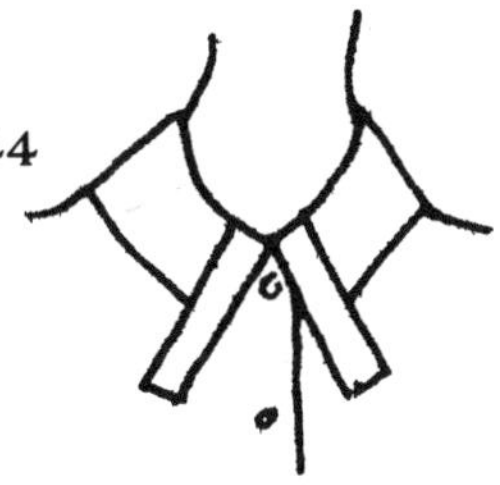

2-245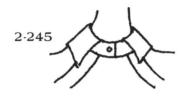

2-246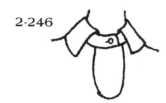

2-247

2-248

VARIED ROLL-TYPE STYLING

2-249

2-250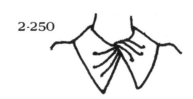

2-251

2-252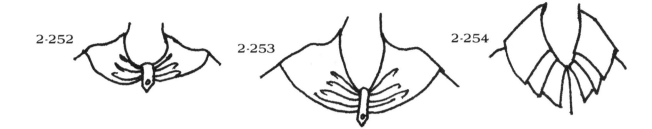

2-253

2-254

2-255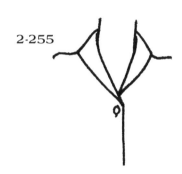

2-256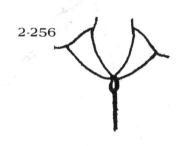

2-257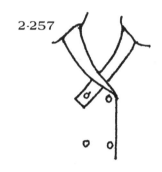

2-258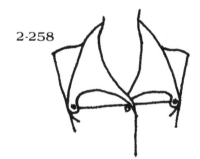

2-259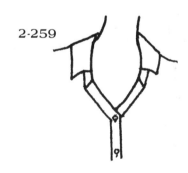

2-260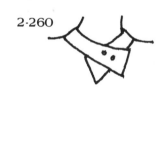

2-261

2-262

2-263

2-264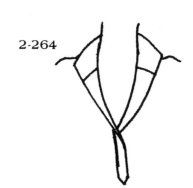

2-265

2-266

2-267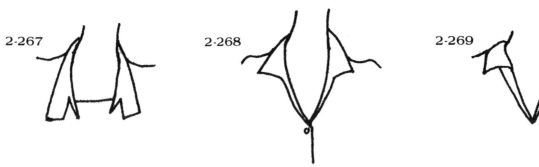

2-268

2-269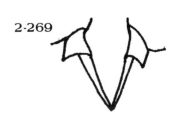

2-270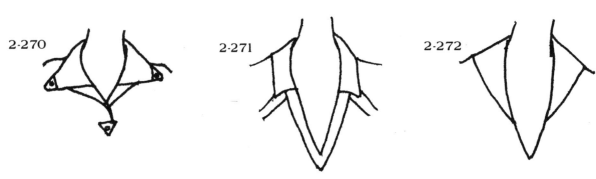

2-271

2-272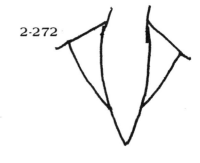

2-273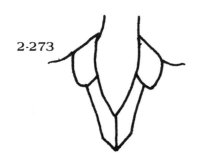

2-274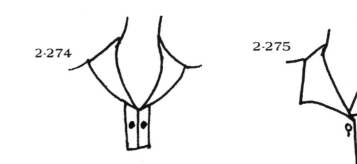

2-275

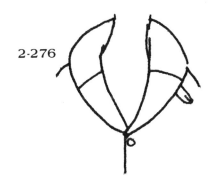

2-276

2-277

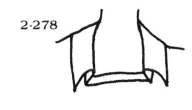

2-278

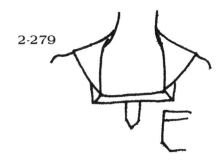

2-279

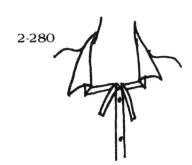

2-280

SHAWL STYLING

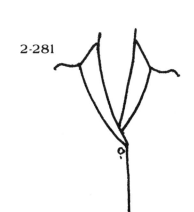

2-281

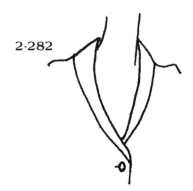

2-282

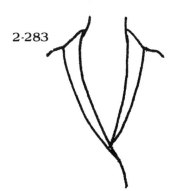

2-283

2-284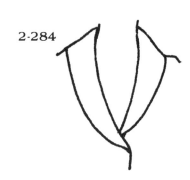

2-285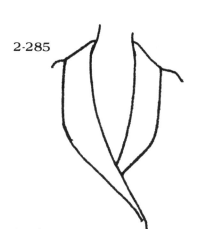

2-286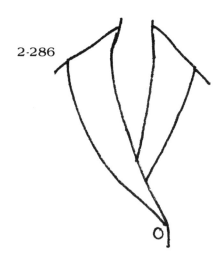

2-287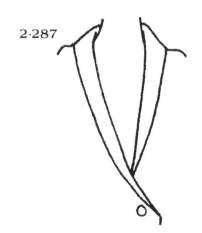

2-288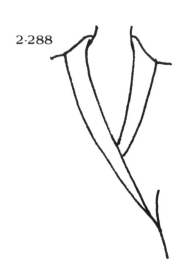

2-289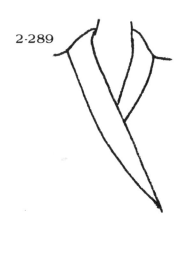

2-290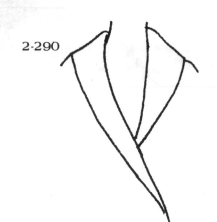

2-291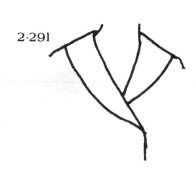

2-292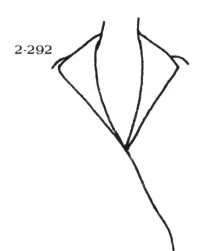

2-293

2-294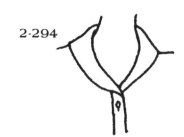

2-295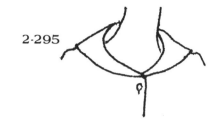

2-296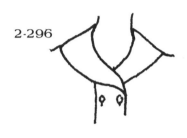

2-297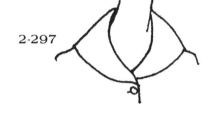

2-298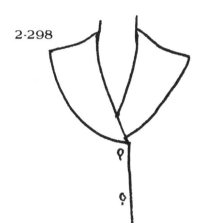

2-299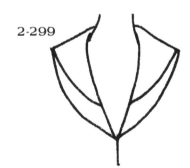

2-300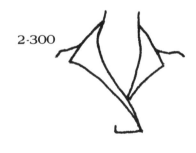

2-301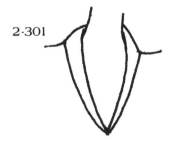

2-302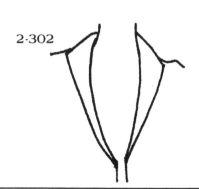

2-303

2-304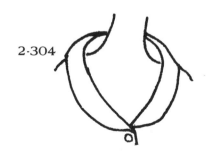

2-305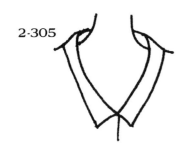

2-306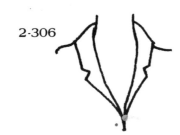

2-307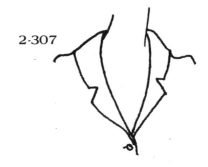

2-308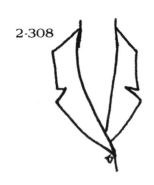

2-309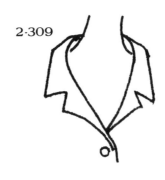

2-310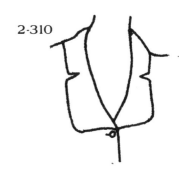

2-311

2-312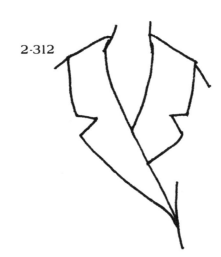

2-313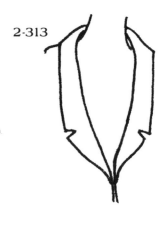

2-314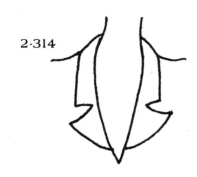

2-315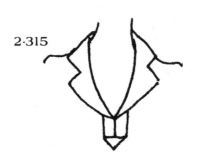

2-316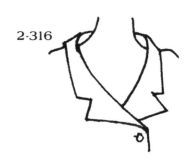

2-317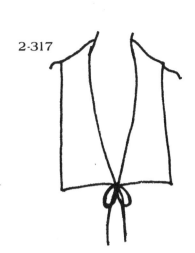

2-318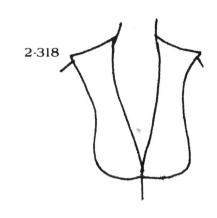

2-319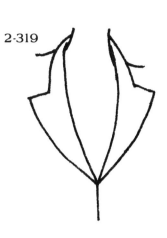

2-320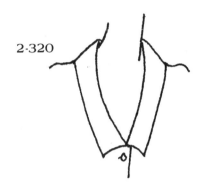

2-321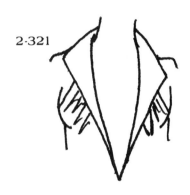

2-322

2-323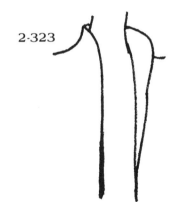

2-324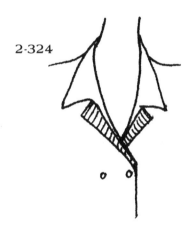

2-325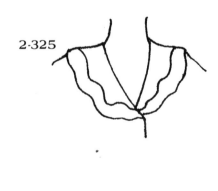

2-326

2-327

2-328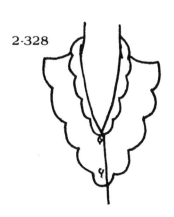

2-329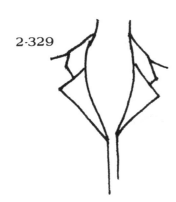

2-330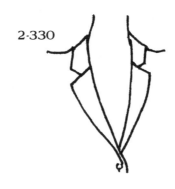

2-331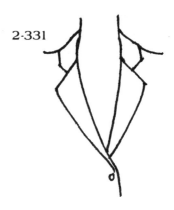

2-332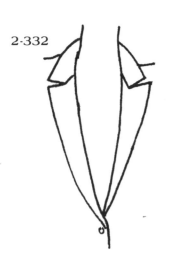

2-333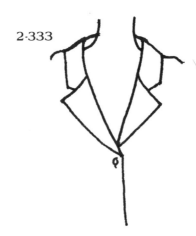

2-334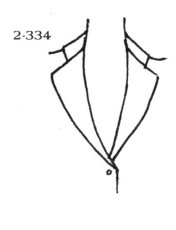

2-335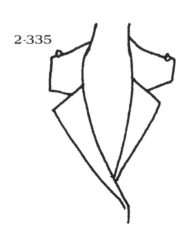

2-336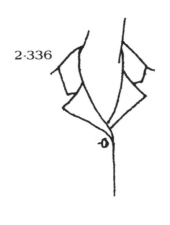

2-337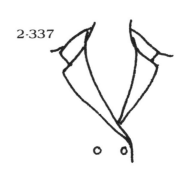

2-338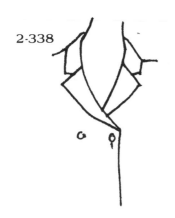

2-339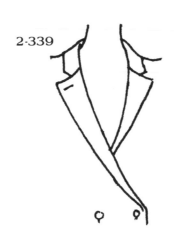

2-340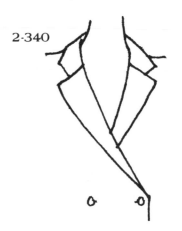

2-341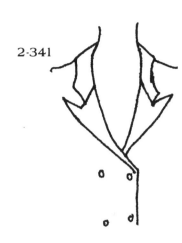

2-342

2-343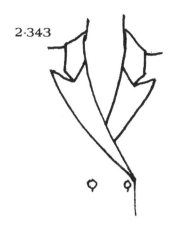

2-344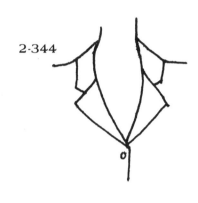

2-345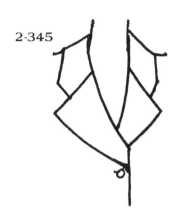

2-346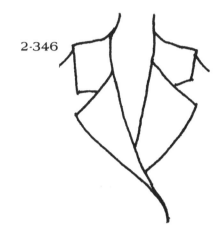

2-347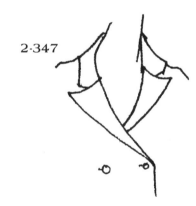

2-348

2-349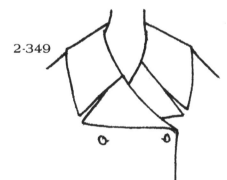

2-350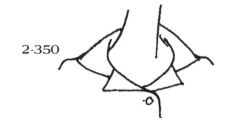

2-351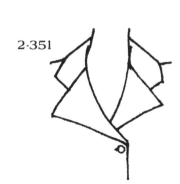

2-352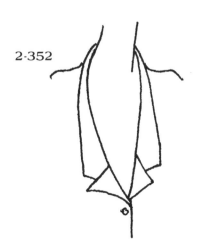

TWO-PIECE NOTCHED STYLING

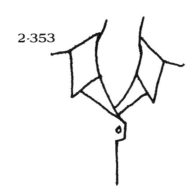
2-353

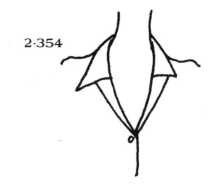
2-354

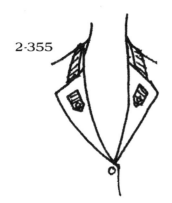
2-355

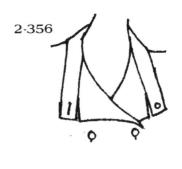
2-356

TWO-PIECE NOTCHED STYLING
WITH ROUND LAPELS

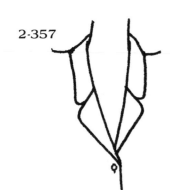
2-357

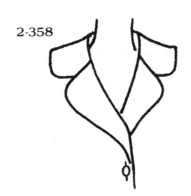
2-358

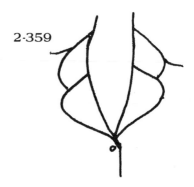
2-359

TWO-PIECE NOTCHED STYLING WITH ROUND LAPELS

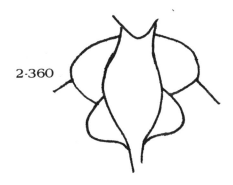

2-360

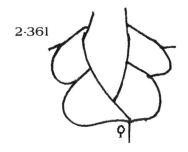

2-361

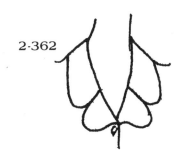

2-362

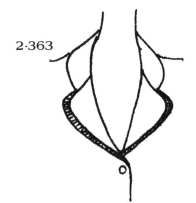

2-363

SAILOR STYLING

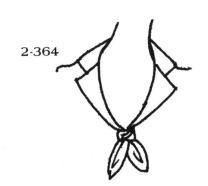

2-364

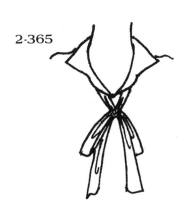

2-365

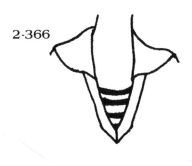

2-366

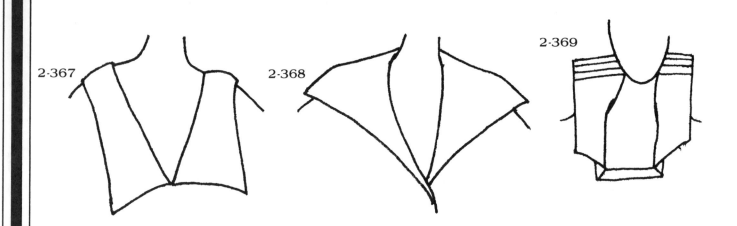

2-367

2-368

2-369

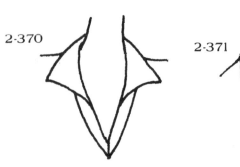

2-370

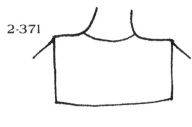

2-371

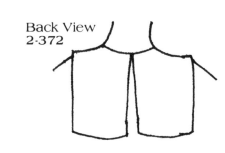

Back View
2-372

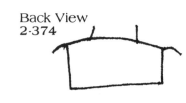

2-373

Back View
2-374

2-375

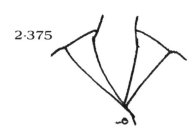

Back View
2-376

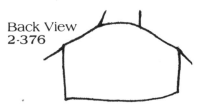

2-377

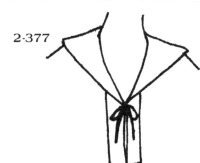

Back View
2-378

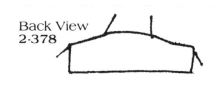

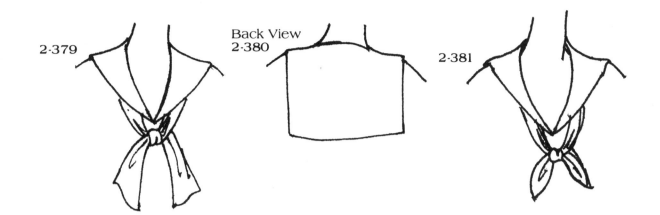

2-379

Back View
2-380

2-381

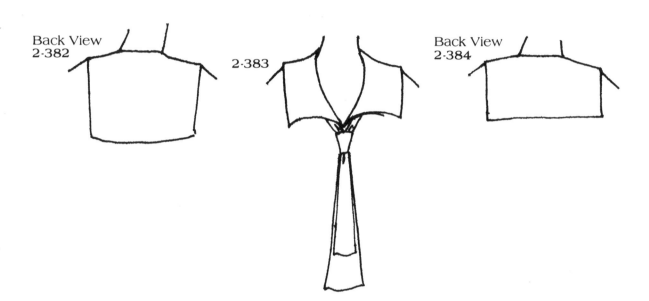

Back View
2-382

2-383

Back View
2-384

VARIED LAPEL STYLING

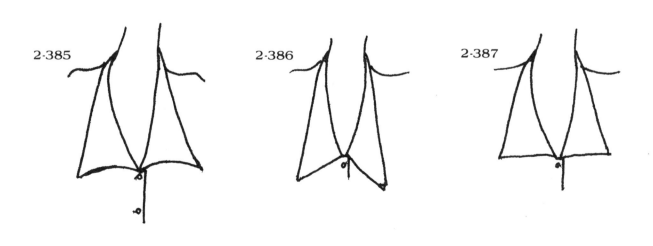

2-385

2-386

2-387

2-388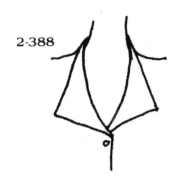

2-389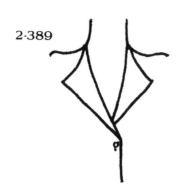

2-390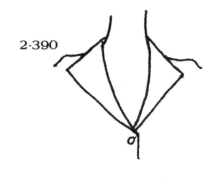

2-391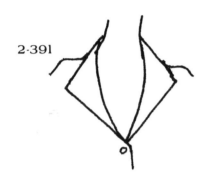

2-392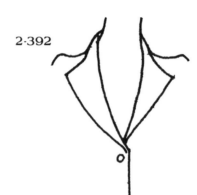

2-393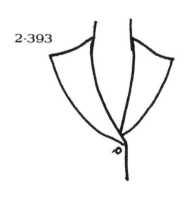

2-394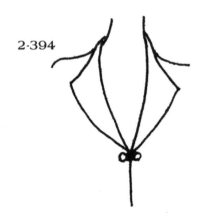

2-395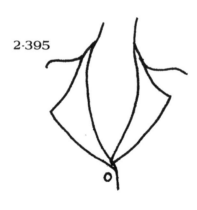

2-396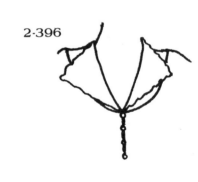

2-397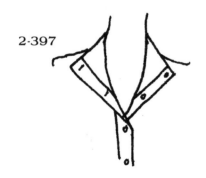

2-398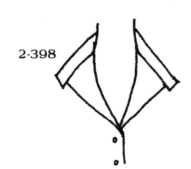

2-399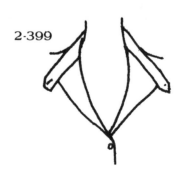

2-400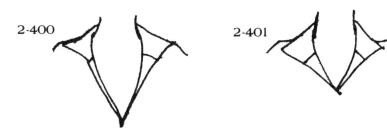

2-401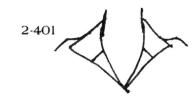

2-402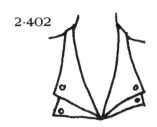

2-403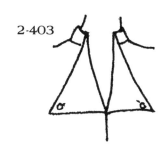

2-404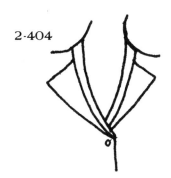

2-405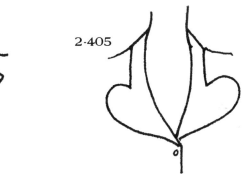

2-406

2-407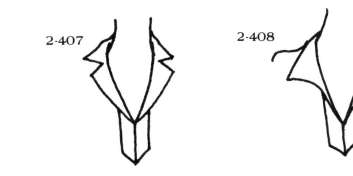

2-408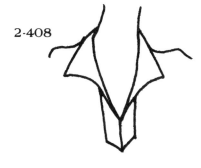

2-409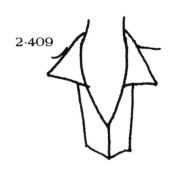

2-410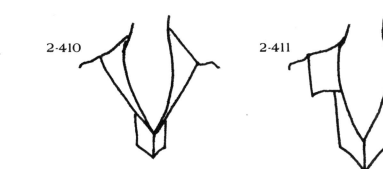

2-411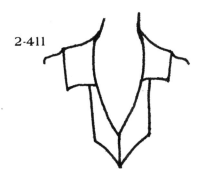

2-412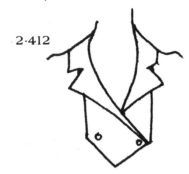

2-413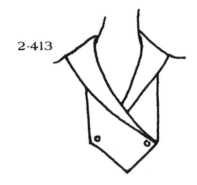

2-414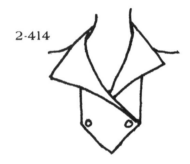

2-415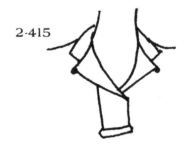

2-416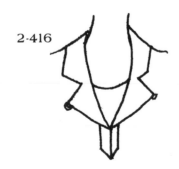

2-417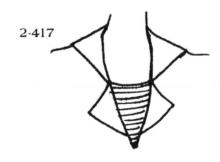

THREE · NECKLINES

3·1

3·2

3·3

3·4

3·5

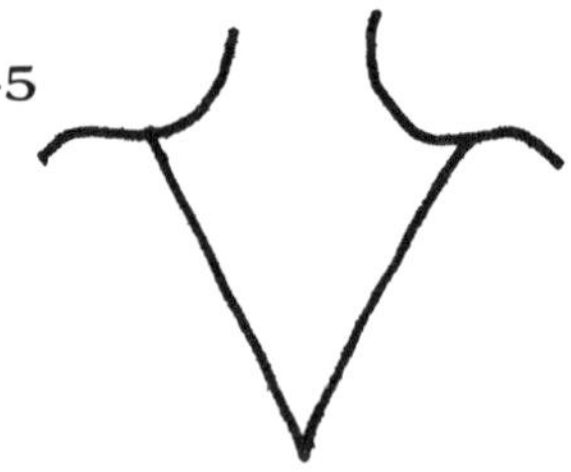

3·6

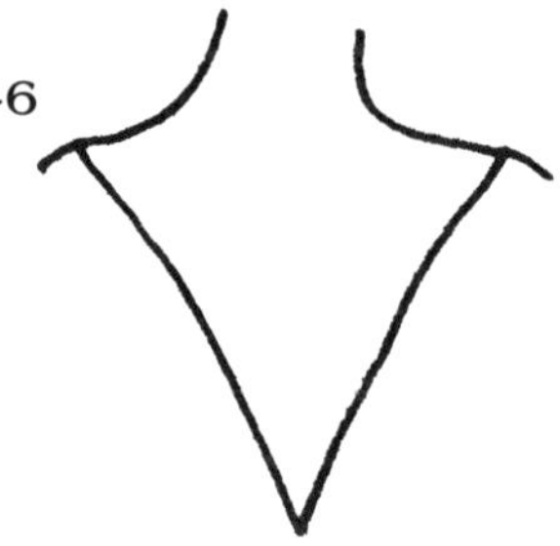

3·7

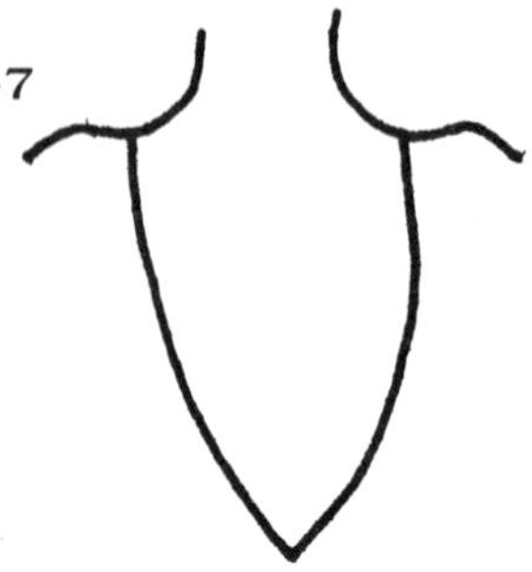

3·8

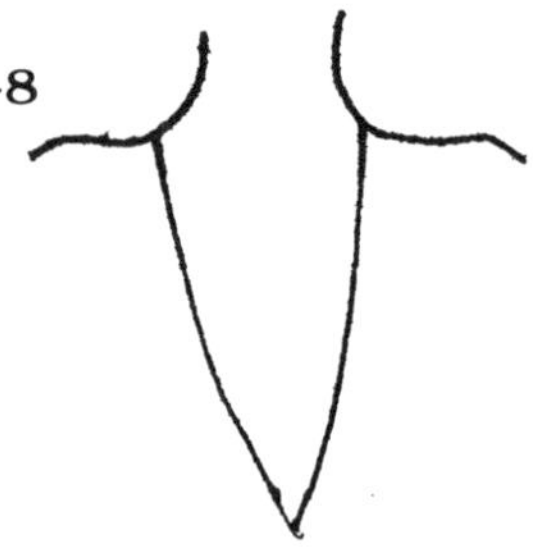

3·9

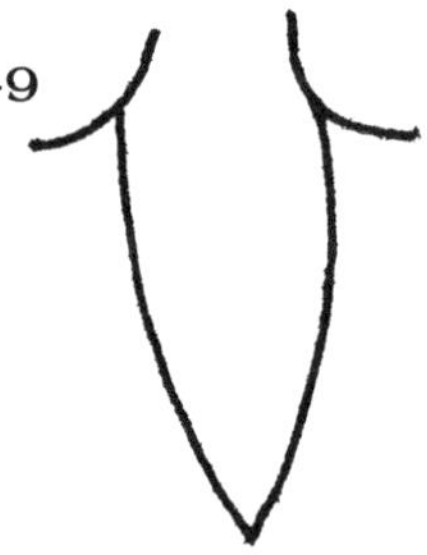

3·10

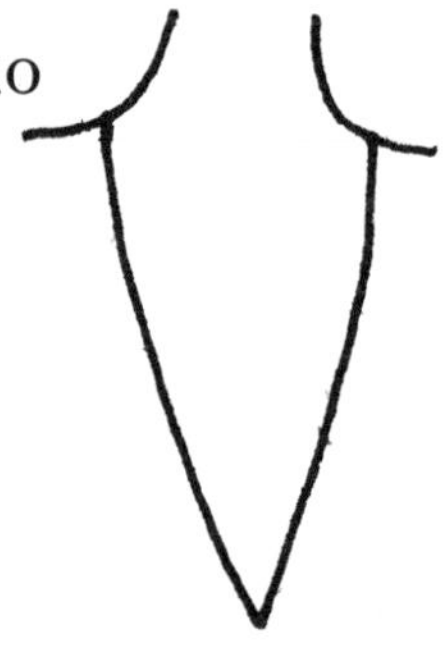

3·11

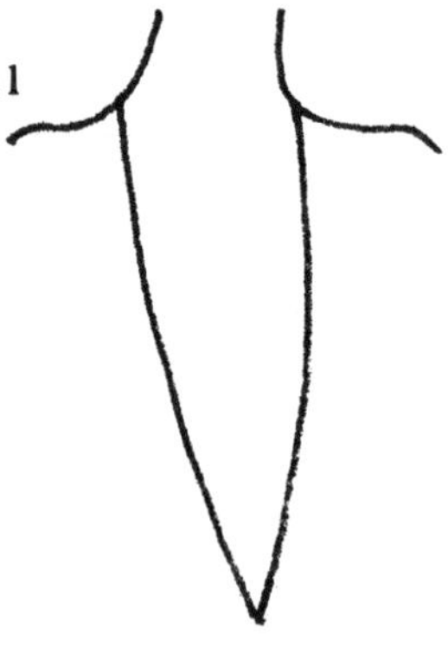

3·12

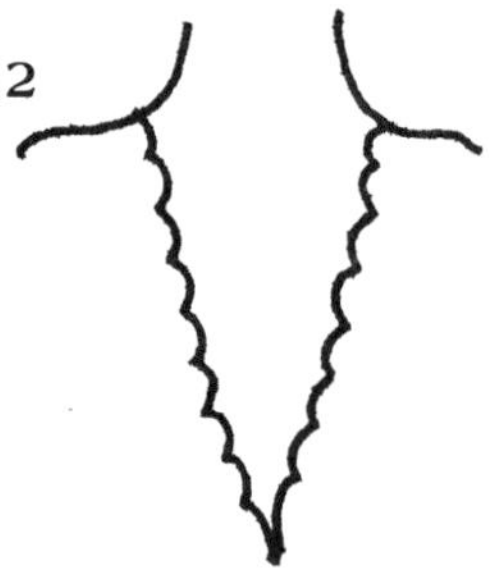

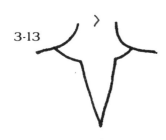

3-13

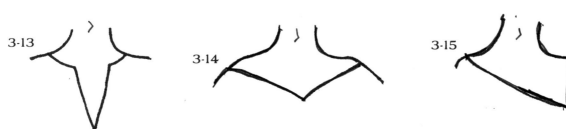

3-14

3-15

3-16

3-17

3-18

3-19

3-20

3-21

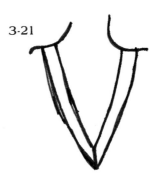

3-22

3-23

3-24

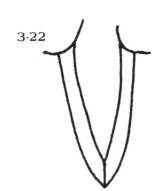

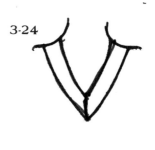

3-25

3-26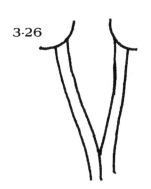

3-27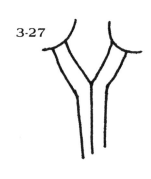

3-28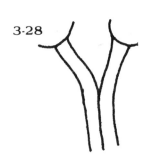

3-29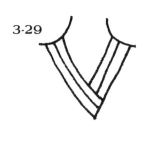

3-30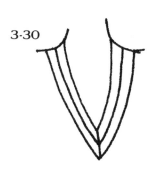

3-31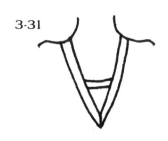

3-32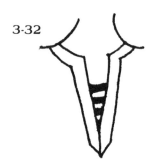

3-33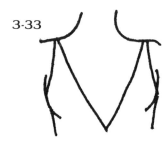

3-34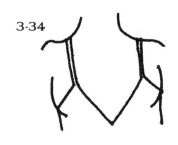

3-35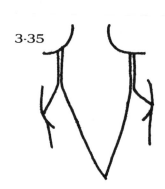

3-36

3-37

3-38

3-39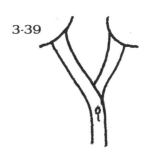

3-40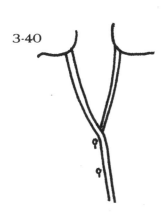

3-41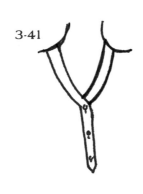

3-42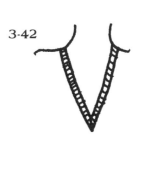

3-43

3-44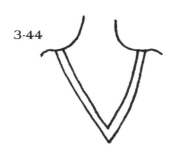

3-45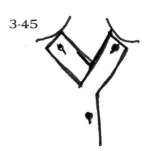

3-46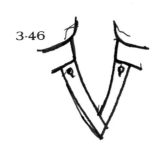

3-47

3-48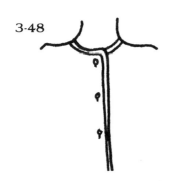

3-49

3-50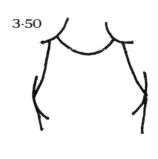

3-51

3-52

3-53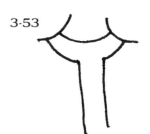

ROUND STYLING

3-54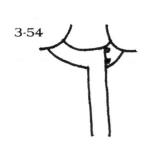

3-55

3-56

3-57

3-58

3-59

LOW ROUND STYLING

3-60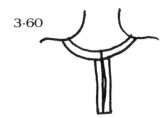

3-61

3-62

3-63

3-64

3-65

3-66

BATEAU/BOAT NECK STYLING

3-67

3-68

3-69

SCOOP/HORSESHOE/"U" STYLING

3-70

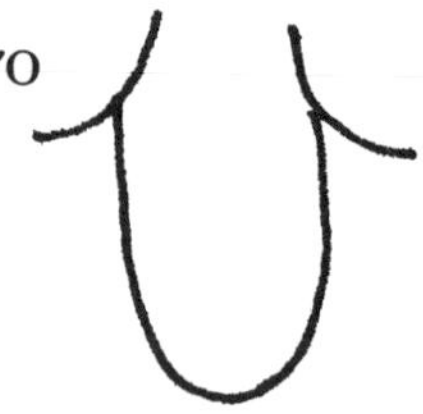

3-71

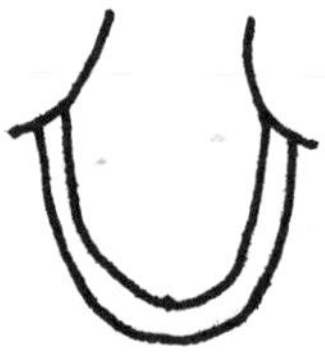

3-72

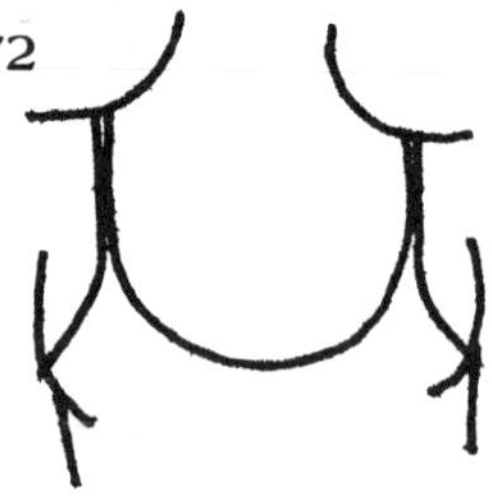

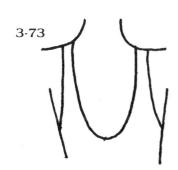

3-73

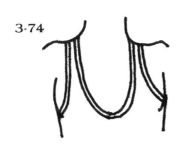

3-74

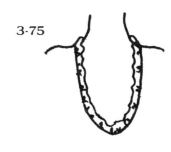

3-75

3-76

3-77

3-78

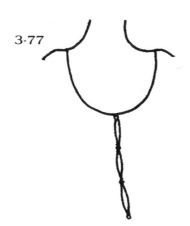

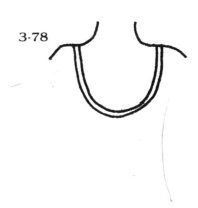

3-79

3-80

3·81

3·82

3·83

3·84

3·85 3·86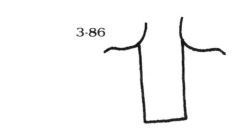

3·87

3·88 3·89

3·90

3·91 3·92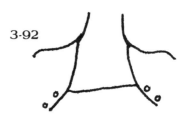

3-93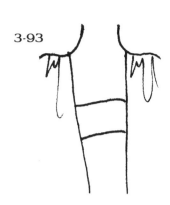

3-94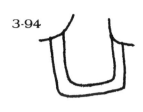

3-95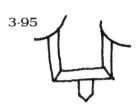

3-96

3-97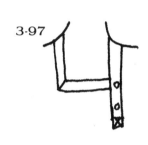

3-98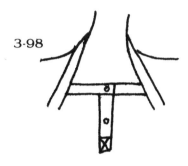

3-99

3-100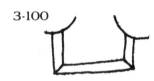

3-101

3-102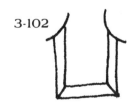

3-103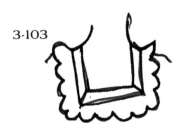

3-104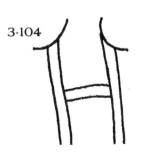

3-105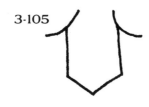

3-106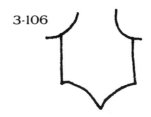

3-107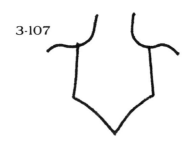

3-108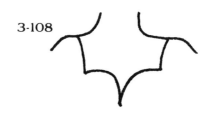

3-109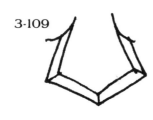

3-110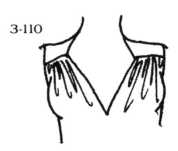

3-111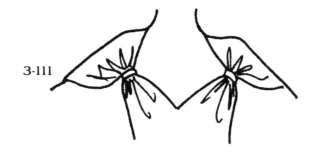

3-112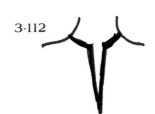

3-113

3-114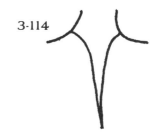

3-115

3-116

3-117

3-118

3-119

3-120

3-121

3-122

3-123

3-124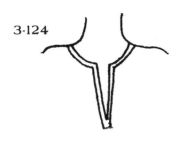

3-125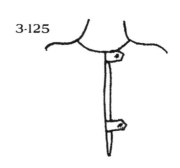

3-126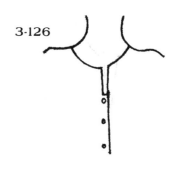

3-127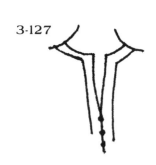

3-128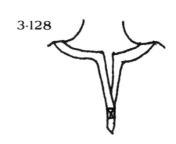

3-129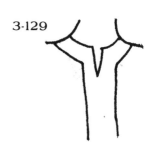

3-130

3-131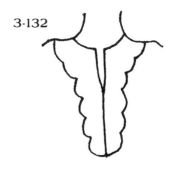

3-132

3-133

3-134

3-135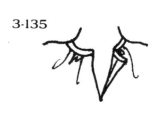

3·136
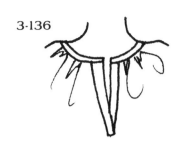

3·137
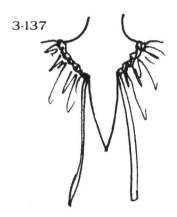

3·138
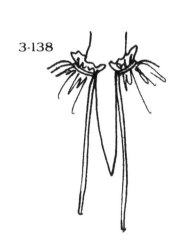

3·139

RAISED NECKLINE STYLING

3·140

3·141

3·142

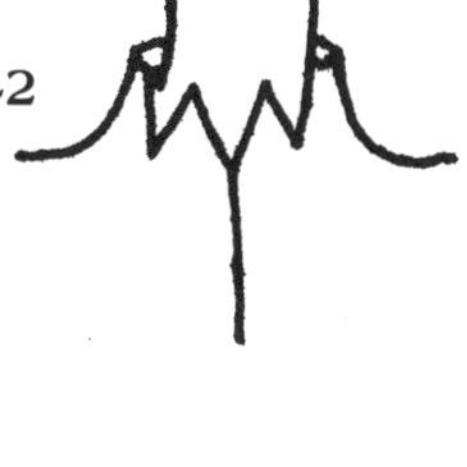

3-143

3-144

3-145

3-146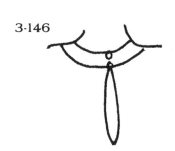

3-147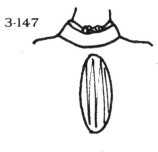

3-148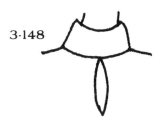

3-149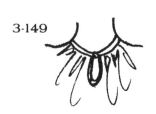

3-150

3-151

3-152

3-153

3-154

3-155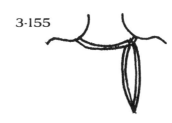

3-156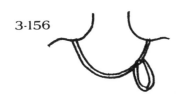

3-157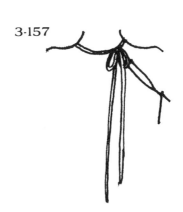

SURPLICE/SIDE-WRAPPED STYLING

3-158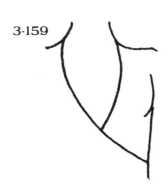

3-159

3-160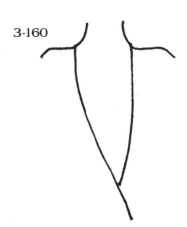

SURPLICE/SIDE-WRAPPED STYLING

3-161

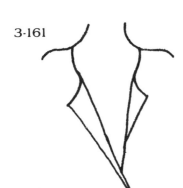

3-162

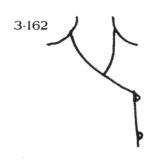

3-163

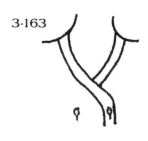

3-164

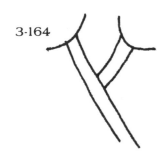

3-165

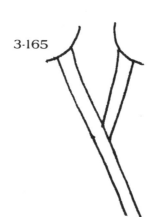

3-166

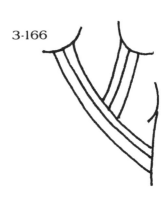

3-167

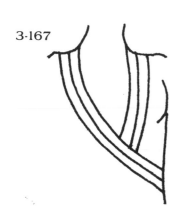

3-168

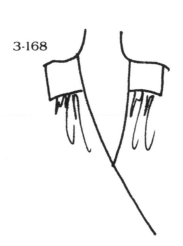

3-169

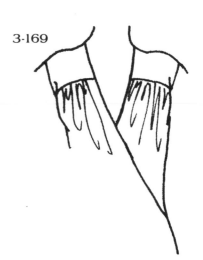

SURPLICE/SIDE-WRAPPED STYLING

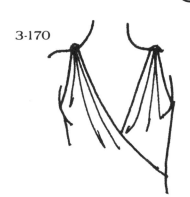

3-170

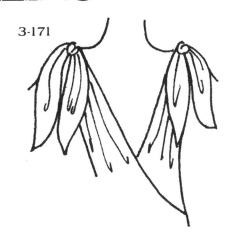

3-171

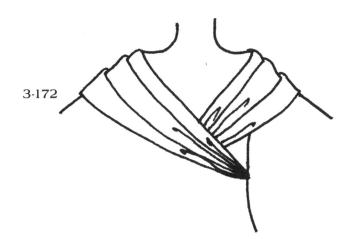

3-172

COWL/COWL DRAPE STYLING

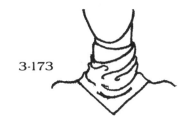

3-173

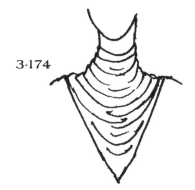

3-174

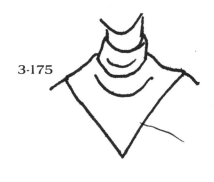

3-175

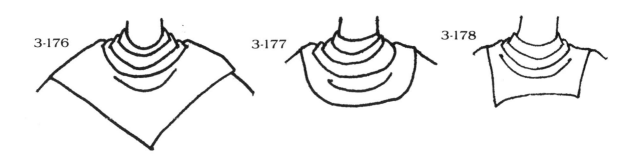

3-176  3-177 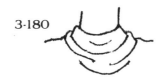 3-178

3-179  3-180 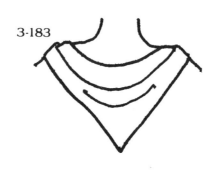 3-181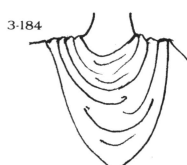

3-182 3-183 3-184

3-185 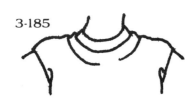 3-186 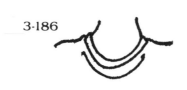 3-187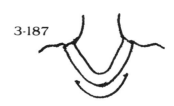

3-188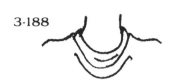

3-189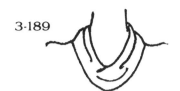

3-190

3-191

3-192

3-193

3-194

3-195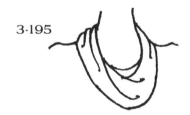

3-196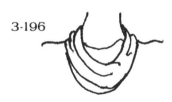

3-197

3-198

3-199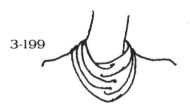

3-200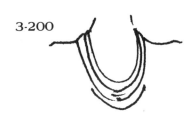

3-201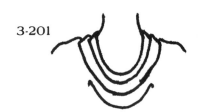

3-202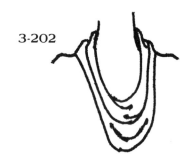

3-203

3-204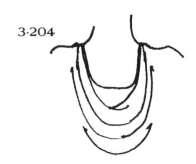

3-205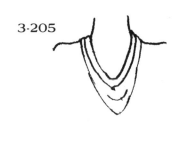

3-206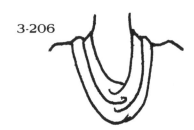

3-207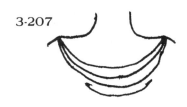

3-208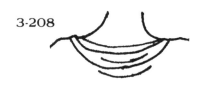

3-209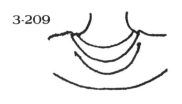

3-210

3-211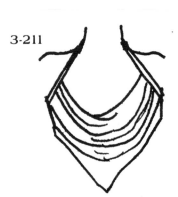

3-212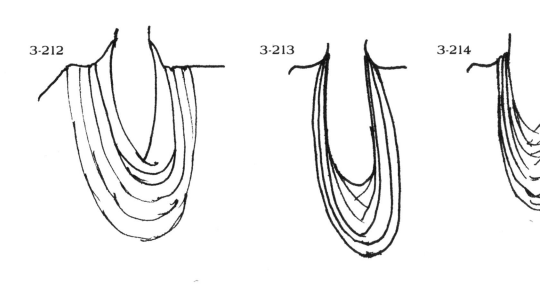

3-213

3-214

3-215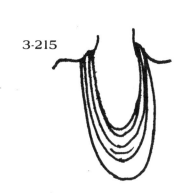

3-216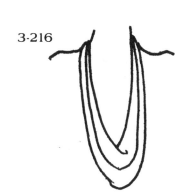

3-217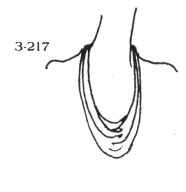

3-218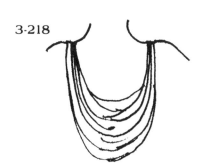

3-219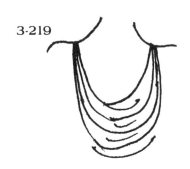

3-220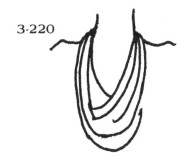

3-221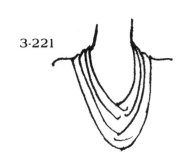

3-222

3-223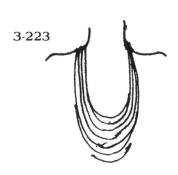

Back View
3-224

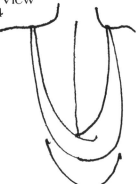

Back View
3-225

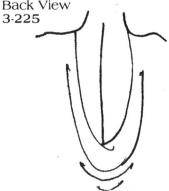

Back View
3-226

Back View
3-227

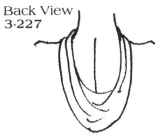

Back View
3-228

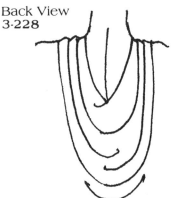

Back View
3-229

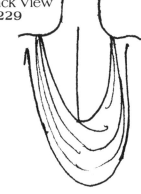

Back View
3-230

Back View
3-231

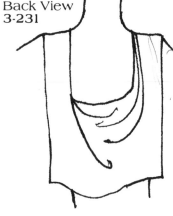

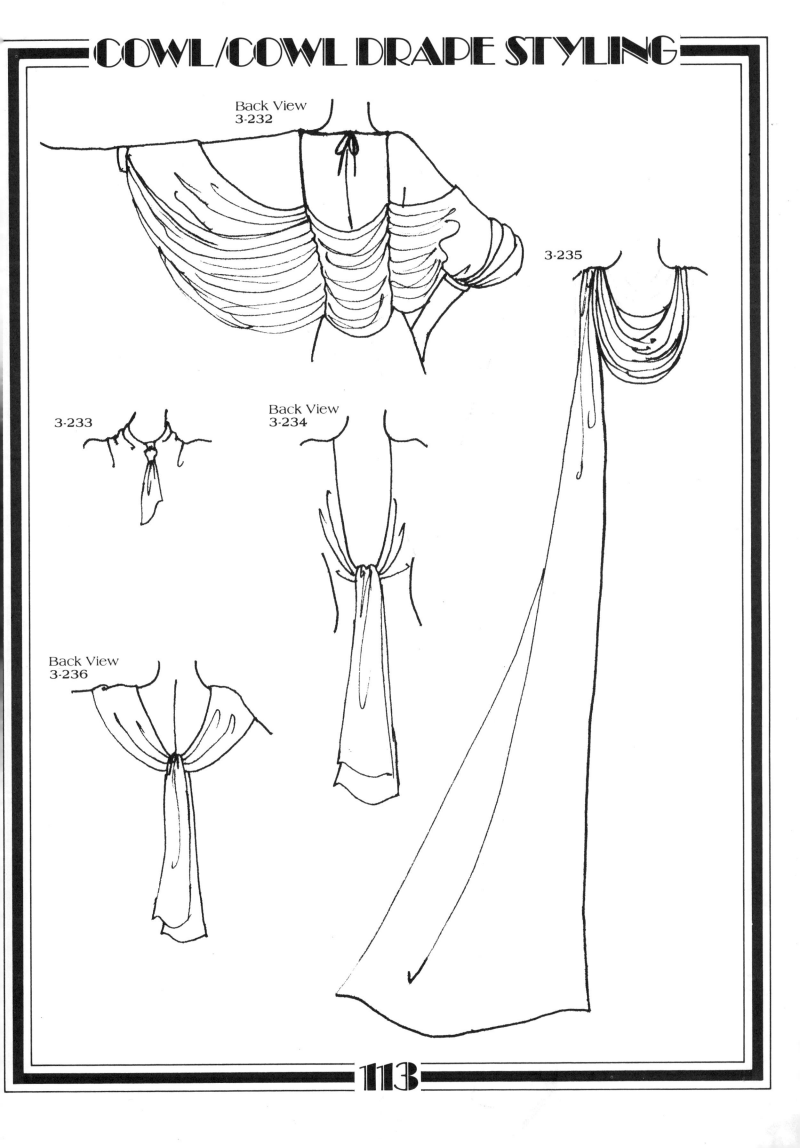

Back View
3-232

3-235

3-233

Back View
3-234

Back View
3-236

3-237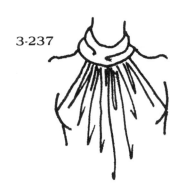

3-238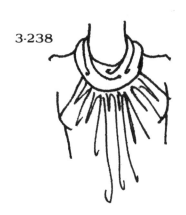

3-239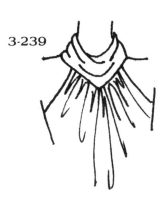

3-240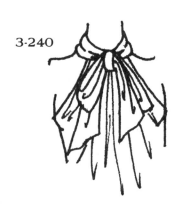

3-241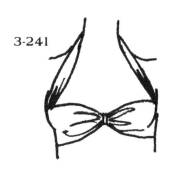

3-242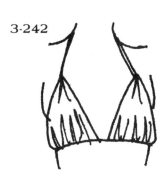

3-243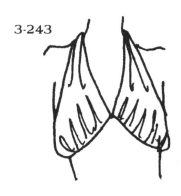

3-244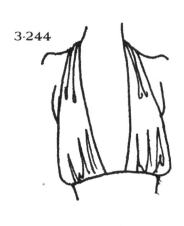

3-245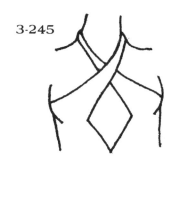

3-246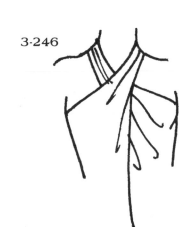

3-247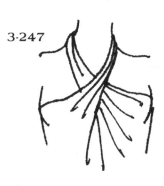

3-248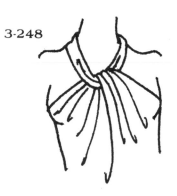

3·249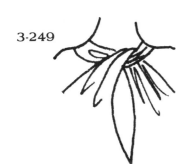

3·250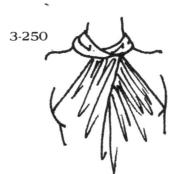

3·251

3·252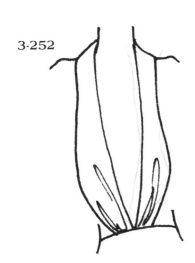

3·253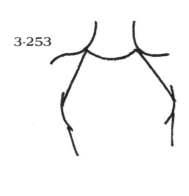

3·254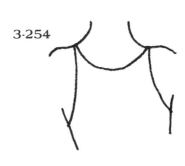

3·255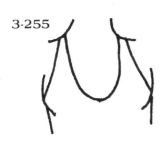

3·256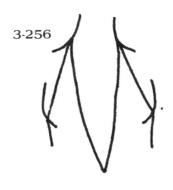

3·257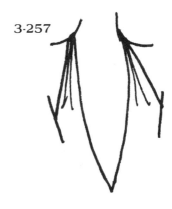

3·258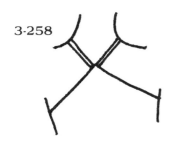

3·259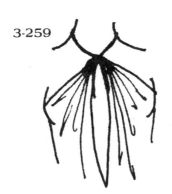

3·260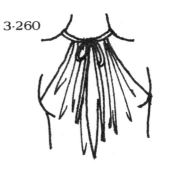

3-261
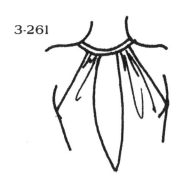

3-262
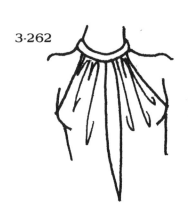

3-263
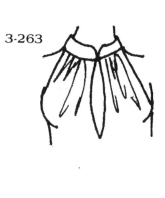

3-264
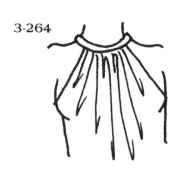

3-265
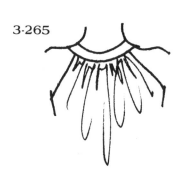

3-266
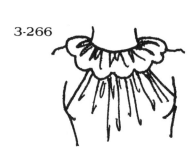

3-267
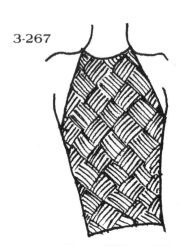

3-268
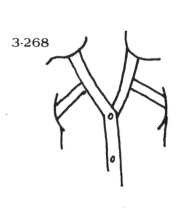

3-269

3-270
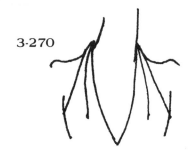

Back View
3-271
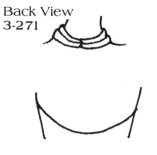

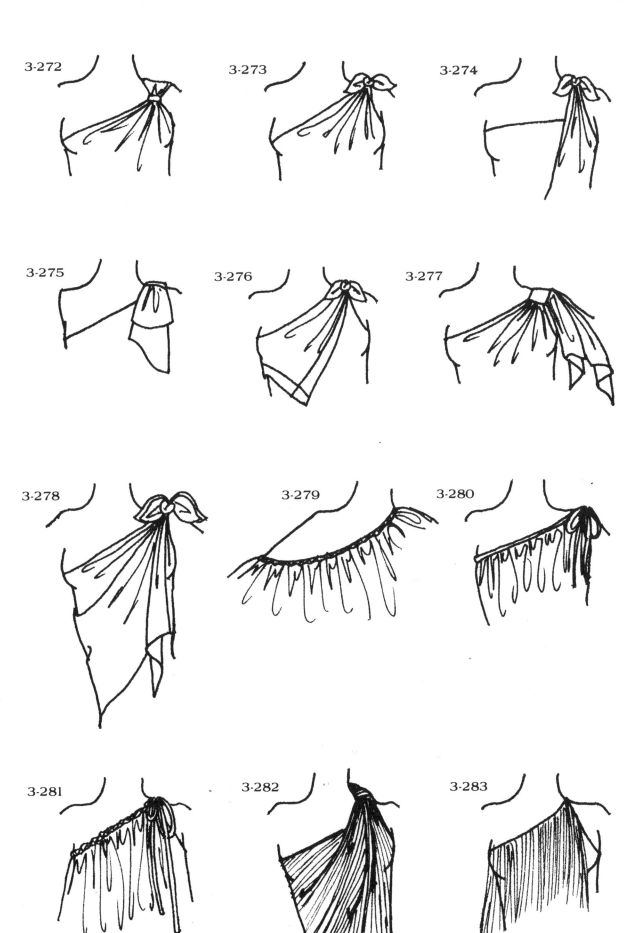

3-272

3-273

3-274

3-275

3-276

3-277

3-278

3-279

3-280

3-281

3-282

3-283

3-284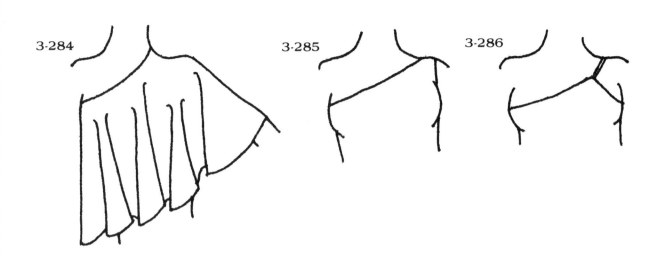

3-285

3-286

3-287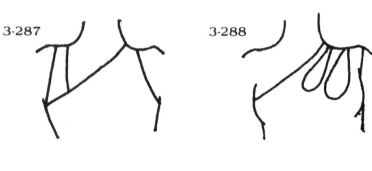

3-288

3-289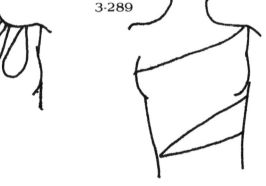

3-290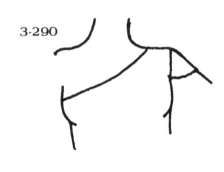

3-291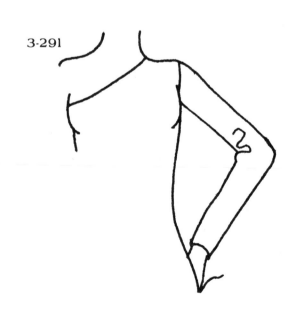

3-292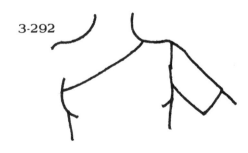

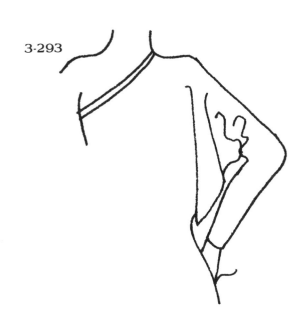

3-293

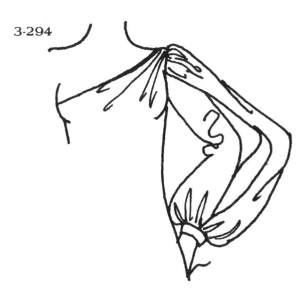

3-294

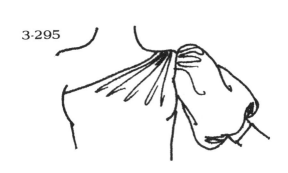

3-295

STRAPLESS STYLING

3-296

3-297

3-298

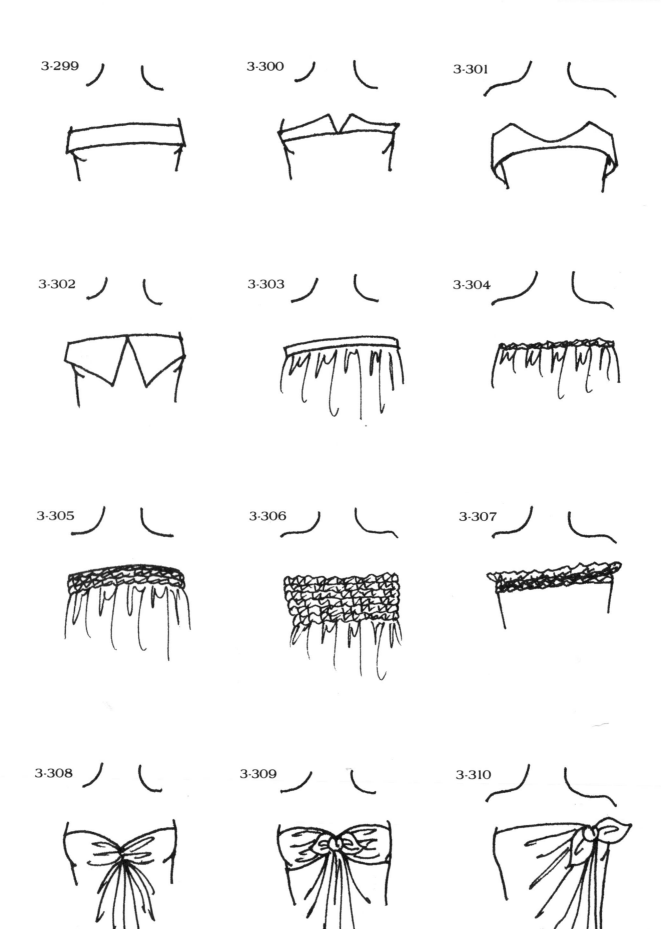

3-299 3-300 3-301

3-302 3-303 3-304

3-305 3-306 3-307

3-308 3-309 3-310

3-311
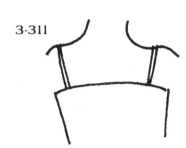

3-312
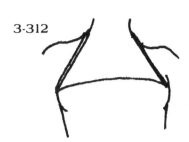

3-313
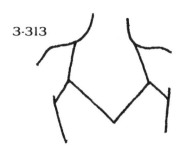

3-314
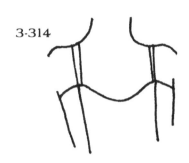

3-315
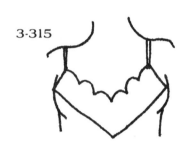

3-316
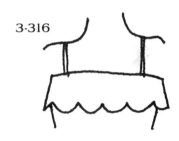

3-317
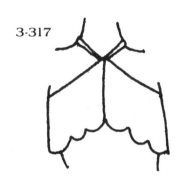

3-318

3-319
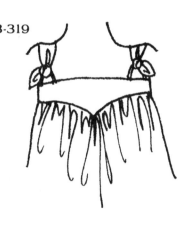

3-320
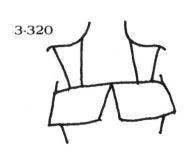

3-321
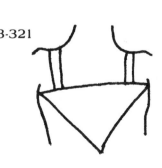

3-322
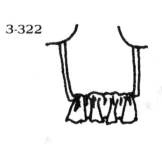

CAMISOLE STYLING

3-323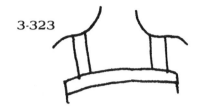

3-324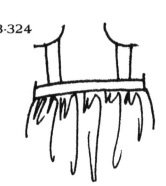

3-325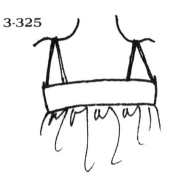

3-326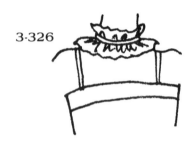

3-327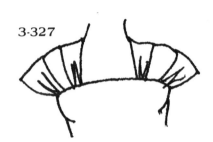

3-328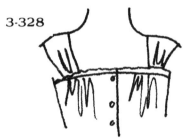

3-329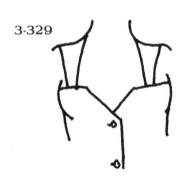

3-330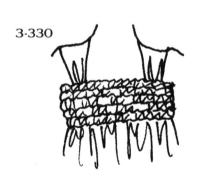

3-331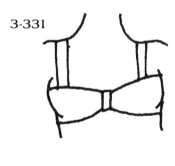

3-332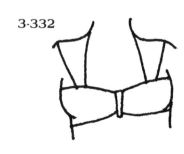

3-333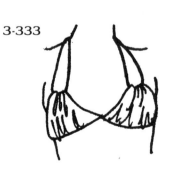

3-334
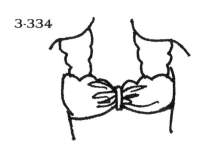

3-335

3-336
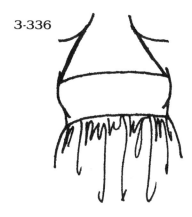

3-337

3-338
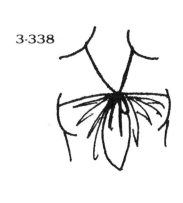

3-339
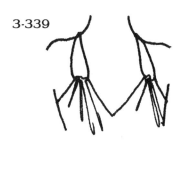

3-340
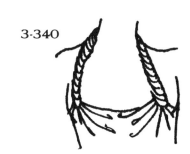

3-341
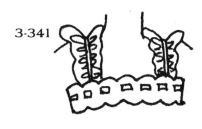

3-342
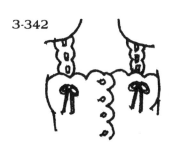

3-343

3-344
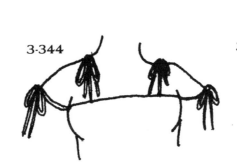

3-345
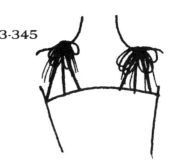

3-346

3-347
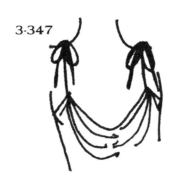

3-348
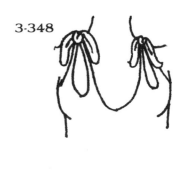

3-349
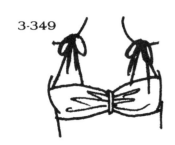

3-350
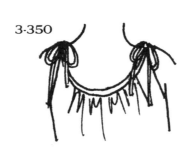

3-351
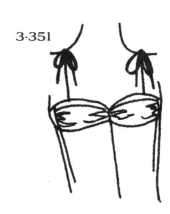

3-352
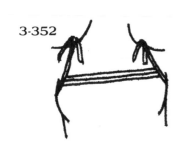

3-353

3-354
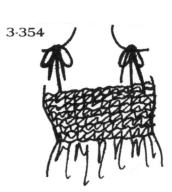

3-355
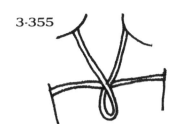

3-356
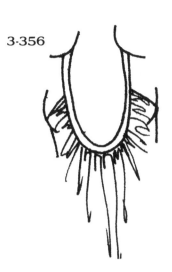

3-357

3-358
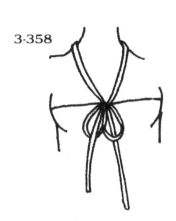

3-359
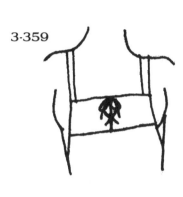

3-360
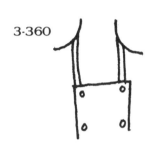

3-361
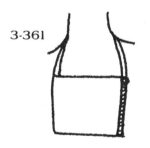

3-362
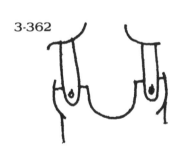

3-363
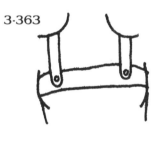

3-364
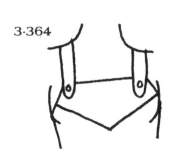

3-365

3-366
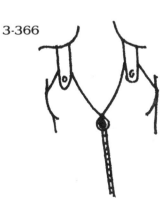

3-367

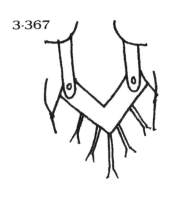

3-368

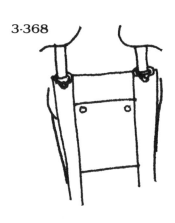

3-369

3-370

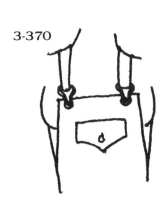

3-371

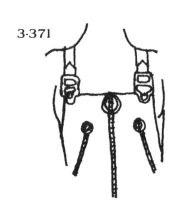

3-372

NECKLINES WITH STRAPWORK DETAILS

3-373

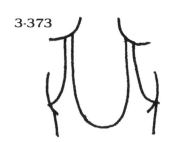

Back View
3-374

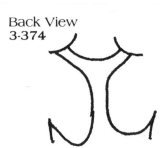

3-375

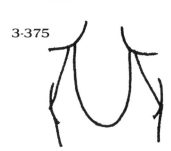

Back View
3-376

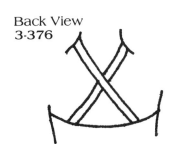

3-377

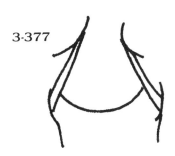

Back View
3-378

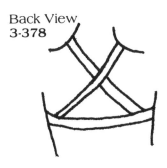

3-379

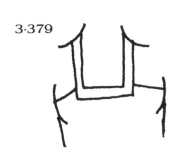

Back View
3-380

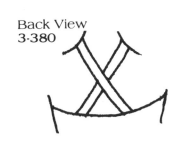

3-381

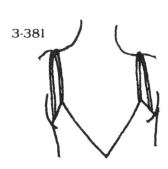

Back View
3-382

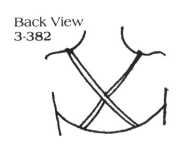

3-383

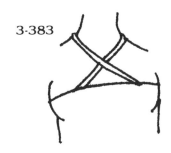

3-384

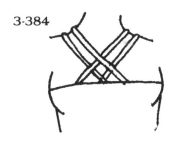

3-385

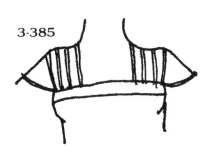

3-386

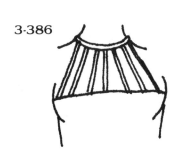

3-387

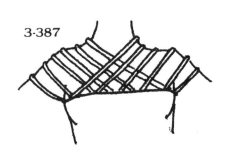

NECKLINES WITH STRAPWORK DETAILS

Back View
3-388

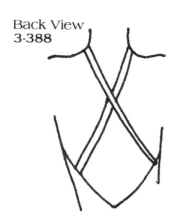

Back View
3-389

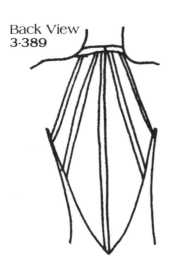

Back View
3-390

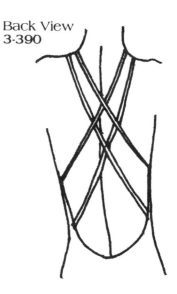

NECKLINES WITH GATHERING OR SHIRRING

3-391

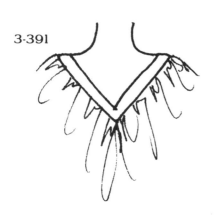

3-392

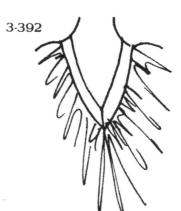

3-393

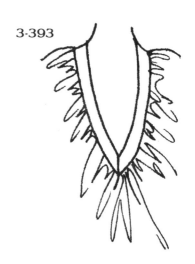

3-394

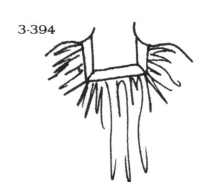

3-395

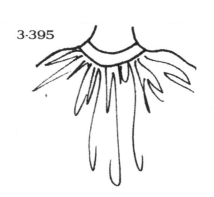

3-396

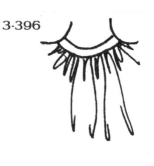

3-397
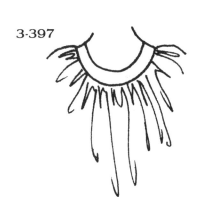

3-398
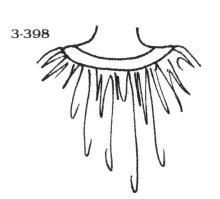

3-399
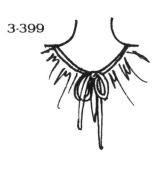

3-400
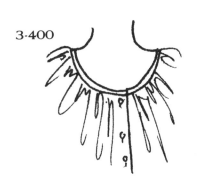

3-401
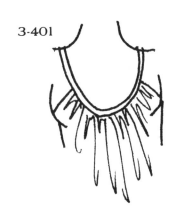

3-402
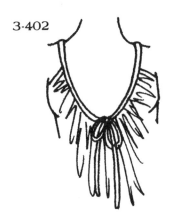

3-403
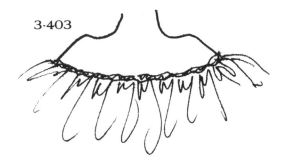

3-404
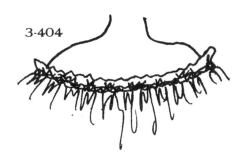

3-405
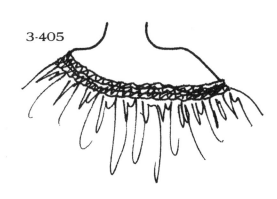

3-406
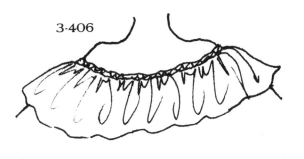

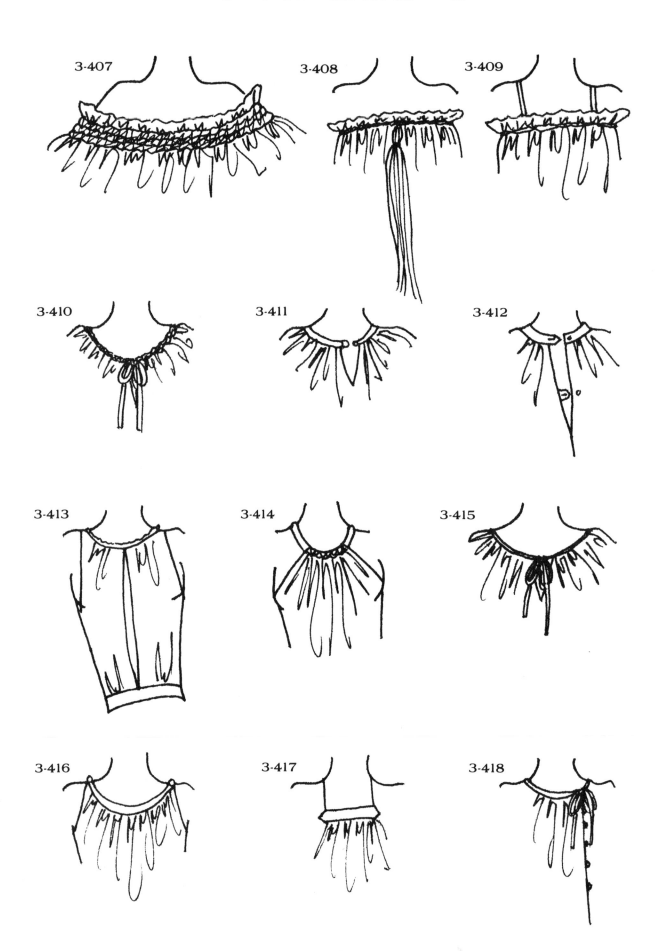

3-407

3-408

3-409

3-410

3-411

3-412

3-413

3-414

3-415

3-416

3-417

3-418

3-419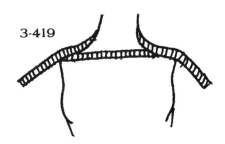

3-420

3-421

3-422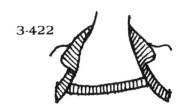

3-423

3-424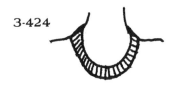

3-425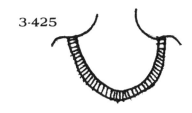

3-426

3-427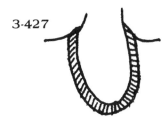

3-428

3-429

3-430

3-431

3-432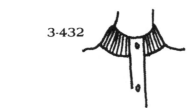

3-433

3-434

3-435

3-436

3-437

3-438

3-439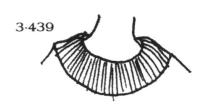

3-440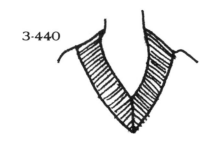

3-441

3-442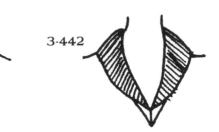

3-443

3-444

3-445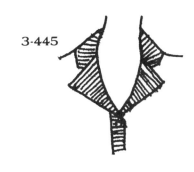

3-446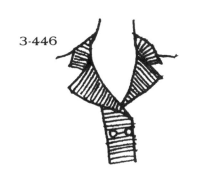

3-447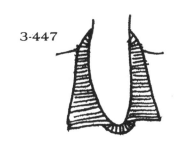

3-448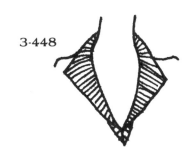

3-449

3-450

3-451

3-452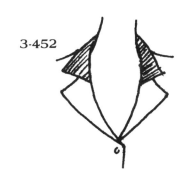

3-453

3-454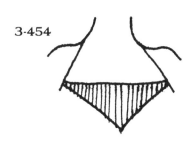

3-455

3-456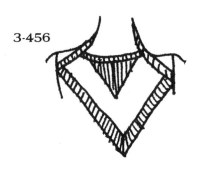

3-457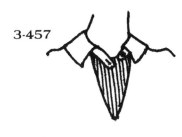

3-458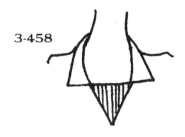

3-459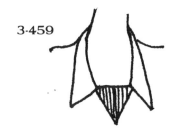

3-460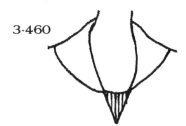

3-461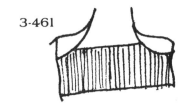

3-462

3-463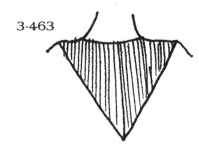

3-464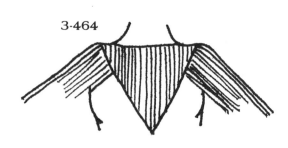

3-465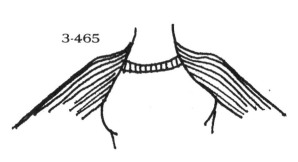

FOUR · NECKLINE DETAILS

4-1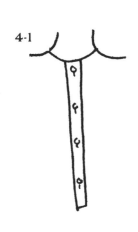

4-2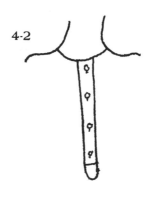

4-3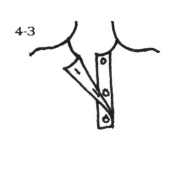

4-4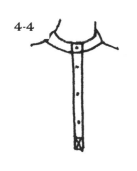

4-5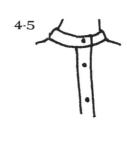

4-6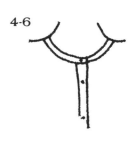

4-7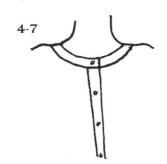

4-8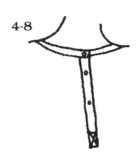

4-9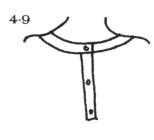

4-10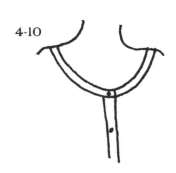

4-11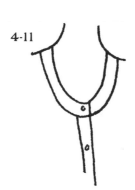

4-12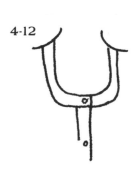

4-13
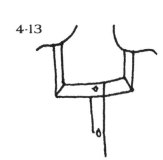

4-14
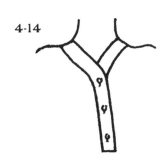

4-15

4-16
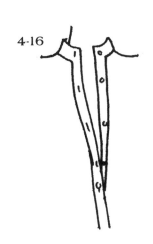

4-17
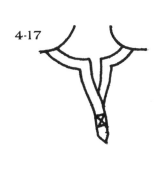

4-18
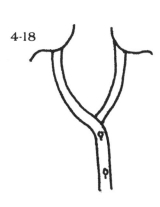

4-19
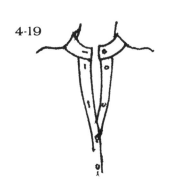

4-20
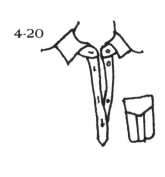

4-21
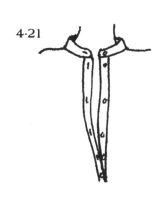

4-22
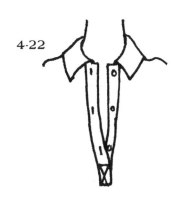

4-23
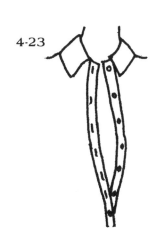

4-24
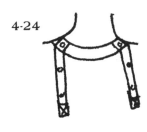

4-25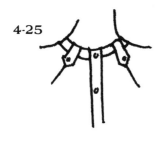

4-26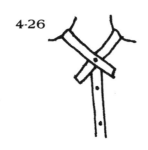

4-27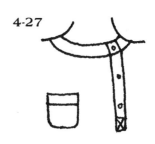

4-28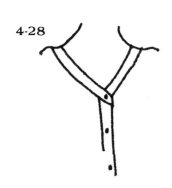

4-29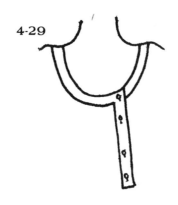

4-30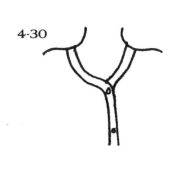

4-31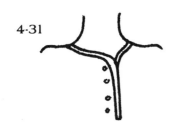

4-32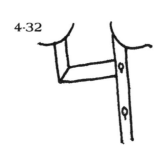

4-33

4-34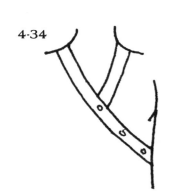

4-35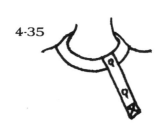

4-36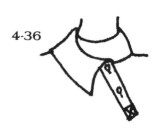

4-37

4-38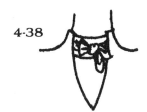

4-39

4-40

4-41

4-42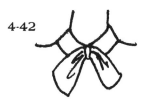

4-43

4-44

4-45

4-46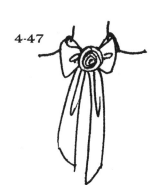

4-47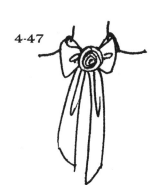

4-48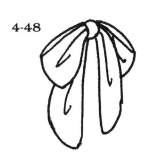

4-49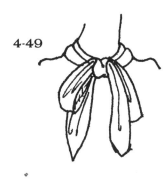

4-50

4-51

4-52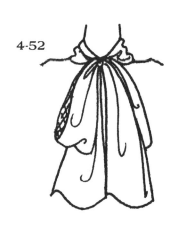

4-53

4-54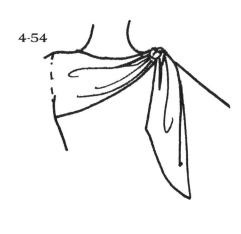

4-55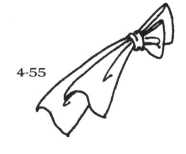

4-56

4-57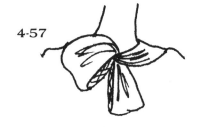

4-58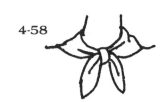

4-59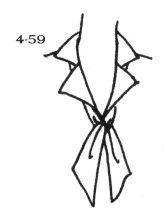

4-60
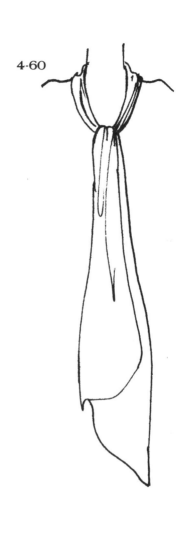

4-61

4-62

4-63
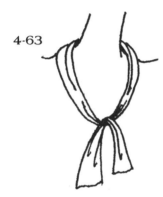

4-64

4-65
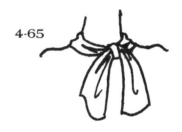

4-66

4-67

4-68
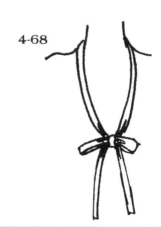

4-69
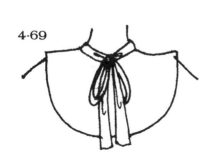

4-70
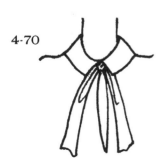

4-71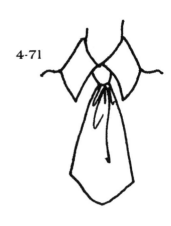

4-72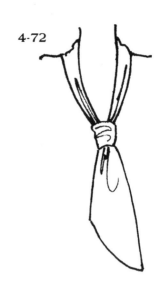

4-73

4-74

4-76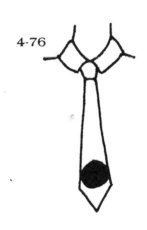

4-77

4-75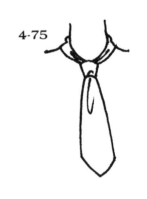

4-78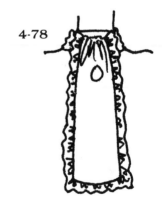

4-79

4-80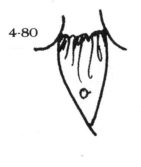

4-81

4-82

4-83
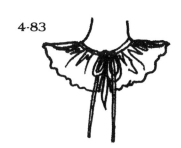

4-84
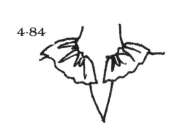

4-85
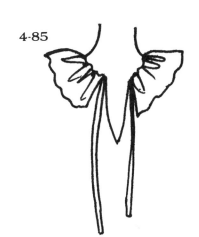

4-86
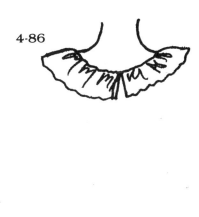

4-87
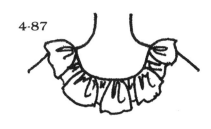

4-88
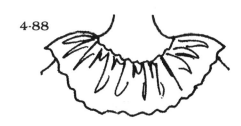

4-89
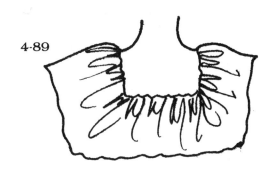

4-90

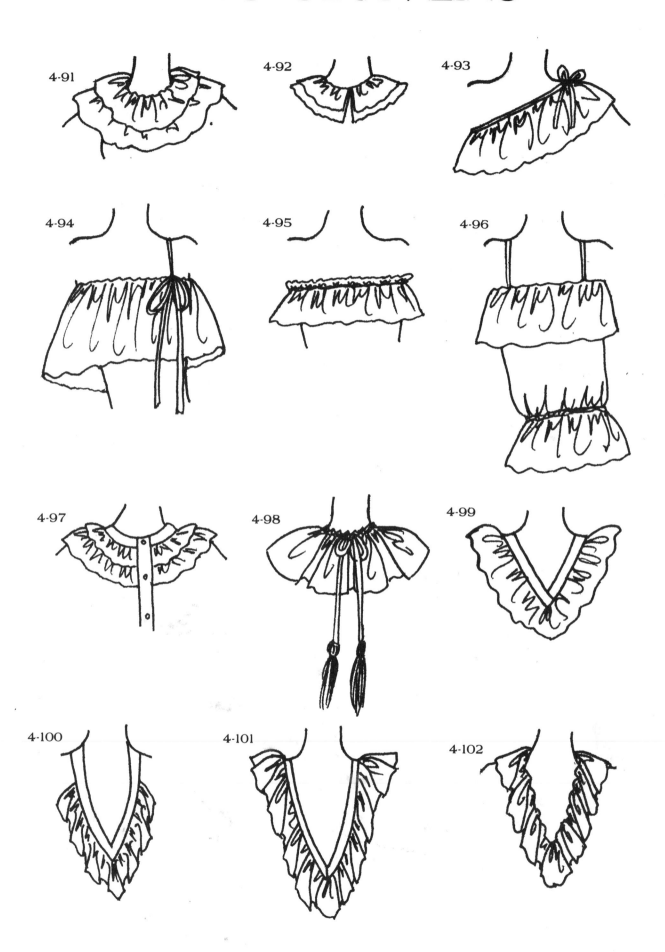

4-91

4-92

4-93

4-94

4-95

4-96

4-97

4-98

4-99

4-100

4-101

4-102

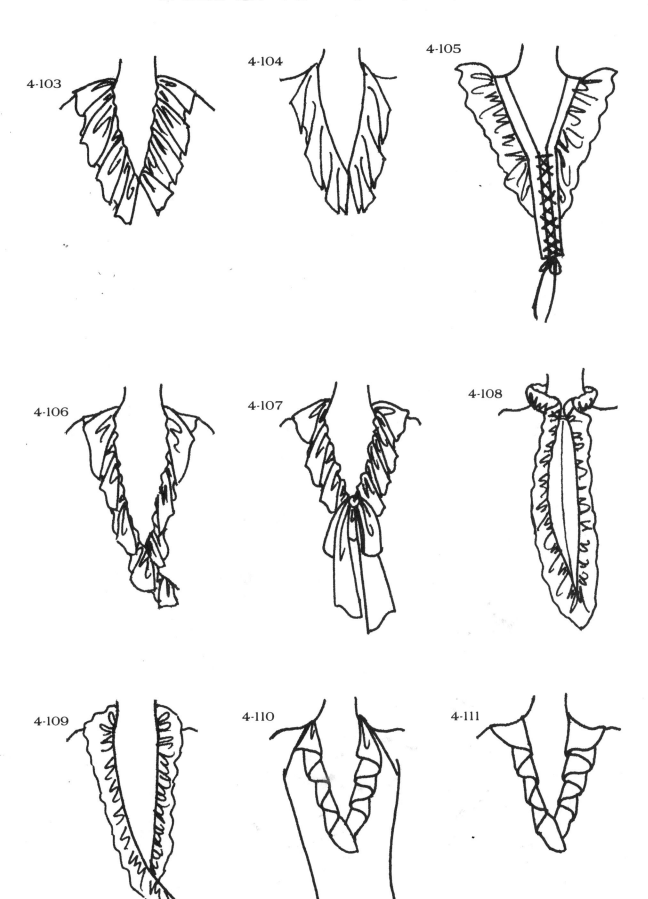

4-103

4-104

4-105

4-106

4-107

4-108

4-109

4-110

4-111

RUFFLED/GATHERED NECKLINE
FLOUNCE STYLING

4-112

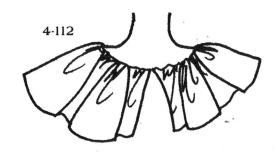

4-113

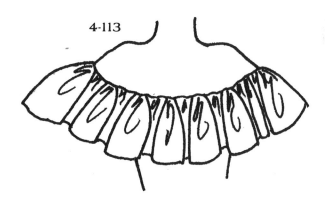

4-114

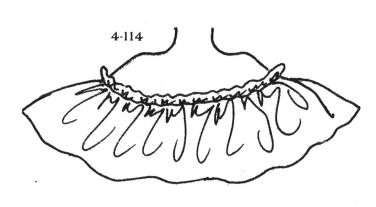

4-115

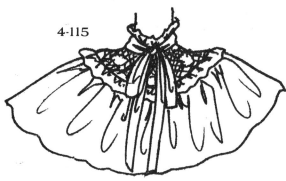

4-116

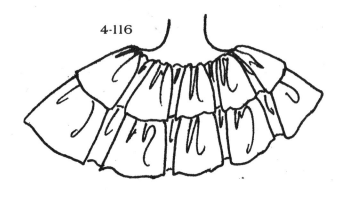

4-117

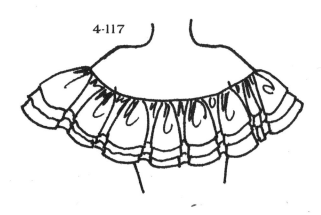

4-118

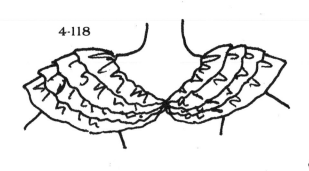

4-119

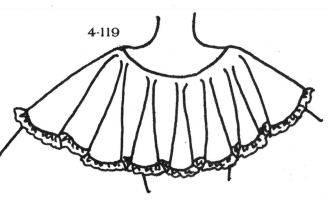

4-120
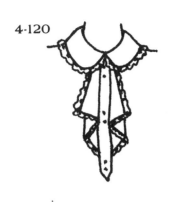

4-121
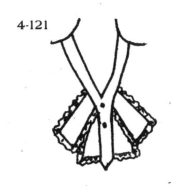

4-122

4-123

4-124
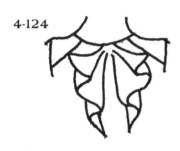

4-125

4-126
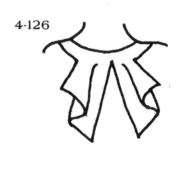

4-127
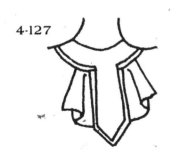

4-128

4-129

4-130
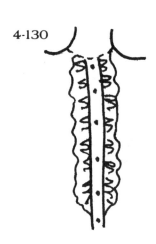

4-131
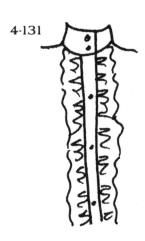

4-132
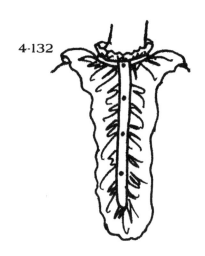

4-133
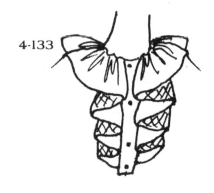

4-134
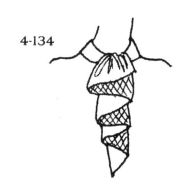

4-135

4-136
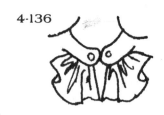

4-137

4-138
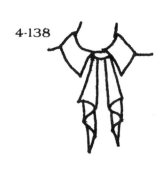

4-139

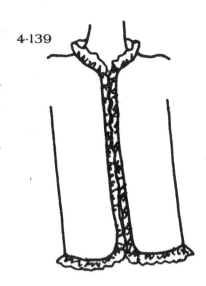

4-140

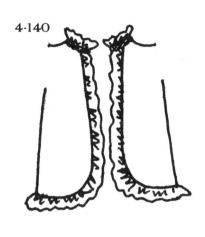

4-141

4-142

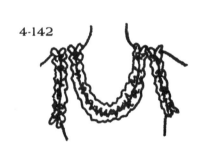

4-143

4-144

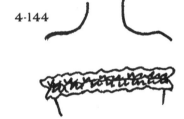

4-145

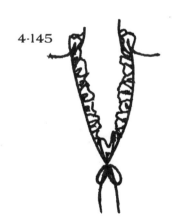

4-146

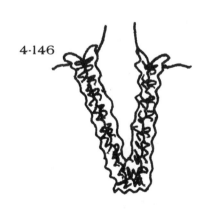

4-147

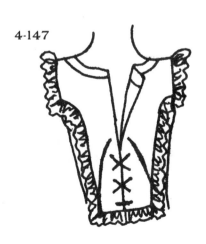

GATHERED LACE TRIMMING (MEDIUM WIDTH)

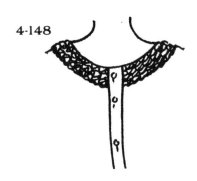

4-148

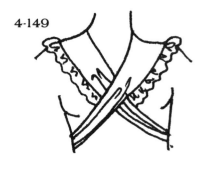

4-149

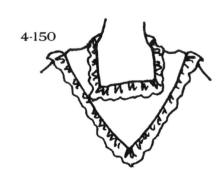

4-150

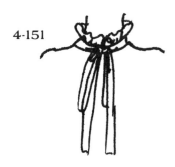

4-151

GATHERED LACE TRIMMING (NARROW WIDTH)

4-152

4-153

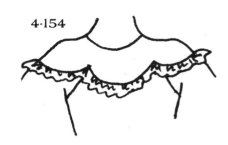

4-154

4-155

4-156

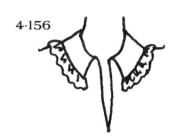

4-157

4-158

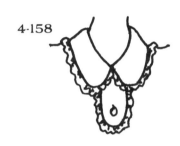

4-159

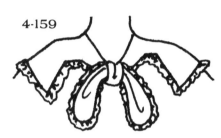

4-160

4-161

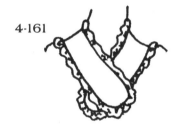

4-162

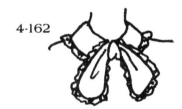

4-163

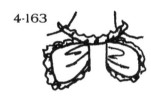

4-164

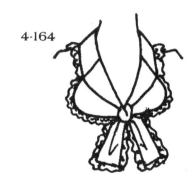

4-165

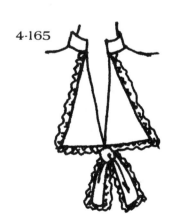

4-166

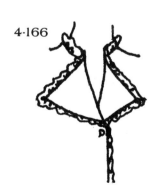

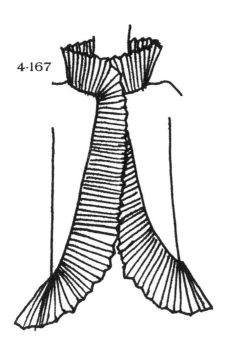

4-167

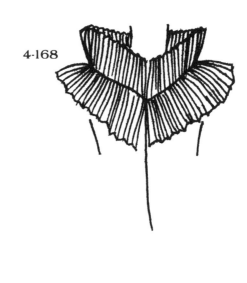

4-168

4-169

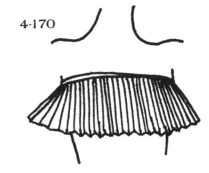

4-170

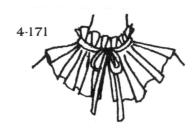

4-171

FIVE·SLEEVES

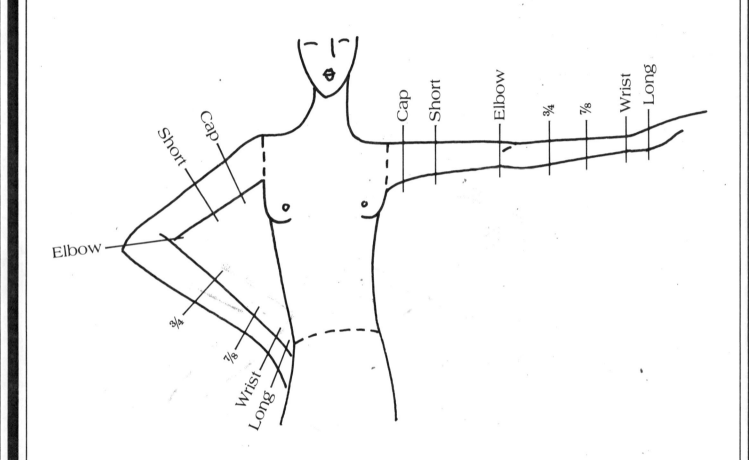

Short
Cap
Elbow
3/4
7/8
Wrist
Long

Cap
Short
Elbow
3/4
7/8
Wrist
Long

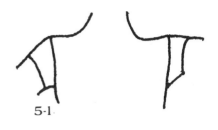

5-1

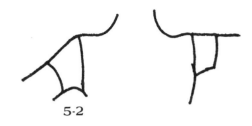

5-2

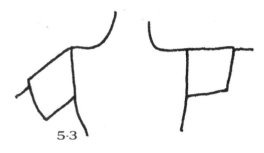

5-3

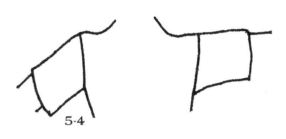

5-4

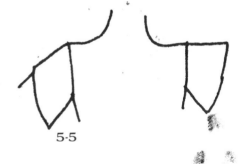

5-5

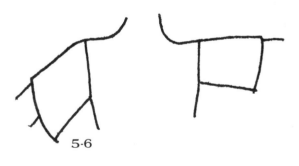

5-6

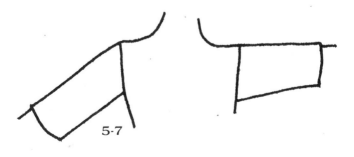

5-7

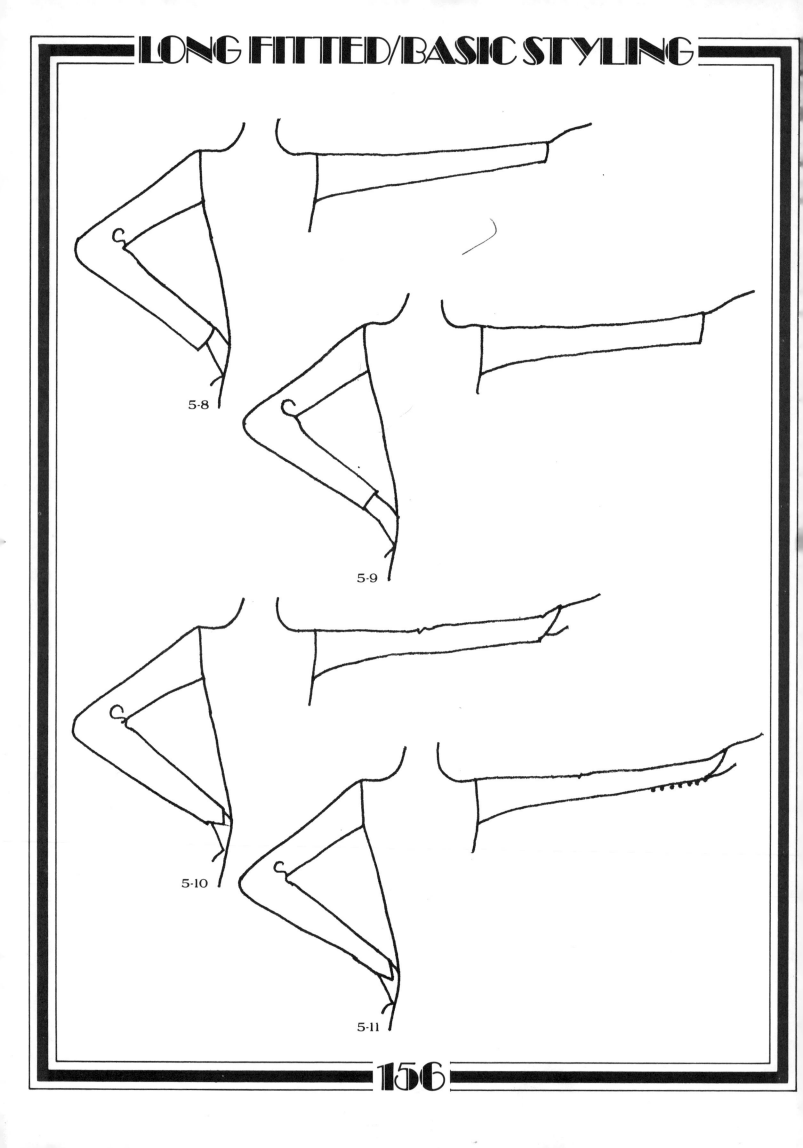

5-8

5-9

5-10

5-11

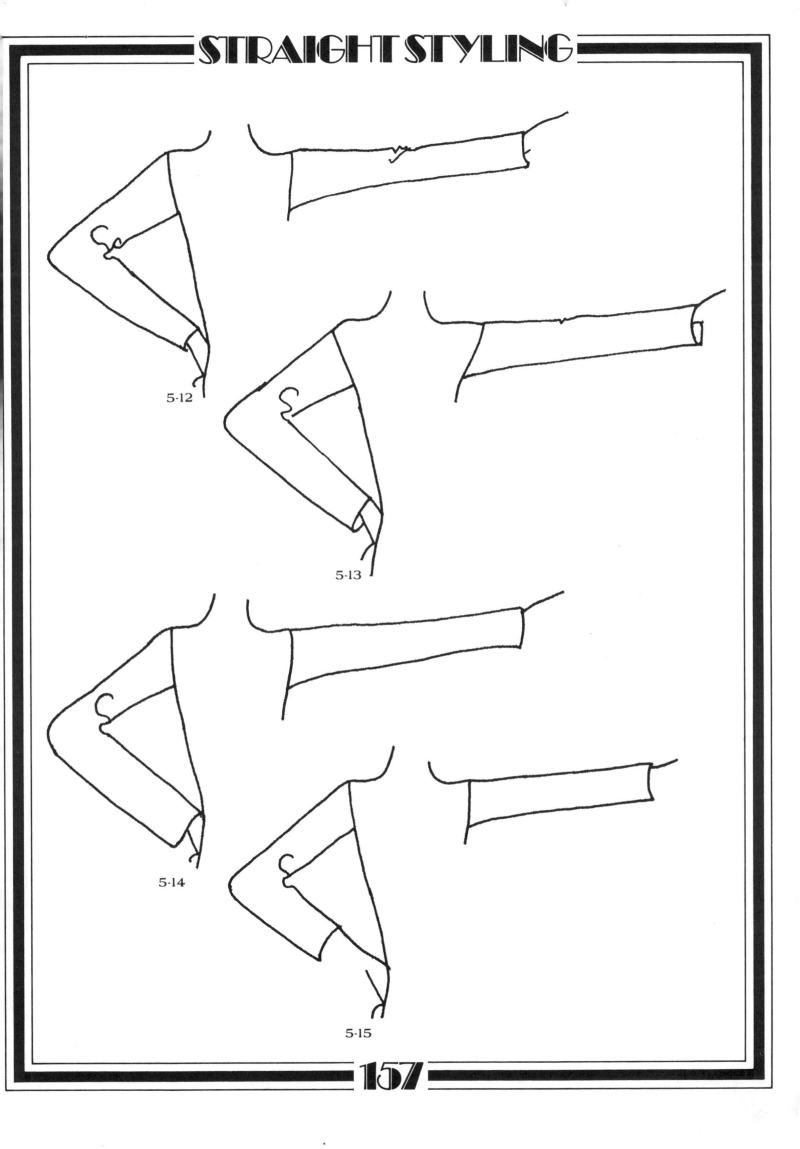

5-12

5-13

5-14

5-15

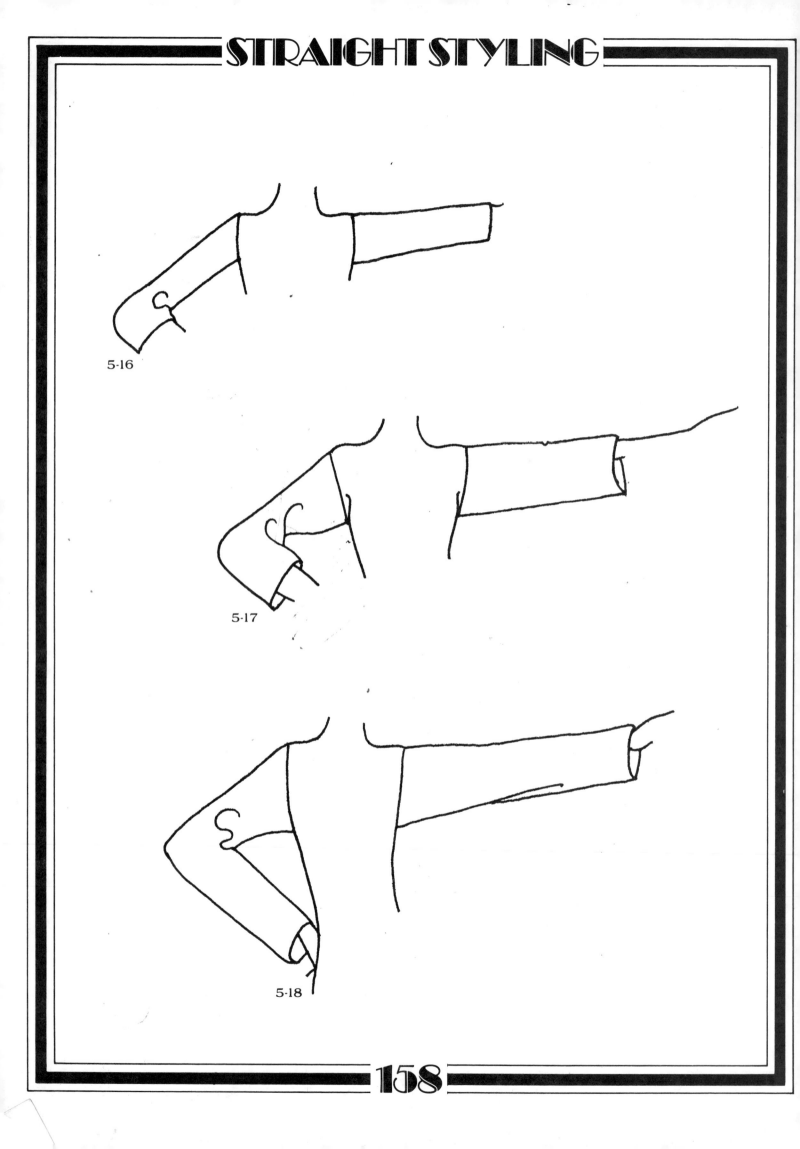

5-16

5-17

5-18

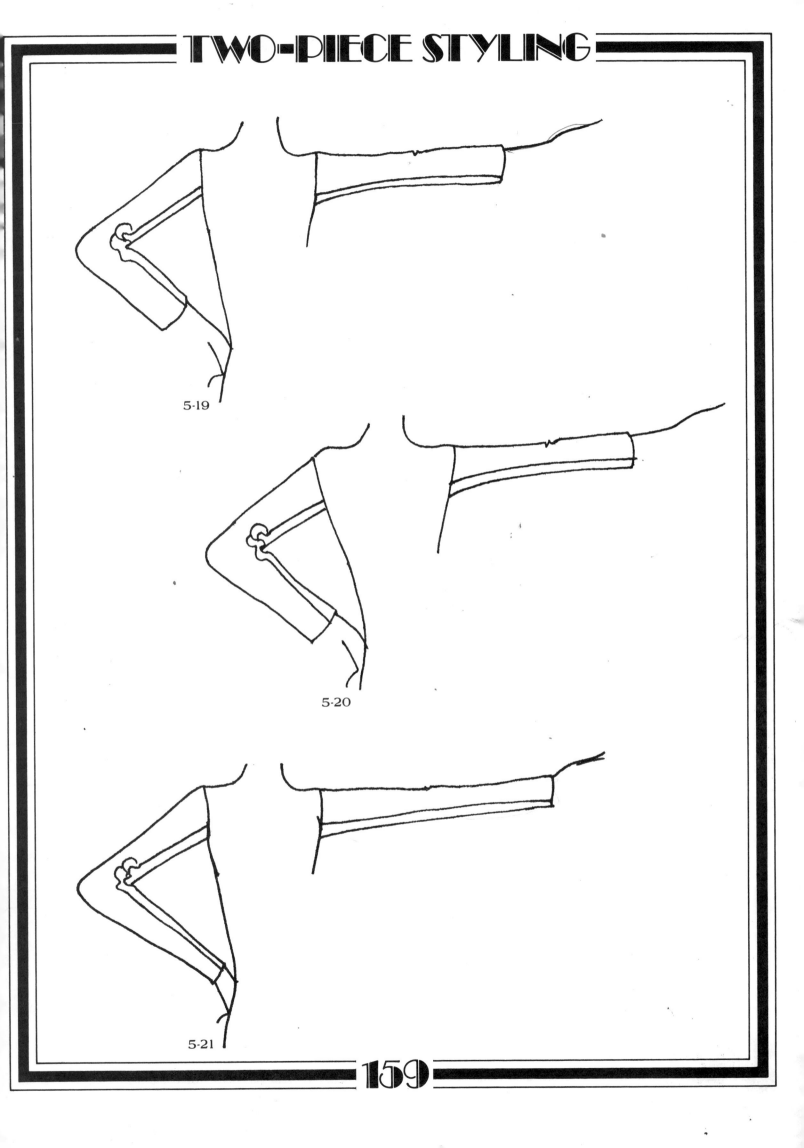

5-19

5-20

5-21

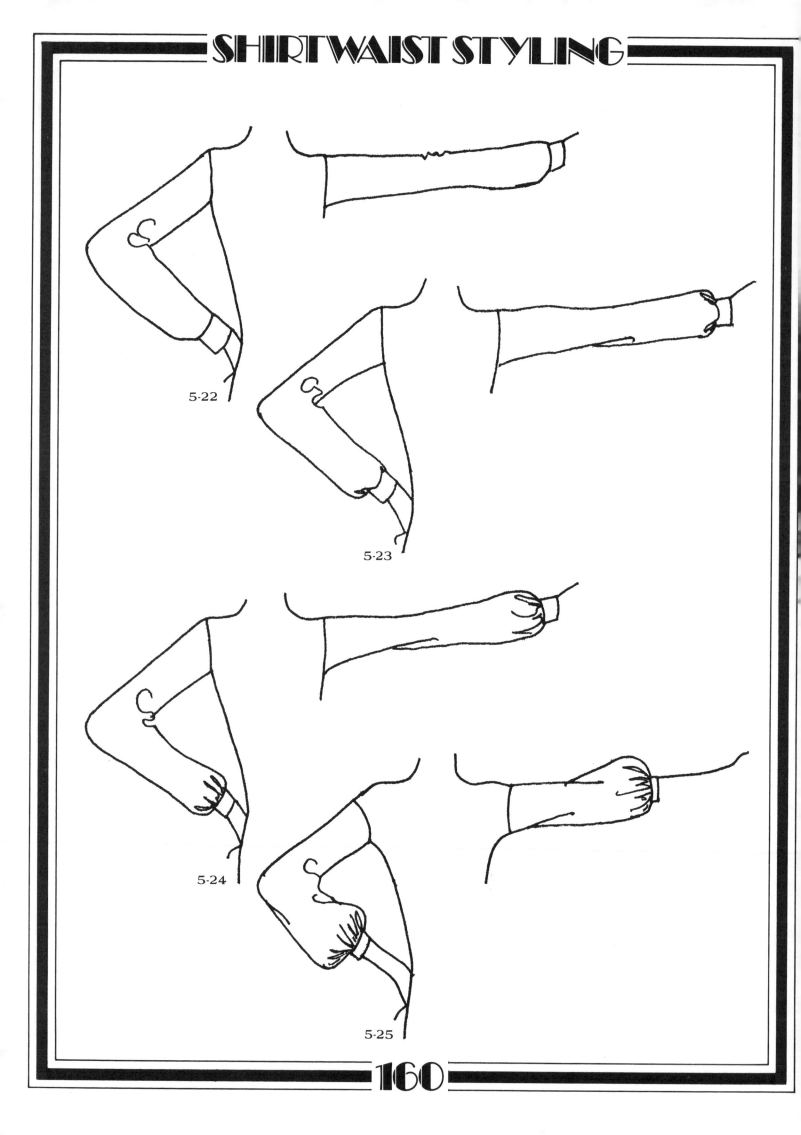

5-22

5-23

5-24

5-25

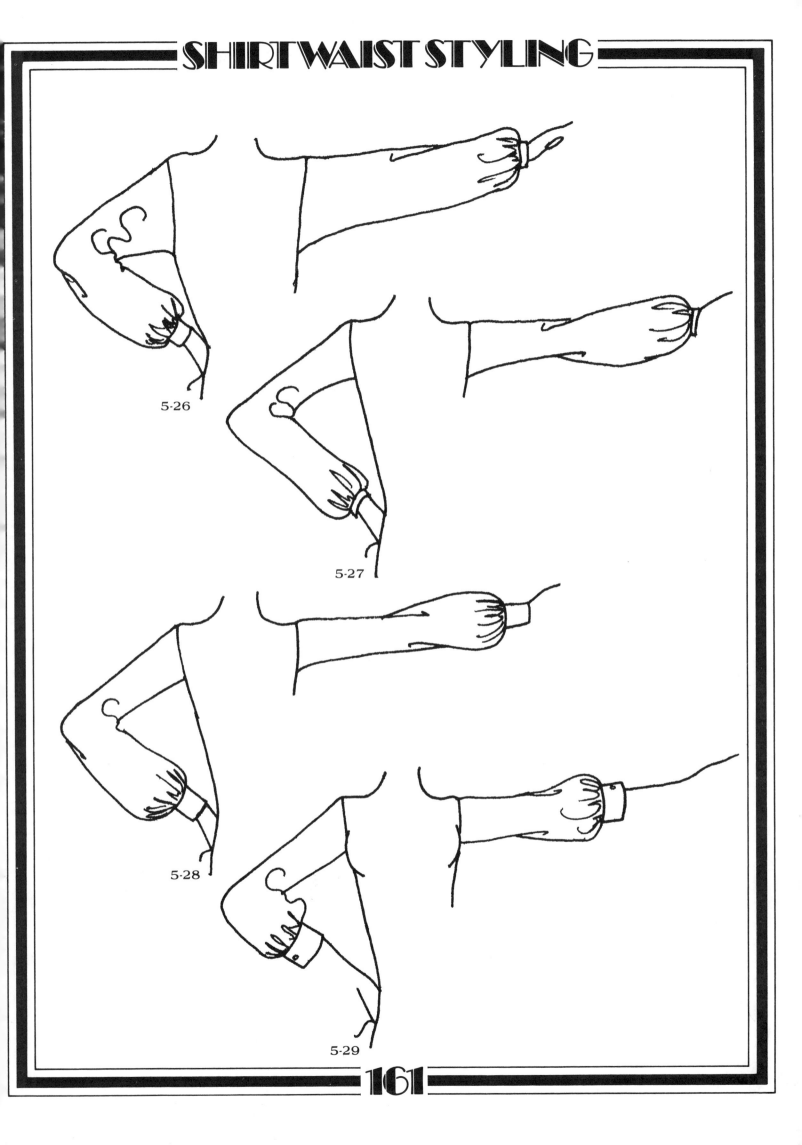

5-26

5-27

5-28

5-29

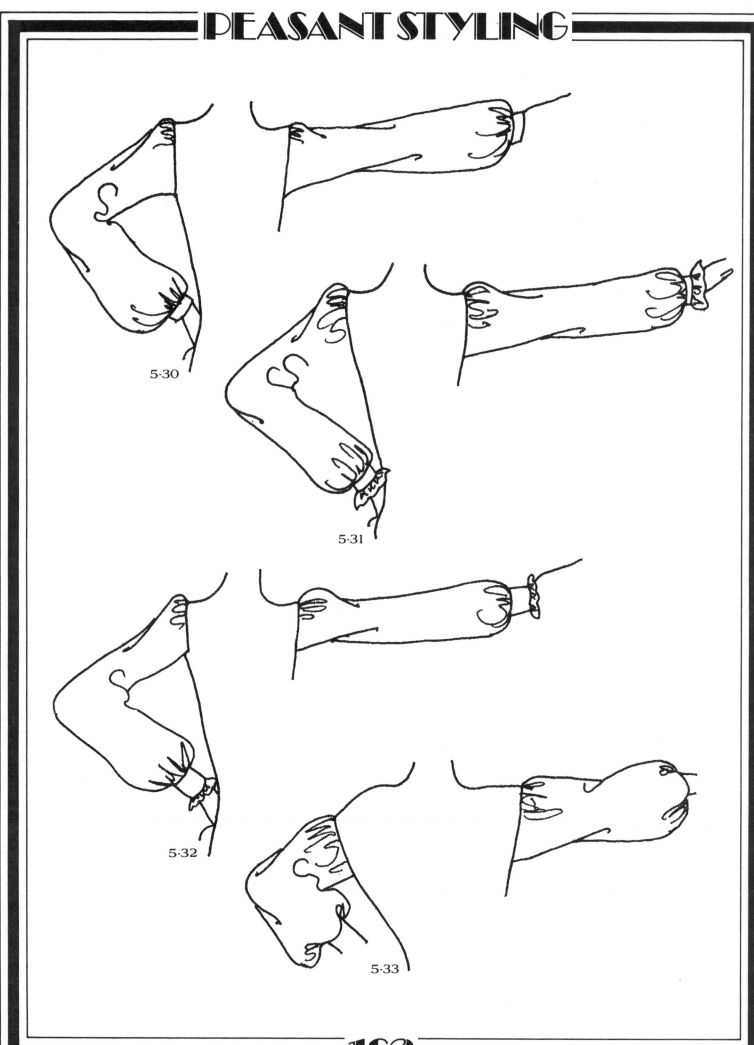

5-30

5-31

5-32

5-33

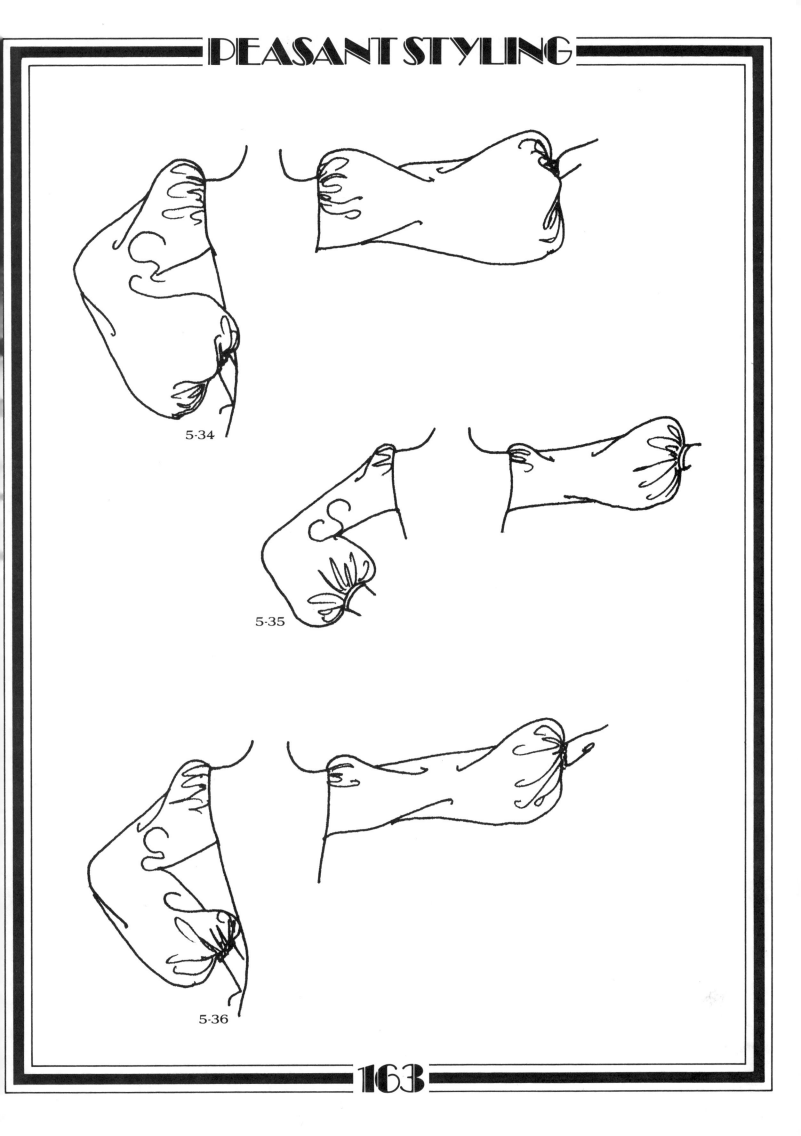

5-34

5-35

5-36

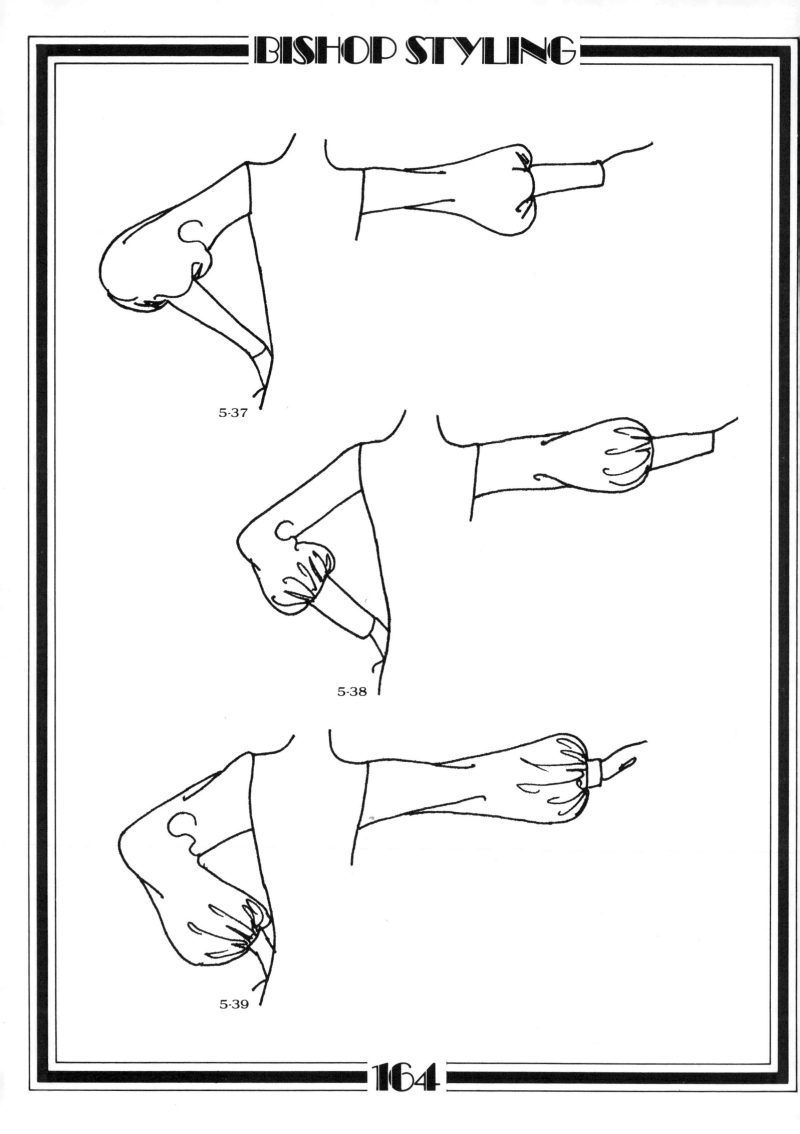

5-37

5-38

5-39

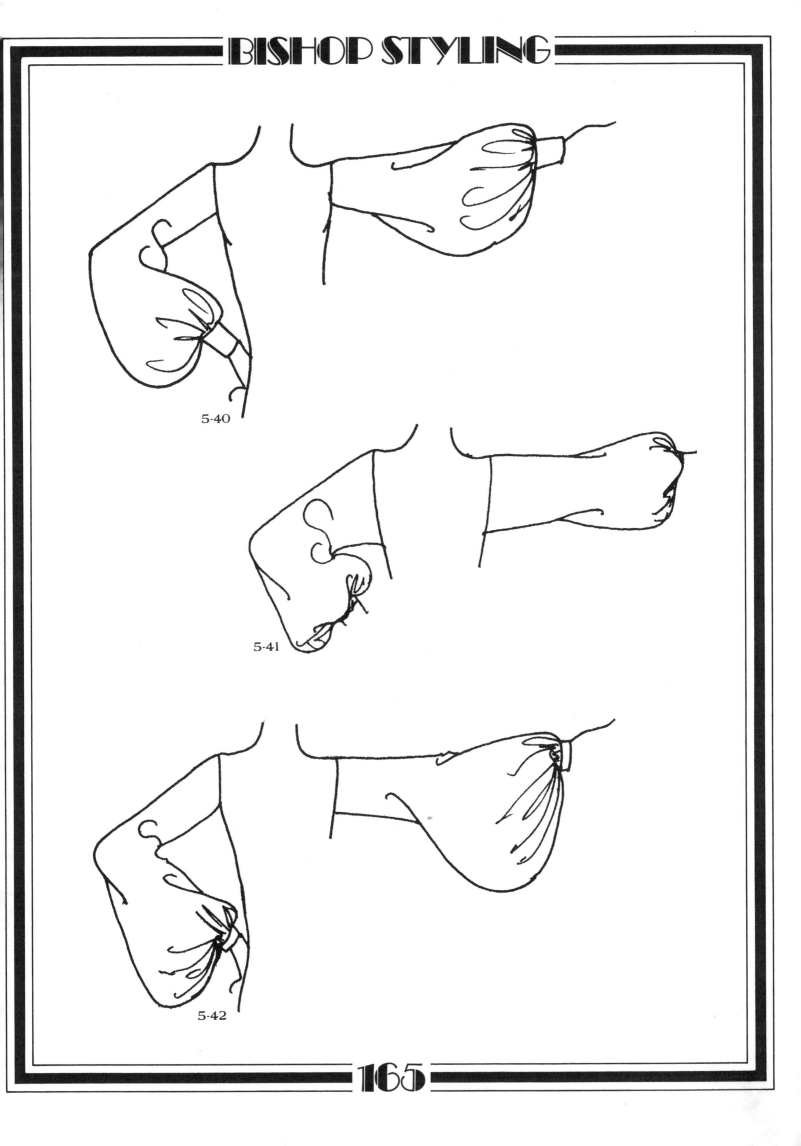

5-40

5-41

5-42

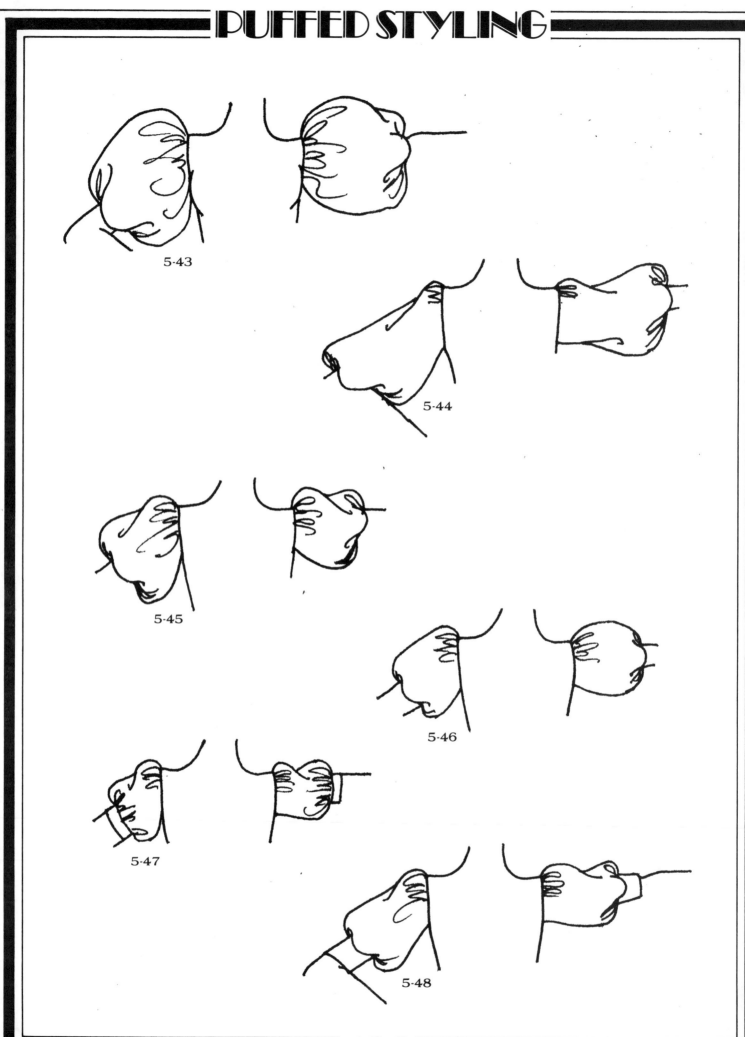

5-43

5-44

5-45

5-46

5-47

5-48

5-49

5-50

5-51

5-52

5-53

5-54

5-55

5-56

5-57

5-58

5-59

5-60

5-61

5-62

5-63

5-64

5-65

5-66

5-67

5-68

5-69

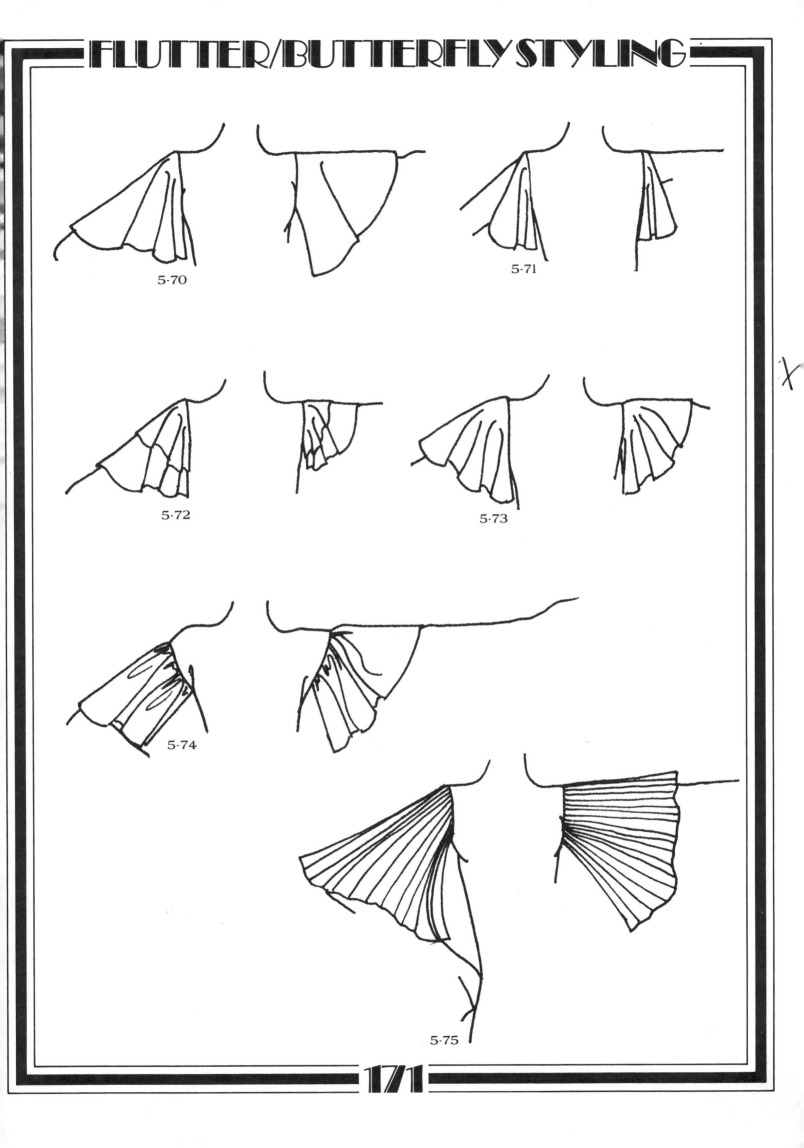

5-70

5-71

5-72

5-73

5-74

5-75

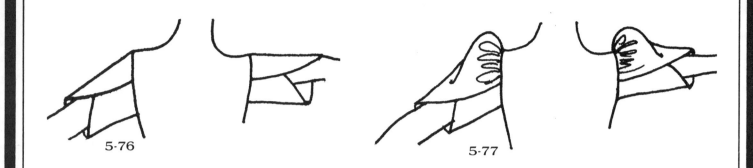

5-76   5-77

MELON STYLING

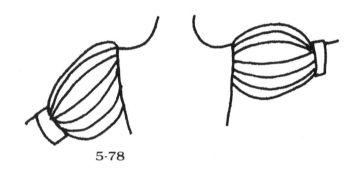

5-78

DRAPED STYLING

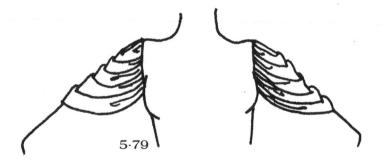

5-79

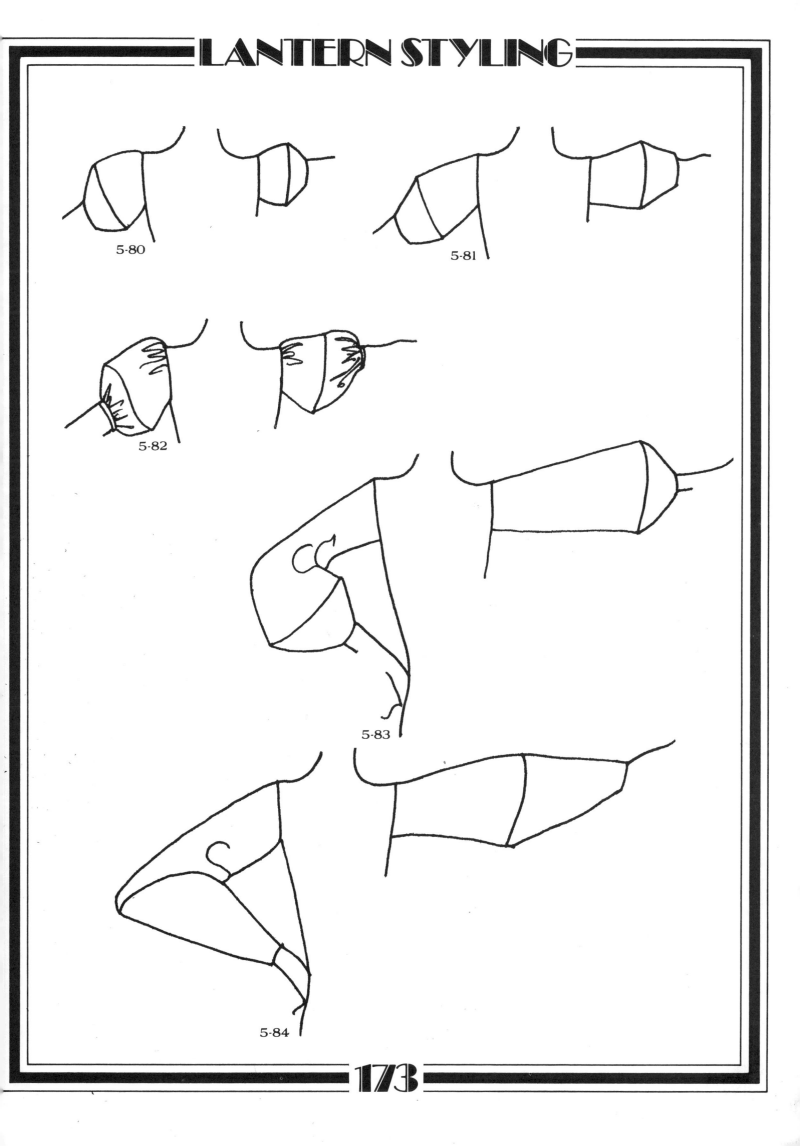

5-80

5-81

5-82

5-83

5-84

5-85

5-86

JULIET STYLING

5-87

5-88

5-89

5-90

5-91

5-92

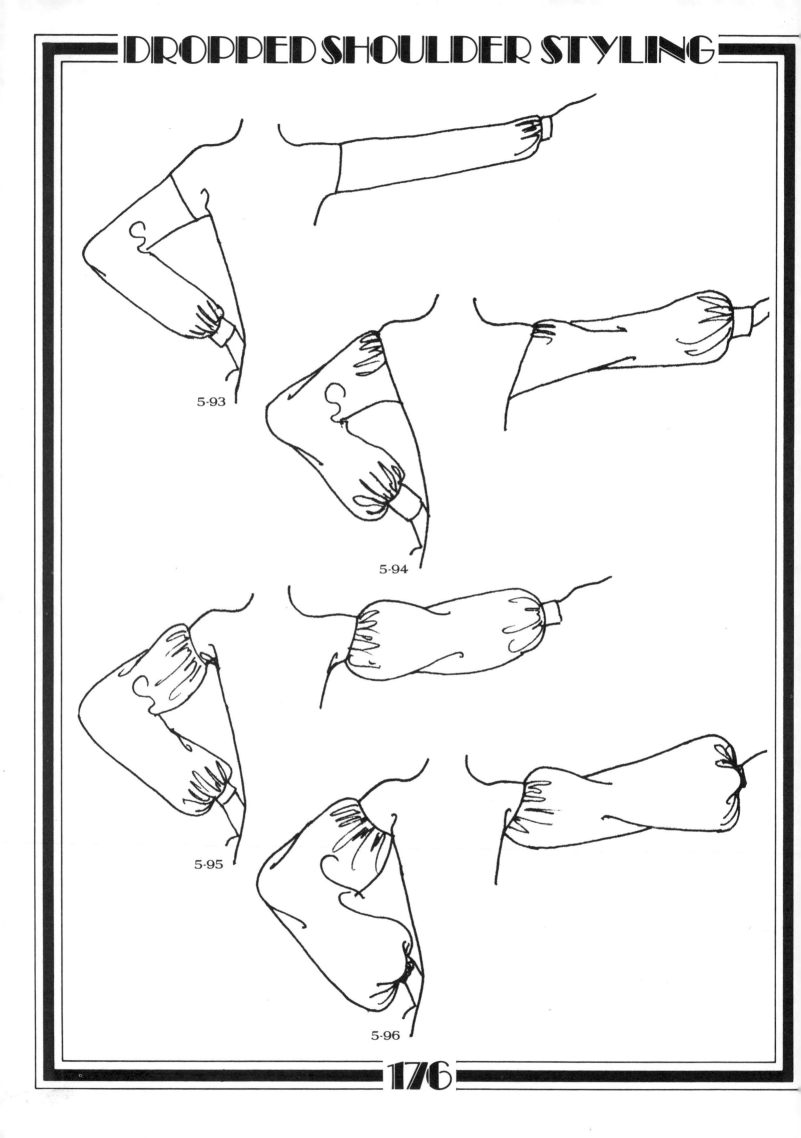

5-93

5-94

5-95

5-96

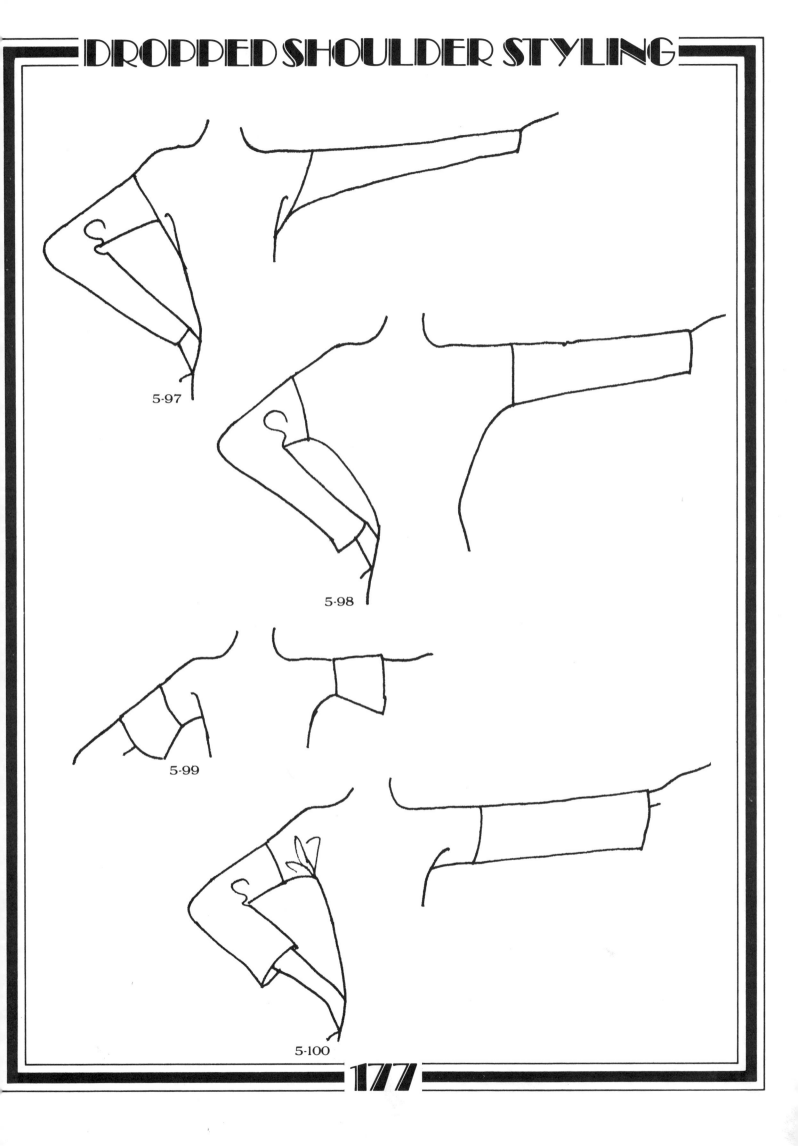

5-97

5-98

5-99

5-100

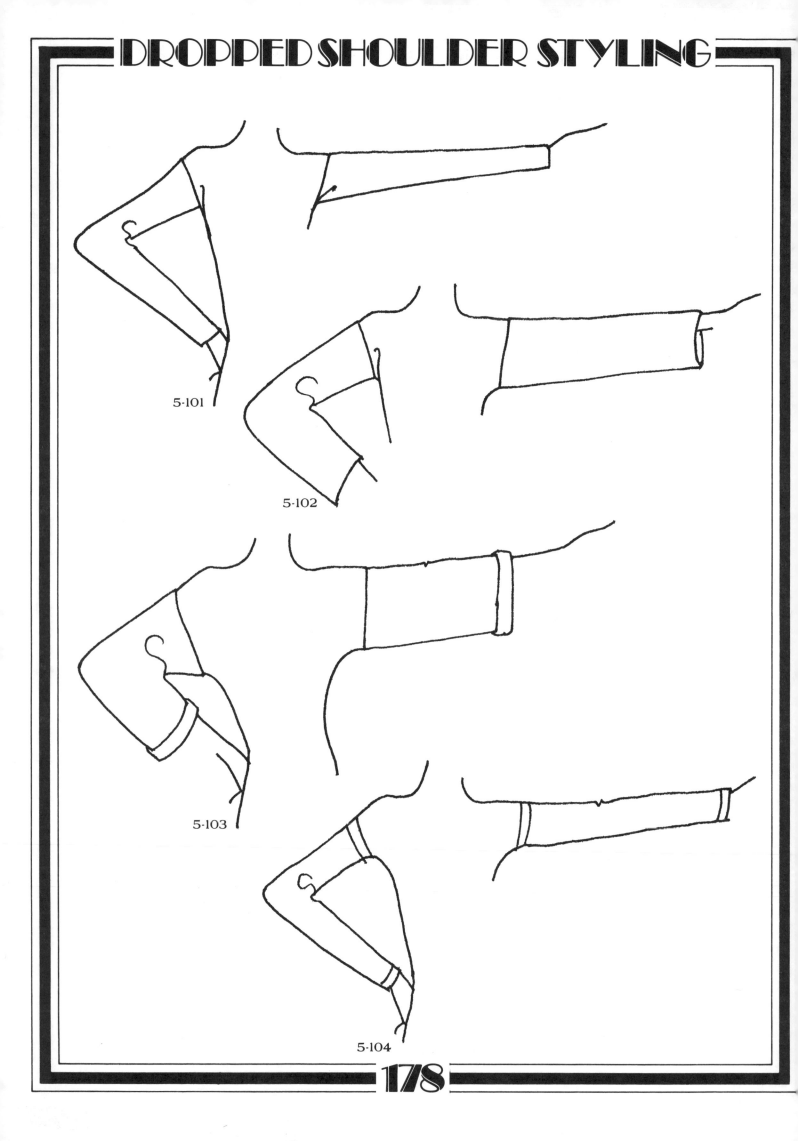

5-101

5-102

5-103

5-104

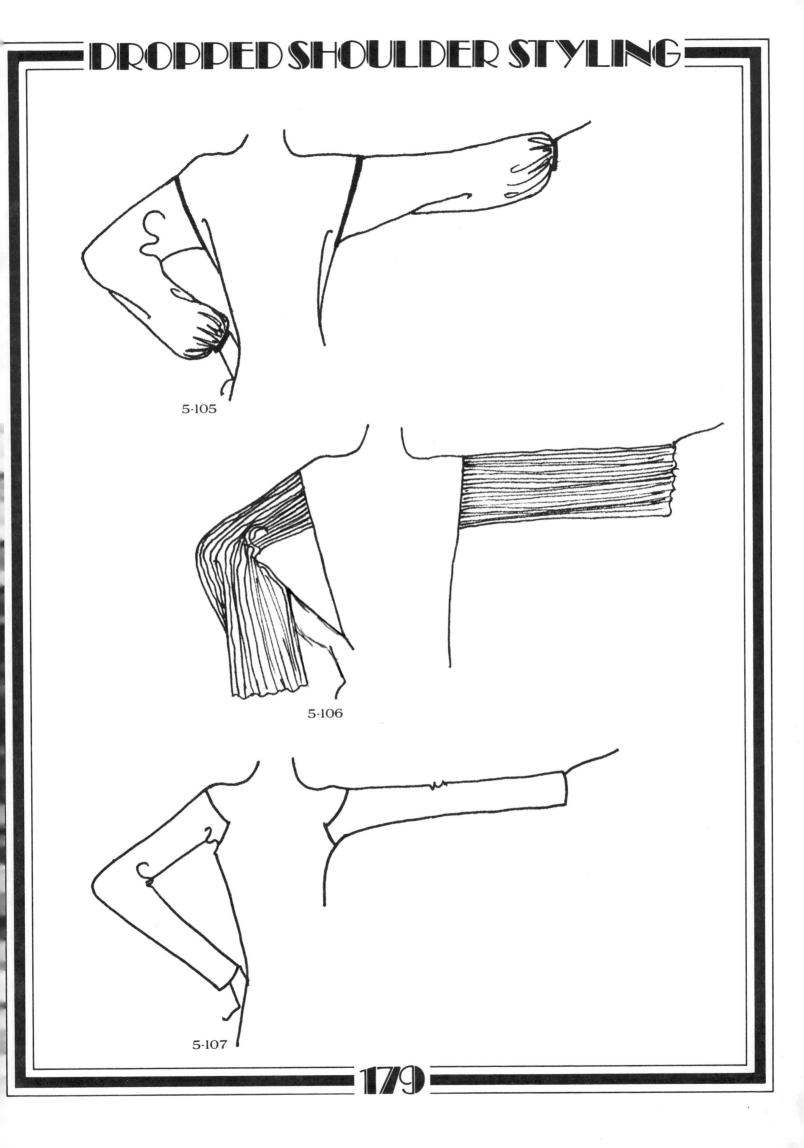

5-105

5-106

5-107

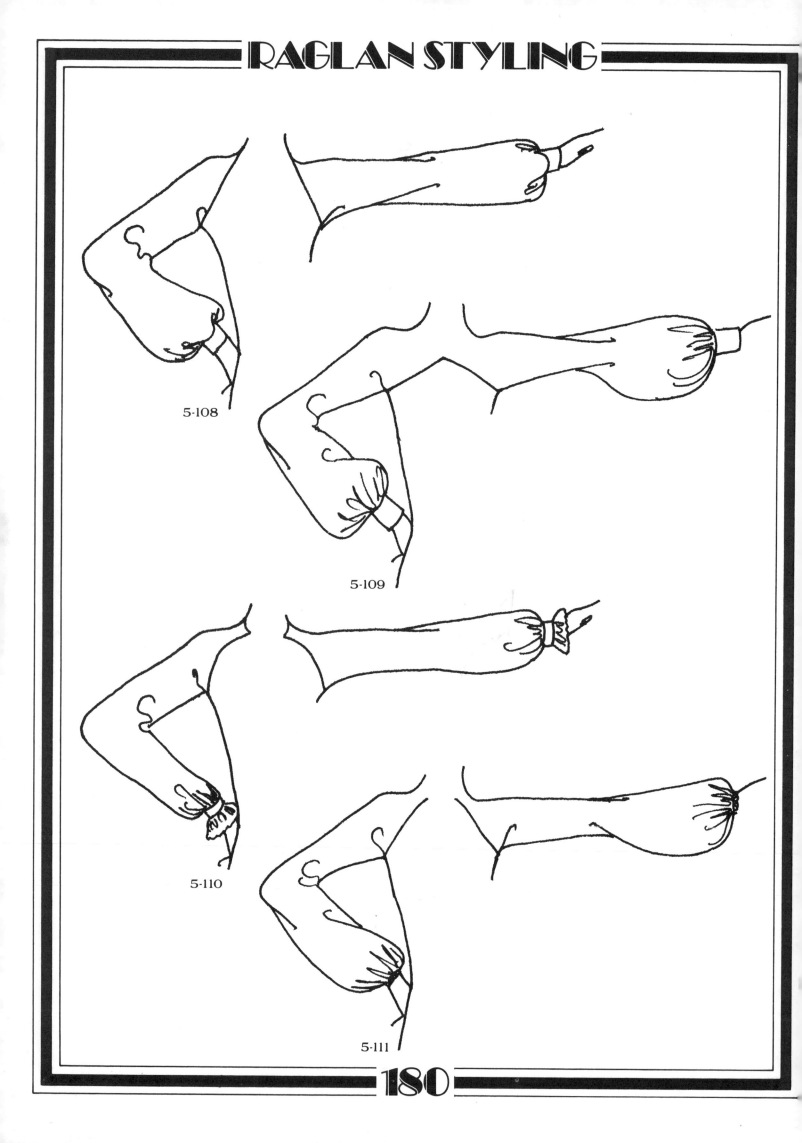

5-108

5-109

5-110

5-111

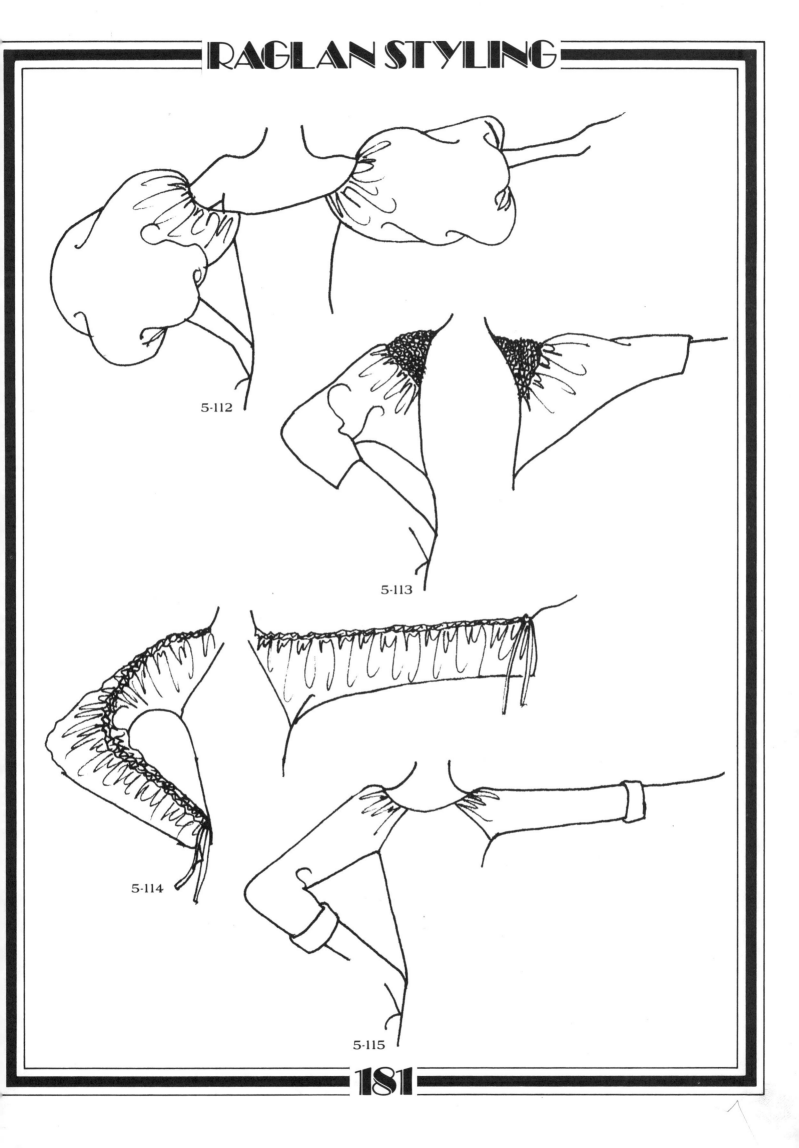

5-112

5-113

5-114

5-115

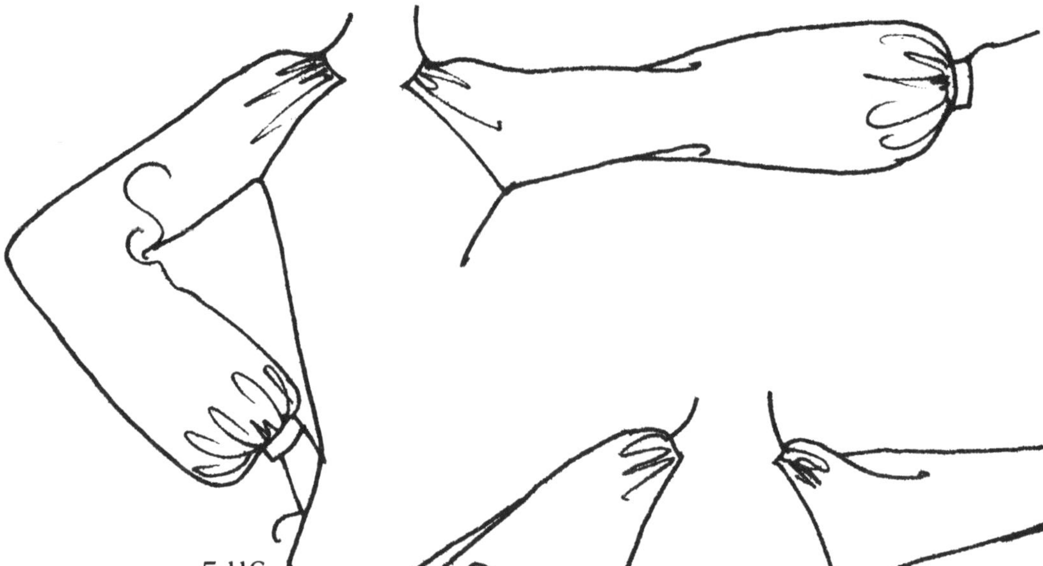

5-116

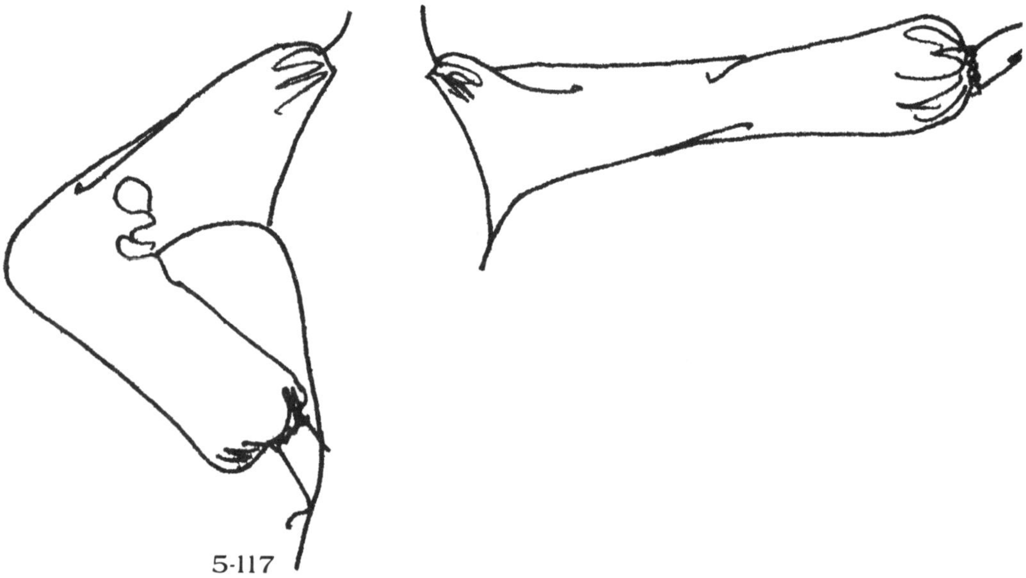

5-117

5-118

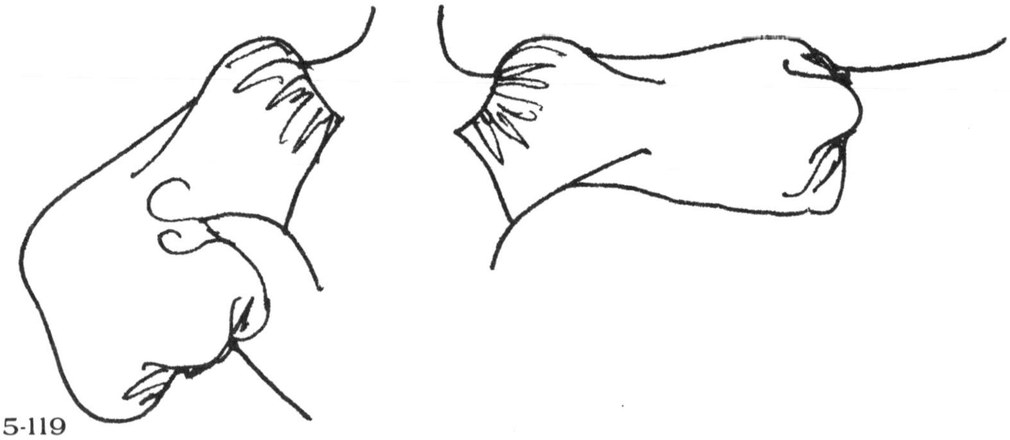

5-119

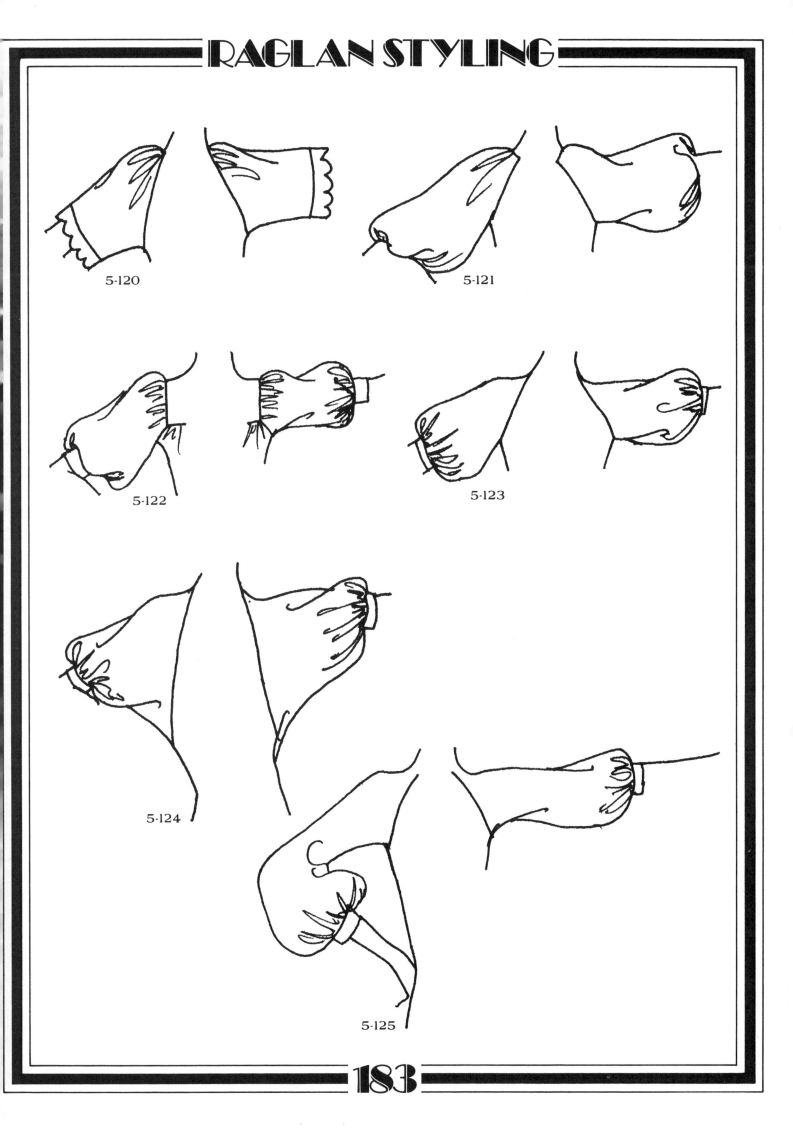

5-120

5-121

5-122

5-123

5-124

5-125

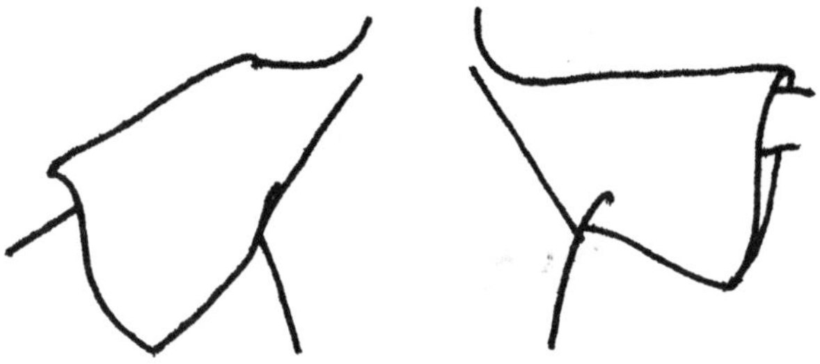

5-126

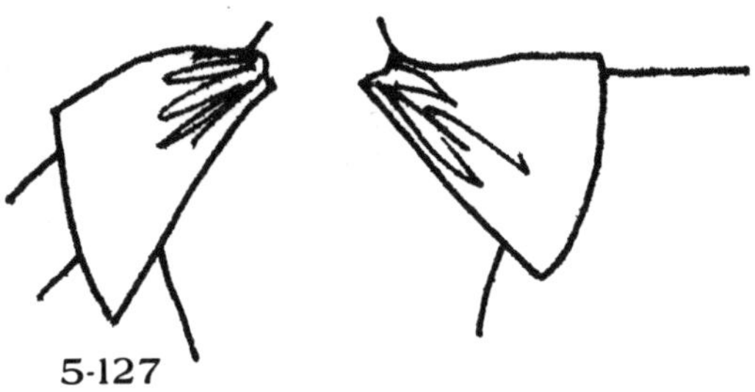

5-127

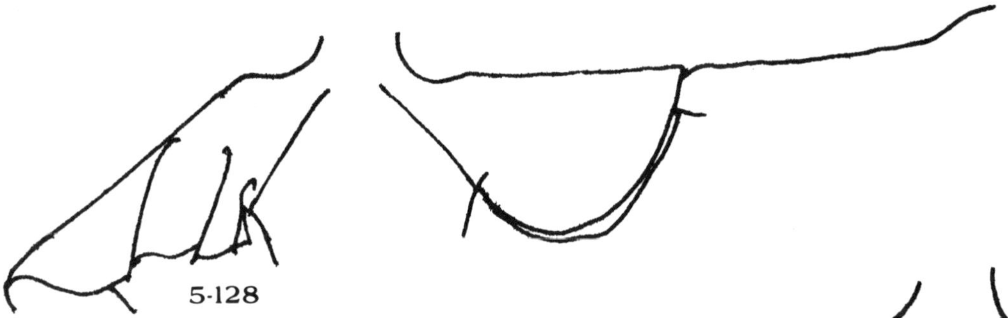

5-128

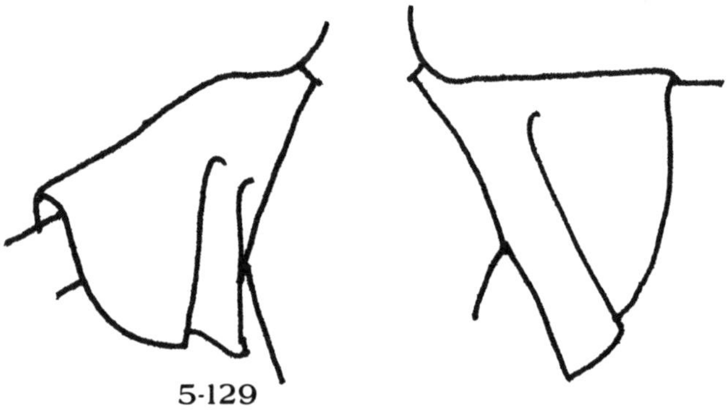

5-129

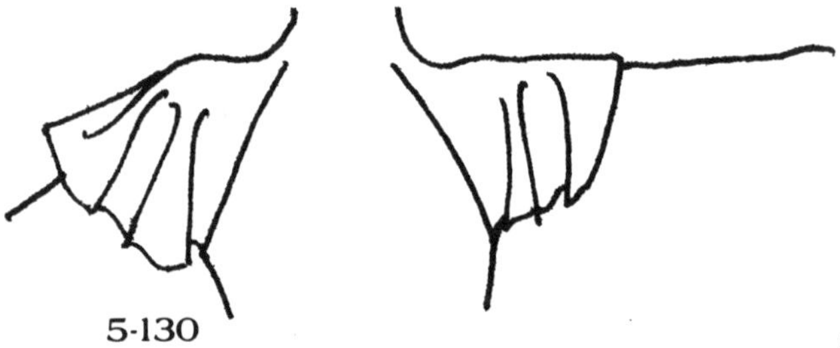

5-130

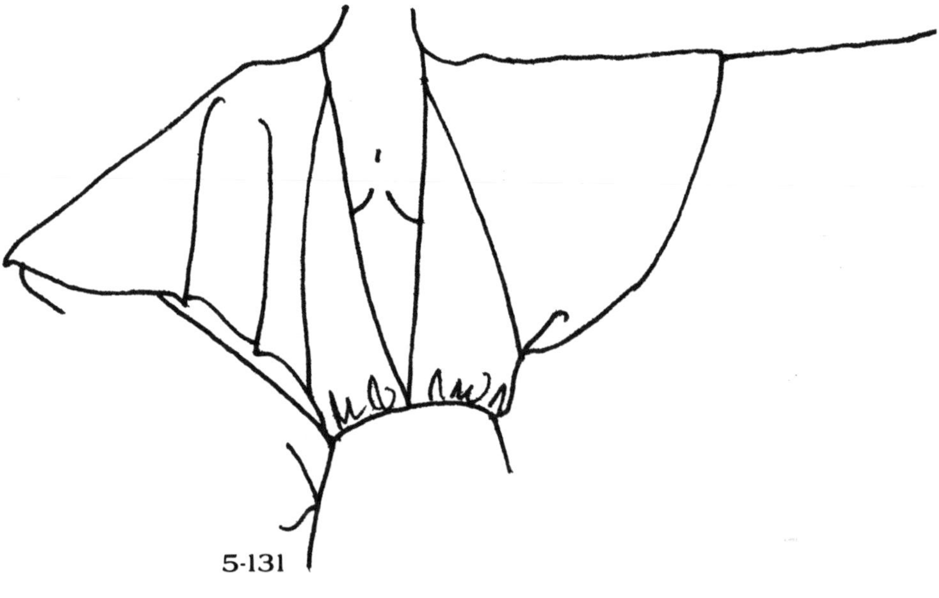

5-131

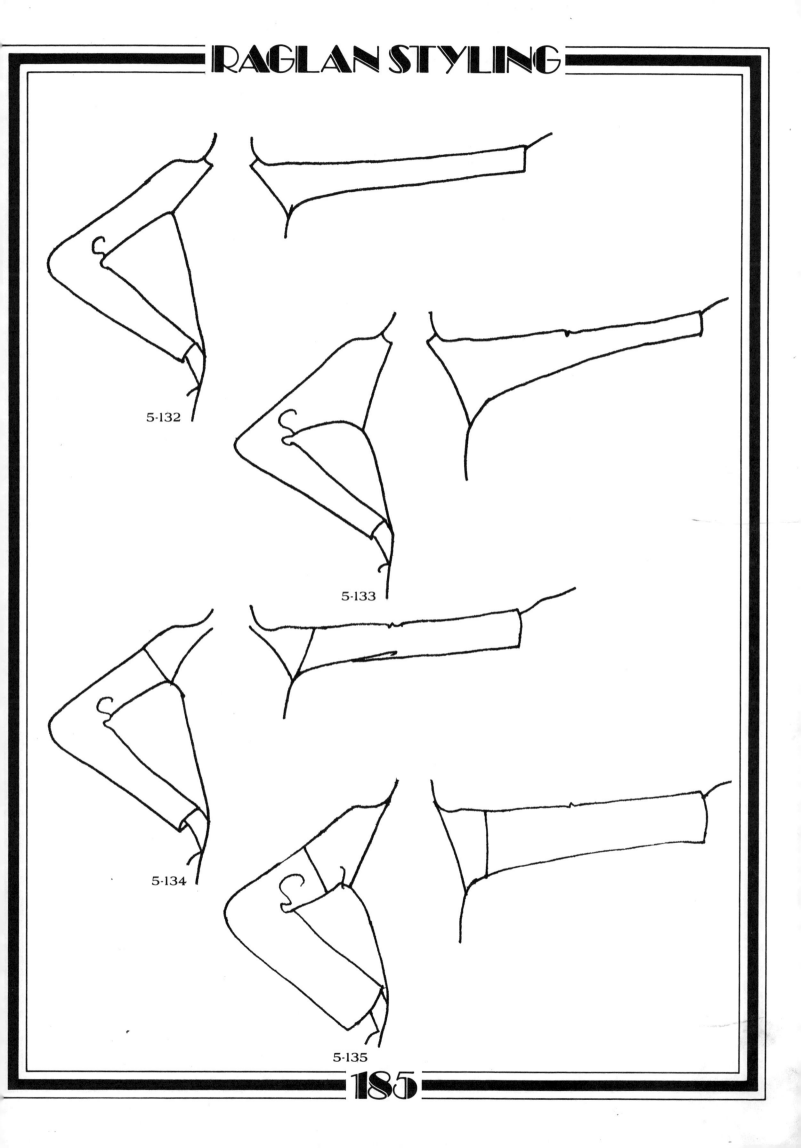

5-132

5-133

5-134

5-135

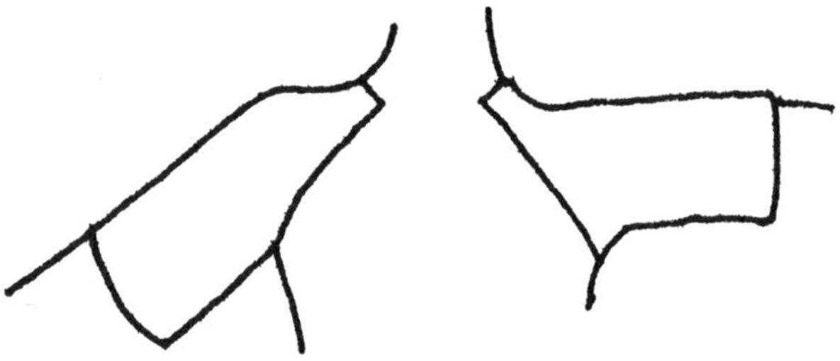

5-136

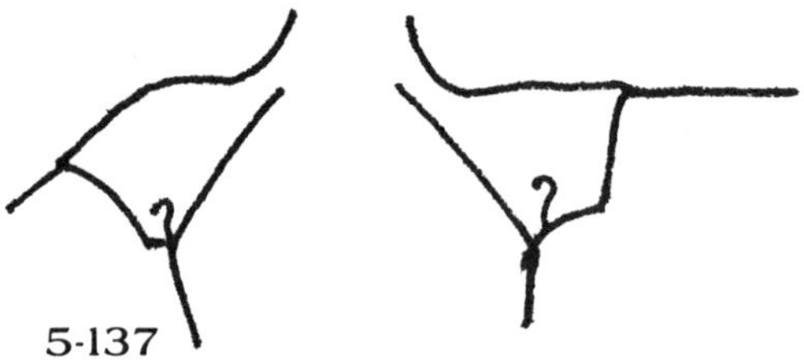

5-137

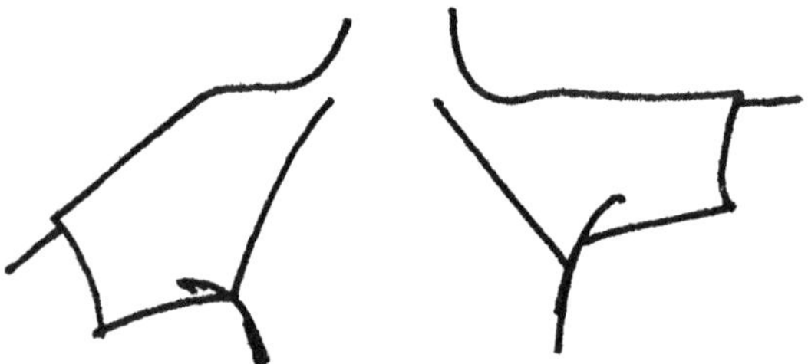

5-138

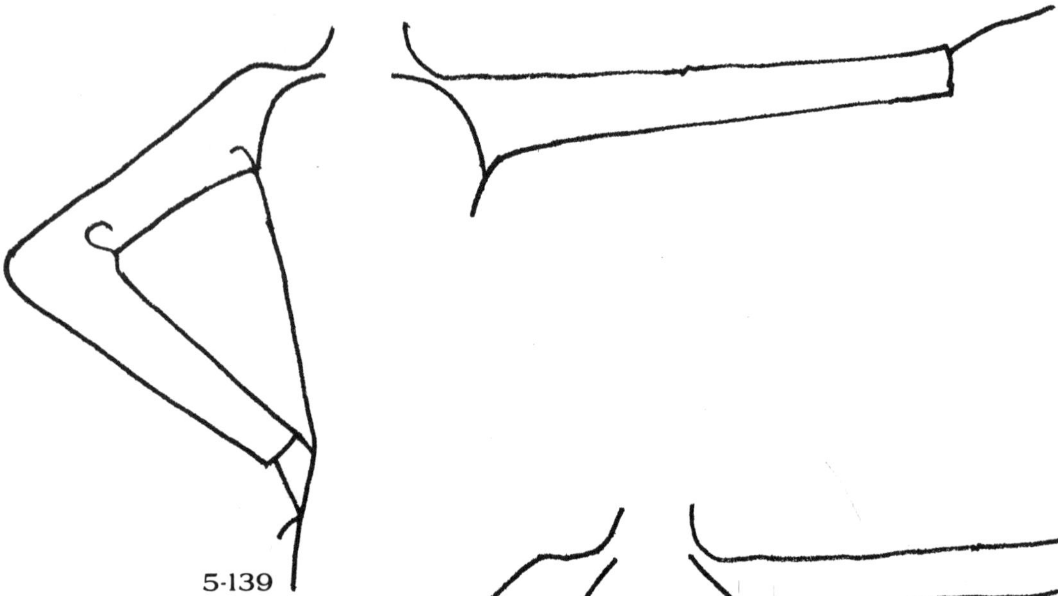

5-139

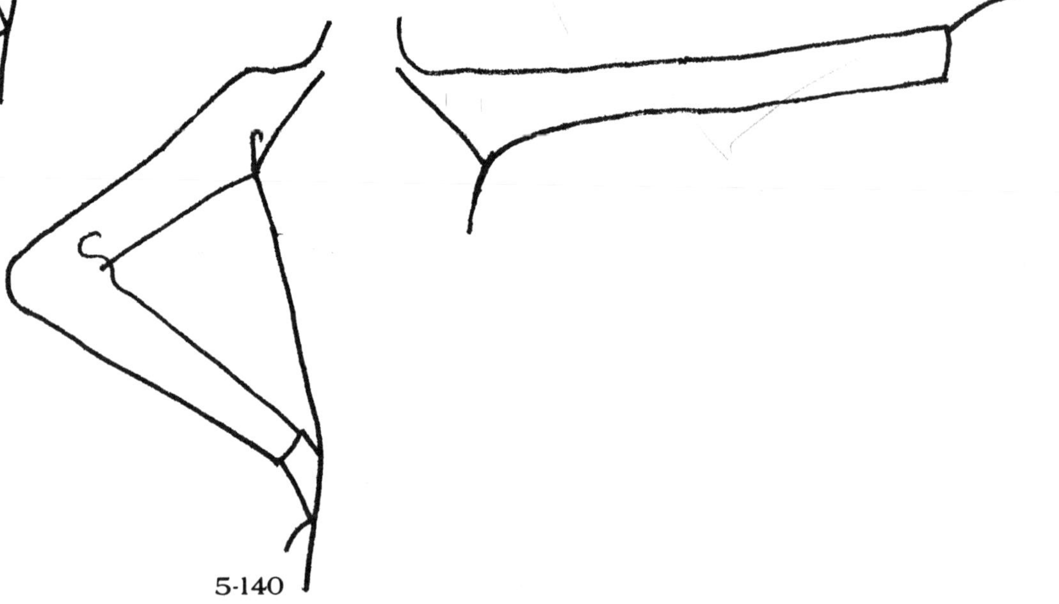

5-140

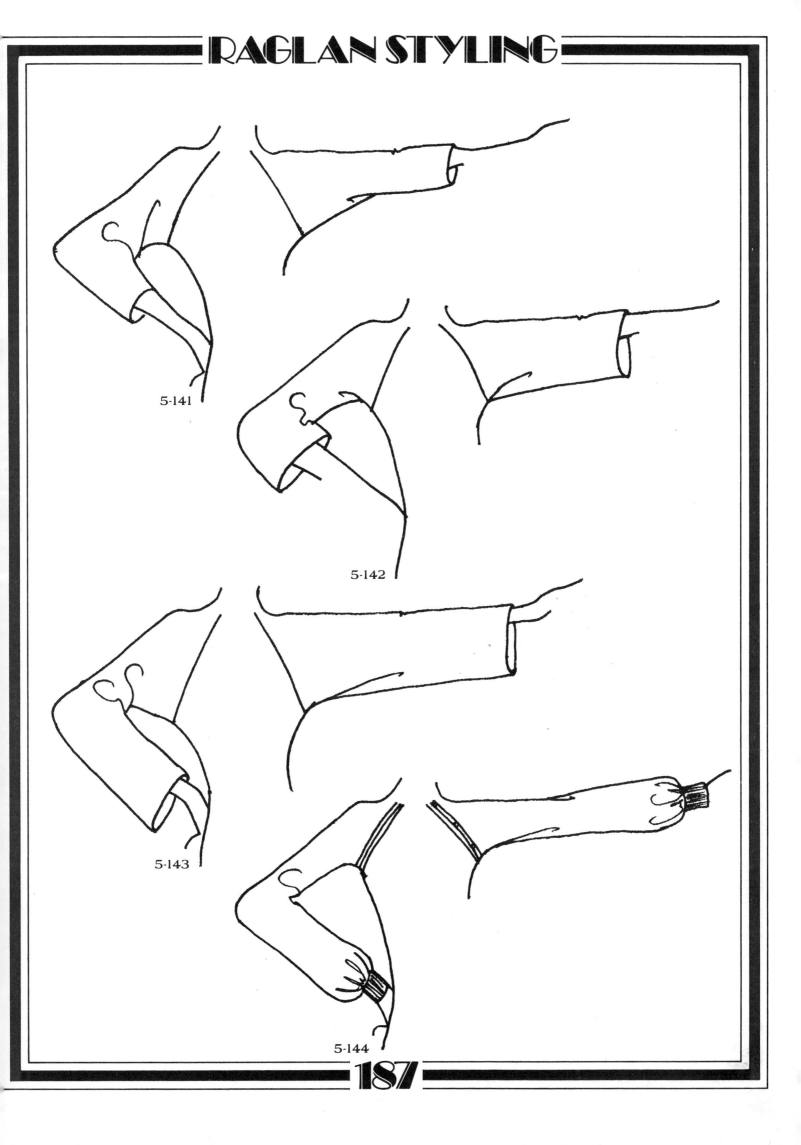

5-141

5-142

5-143

5-144

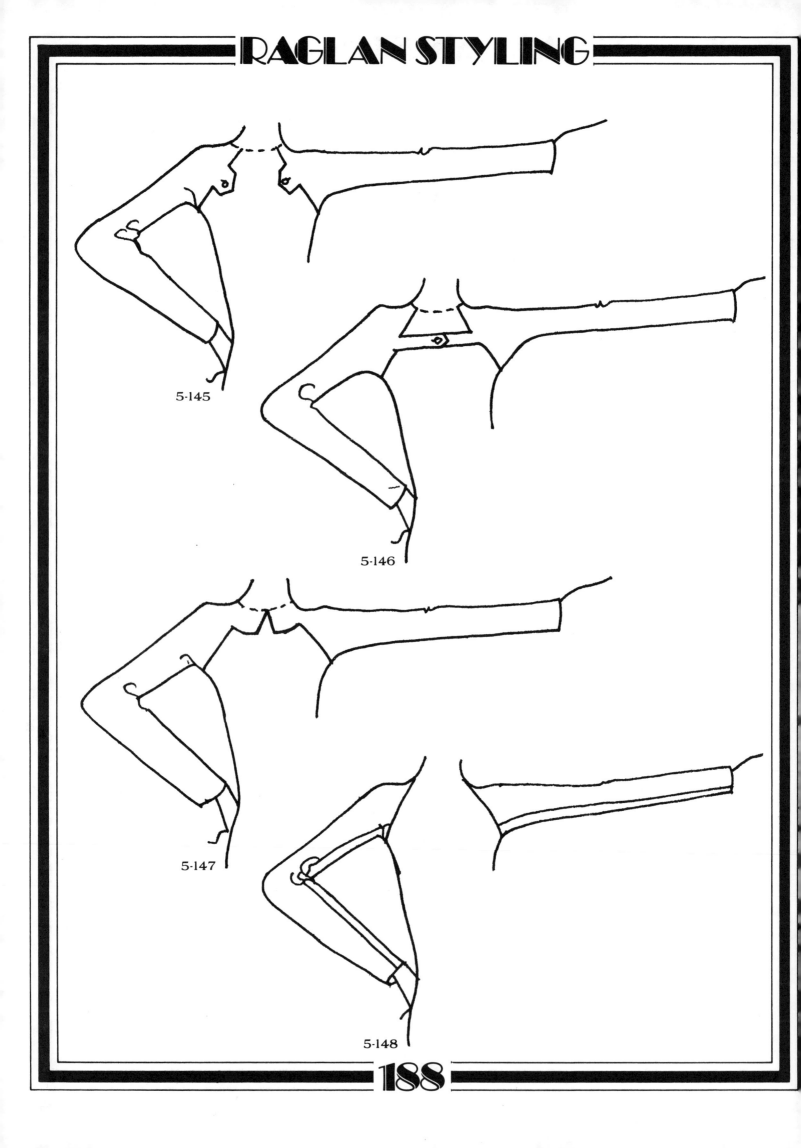

5-145

5-146

5-147

5-148

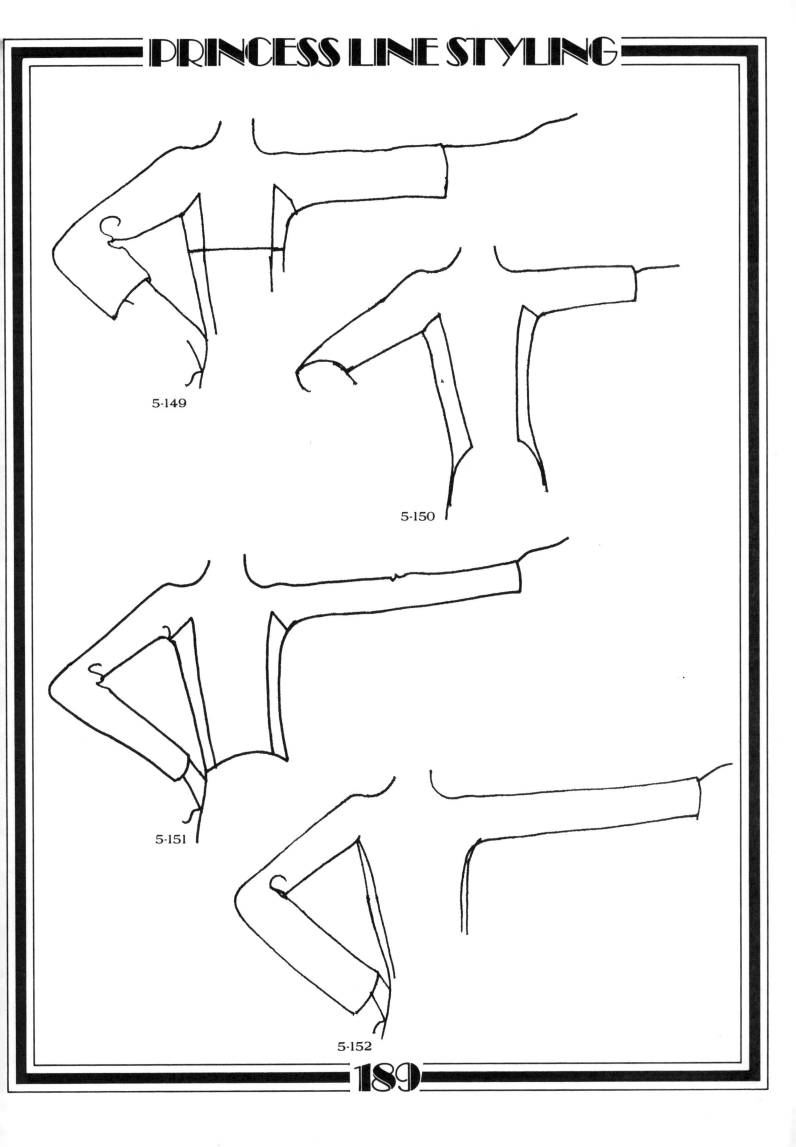

5-149

5-150

5-151

5-152

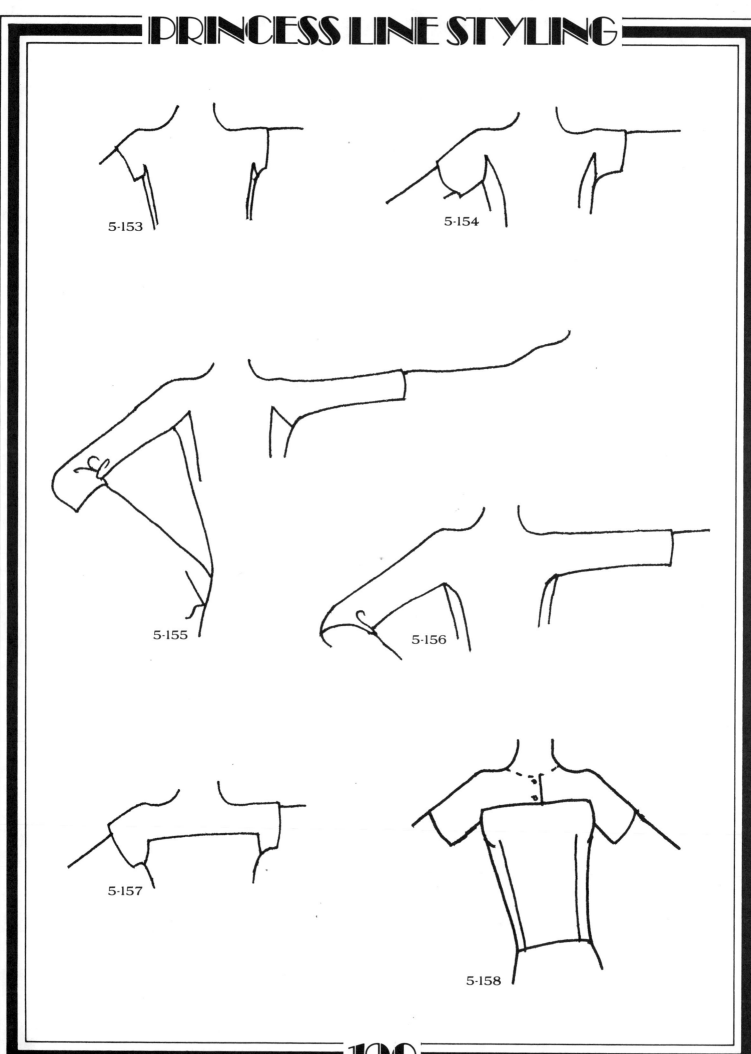

5-153

5-154

5-155

5-156

5-157

5-158

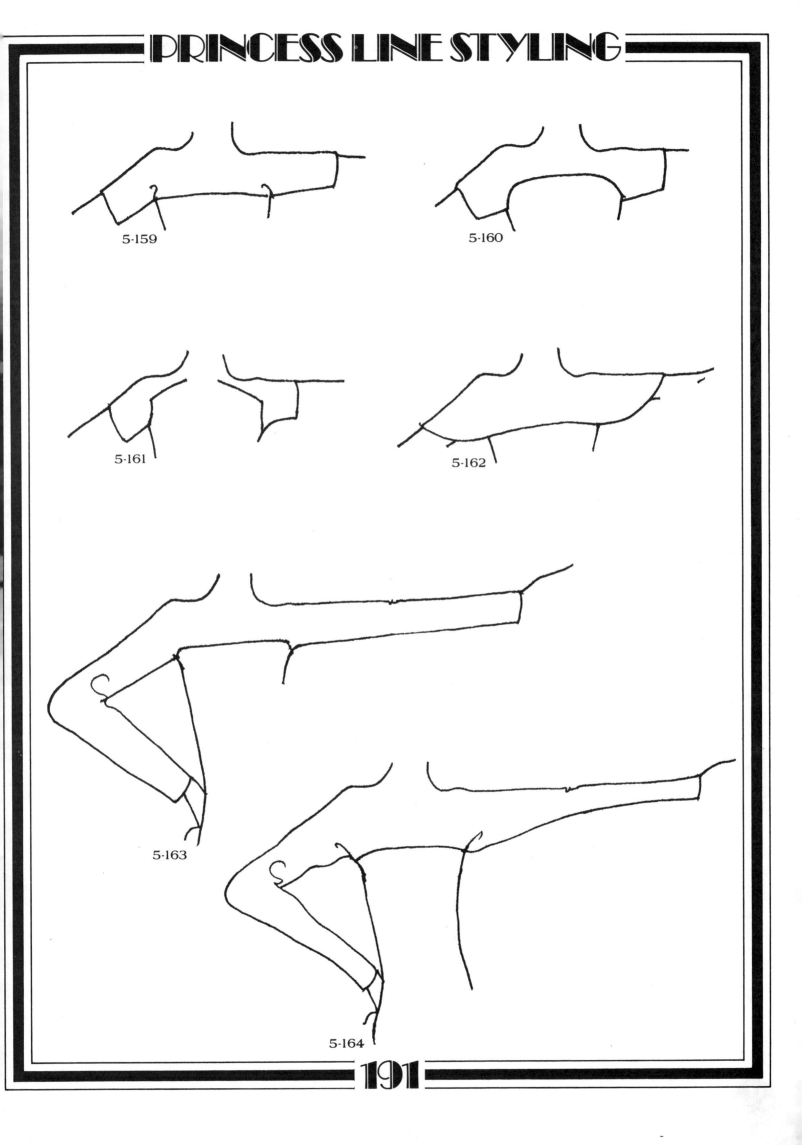

5-159

5-160

5-161

5-162

5-163

5-164

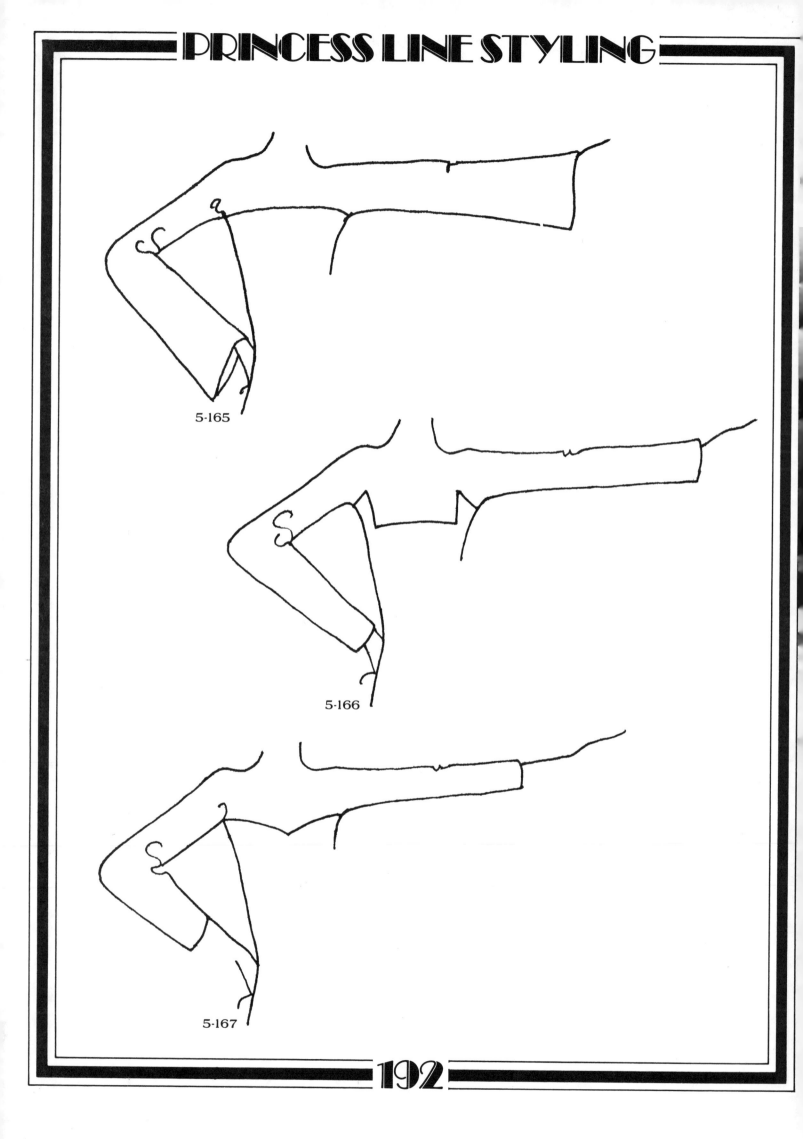

5-165

5-166

5-167

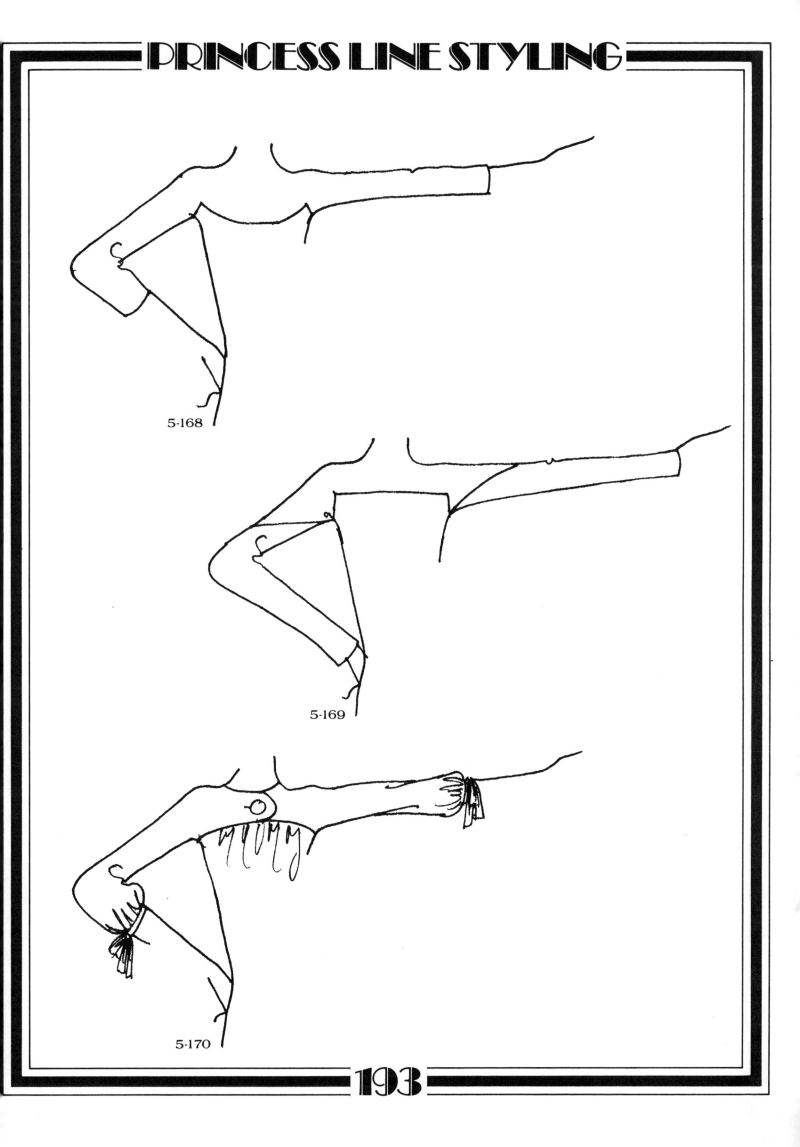

5-168

5-169

5-170

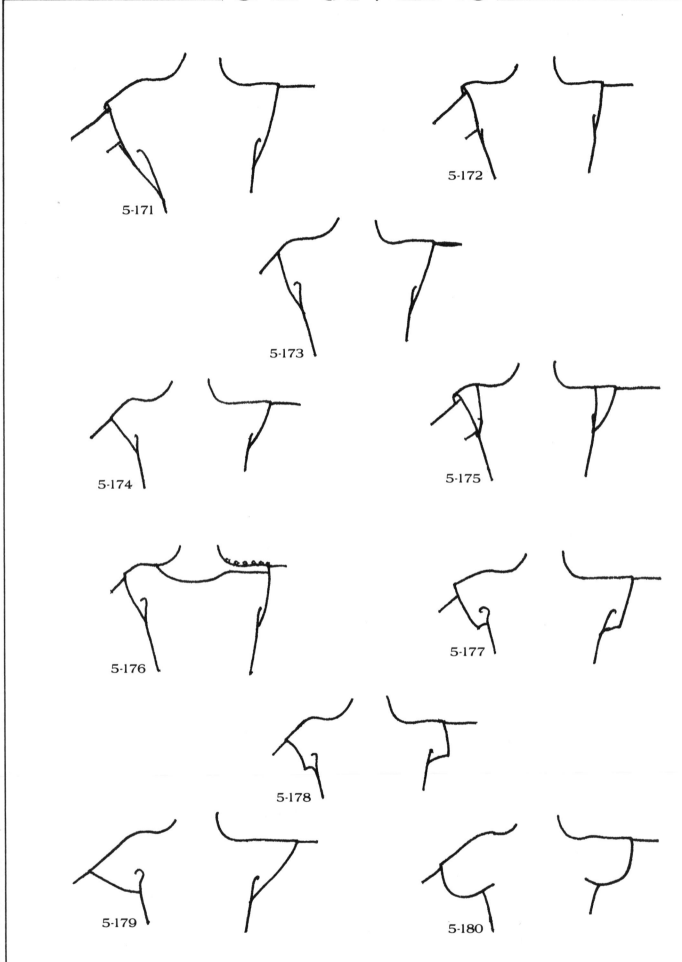

5·171

5·172

5·173

5·174

5·175

5·176

5·177

5·178

5·179

5·180

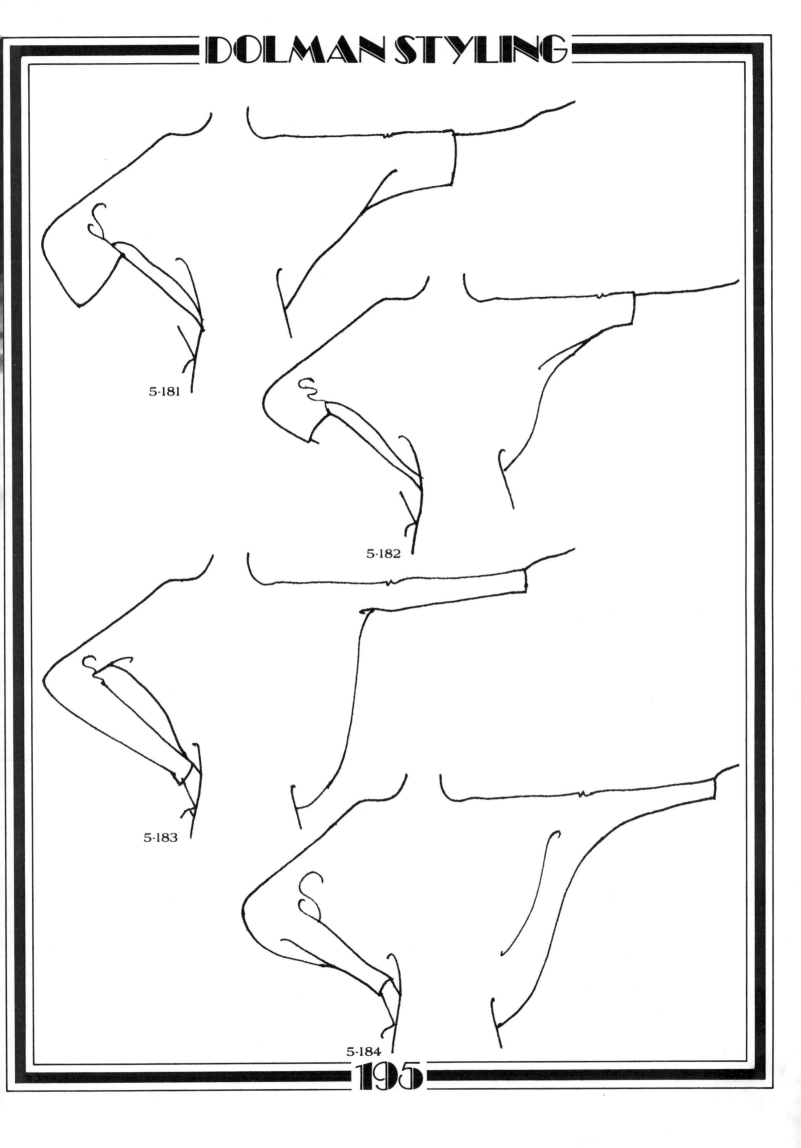

5-181

5-182

5-183

5-184

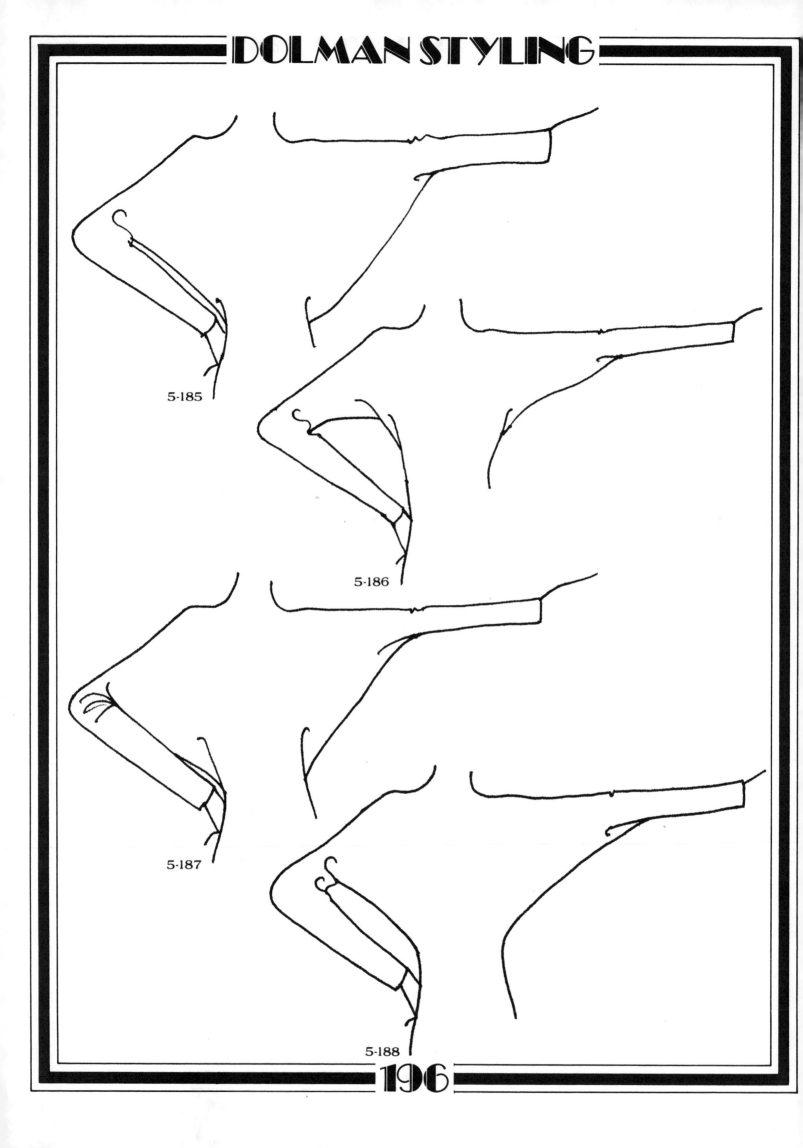

5-185

5-186

5-187

5-188

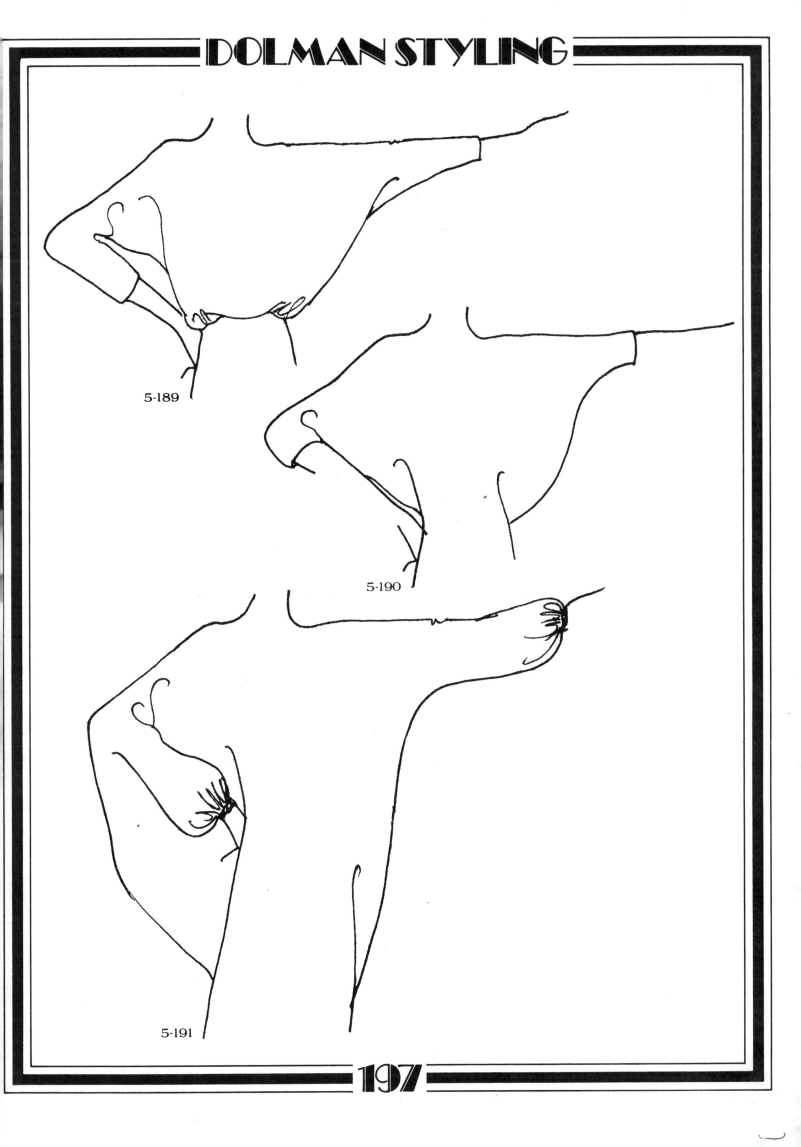

5-189

5-190

5-191

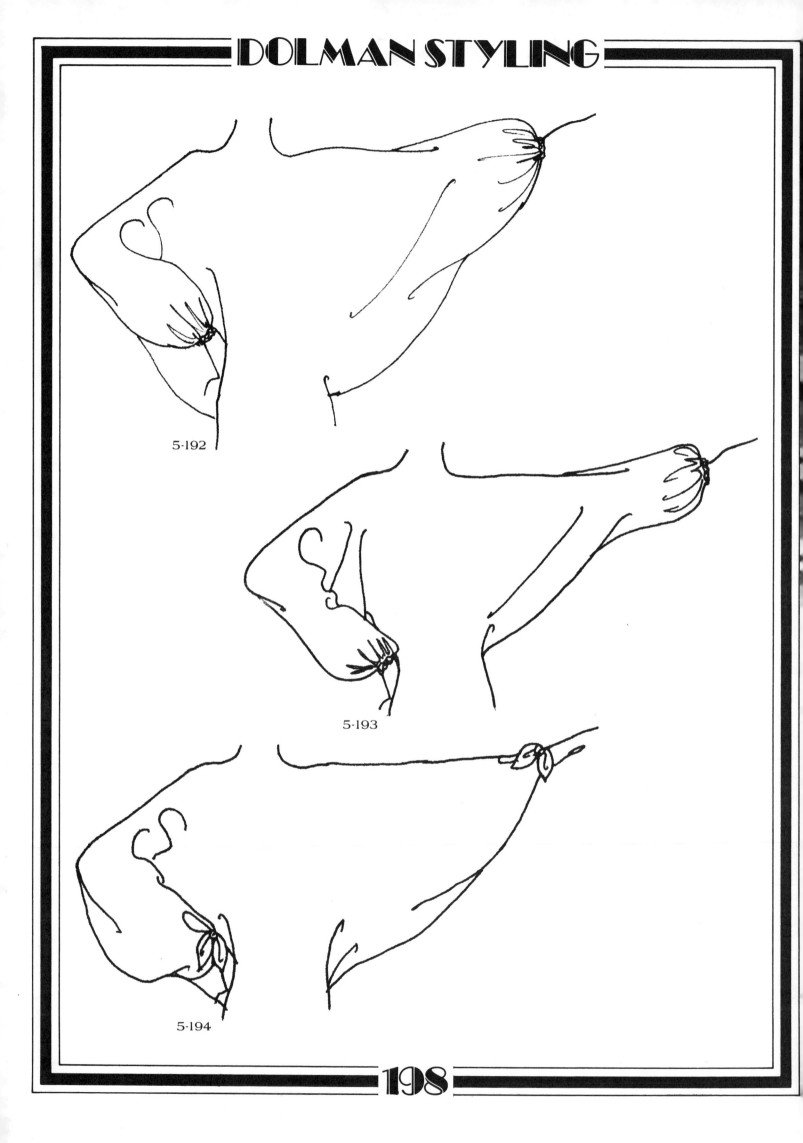

5-192

5-193

5-194

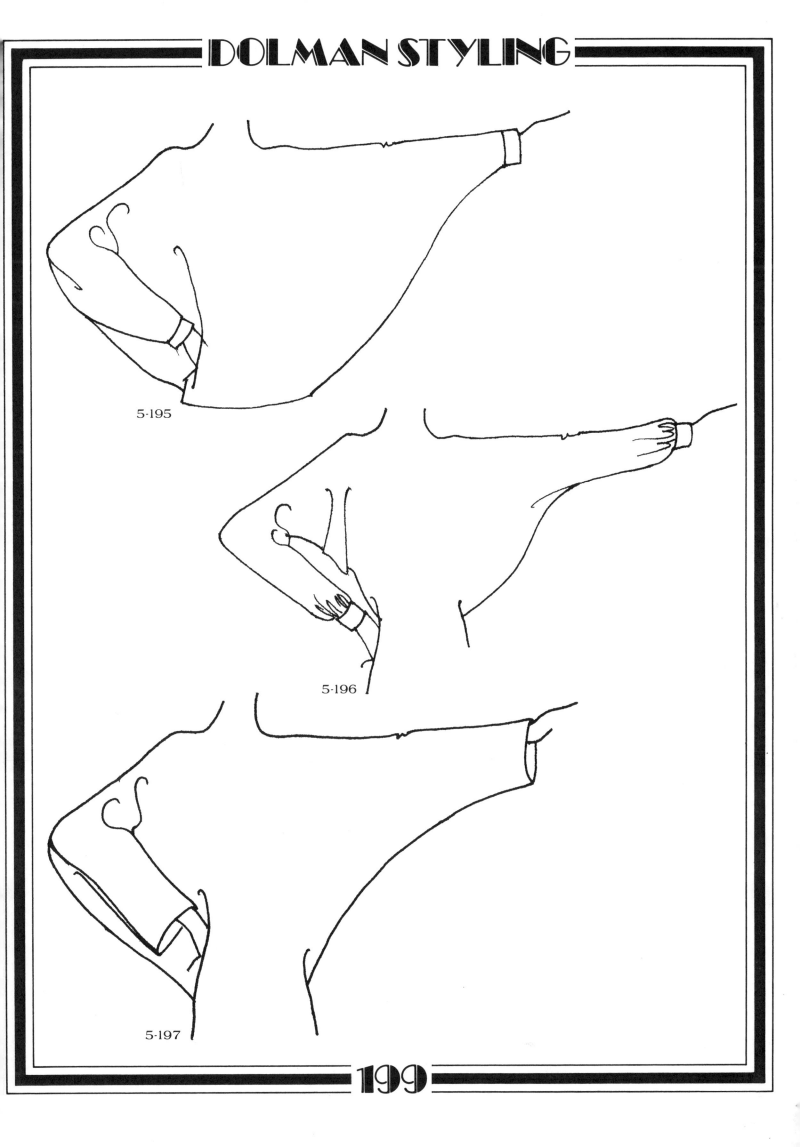

5-195

5-196

5-197

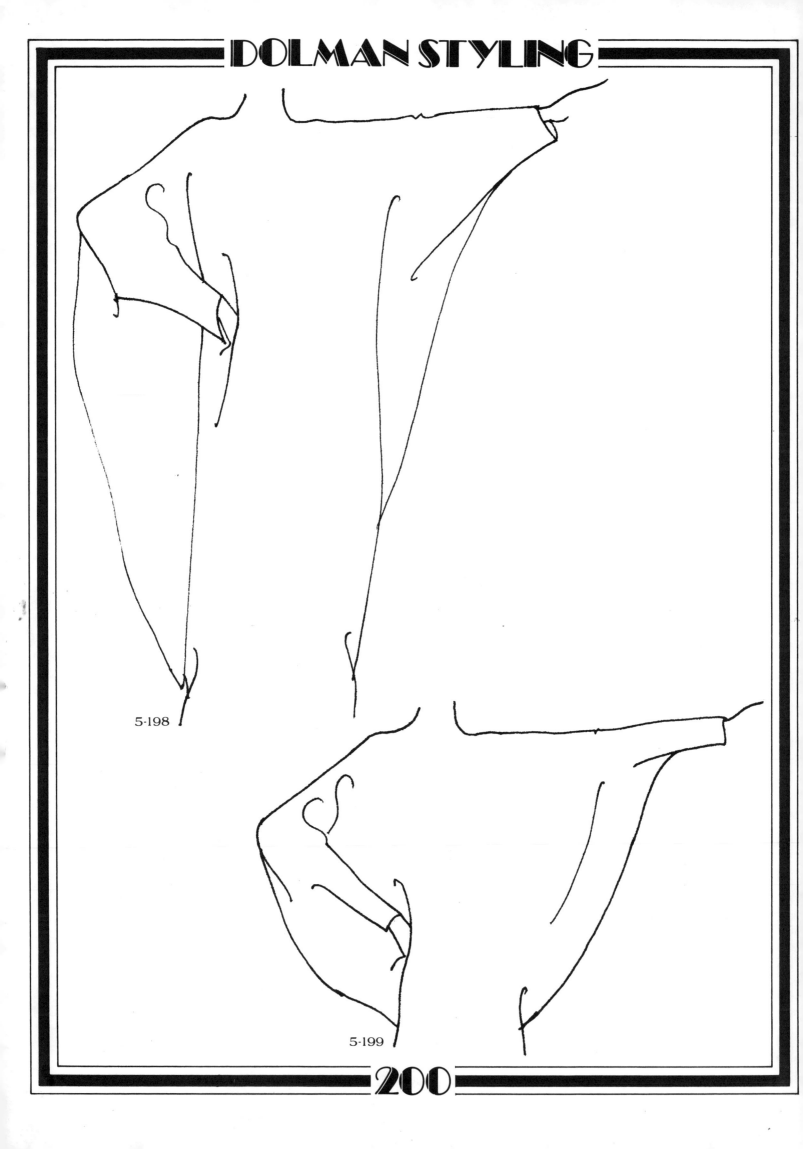

5-198

5-199

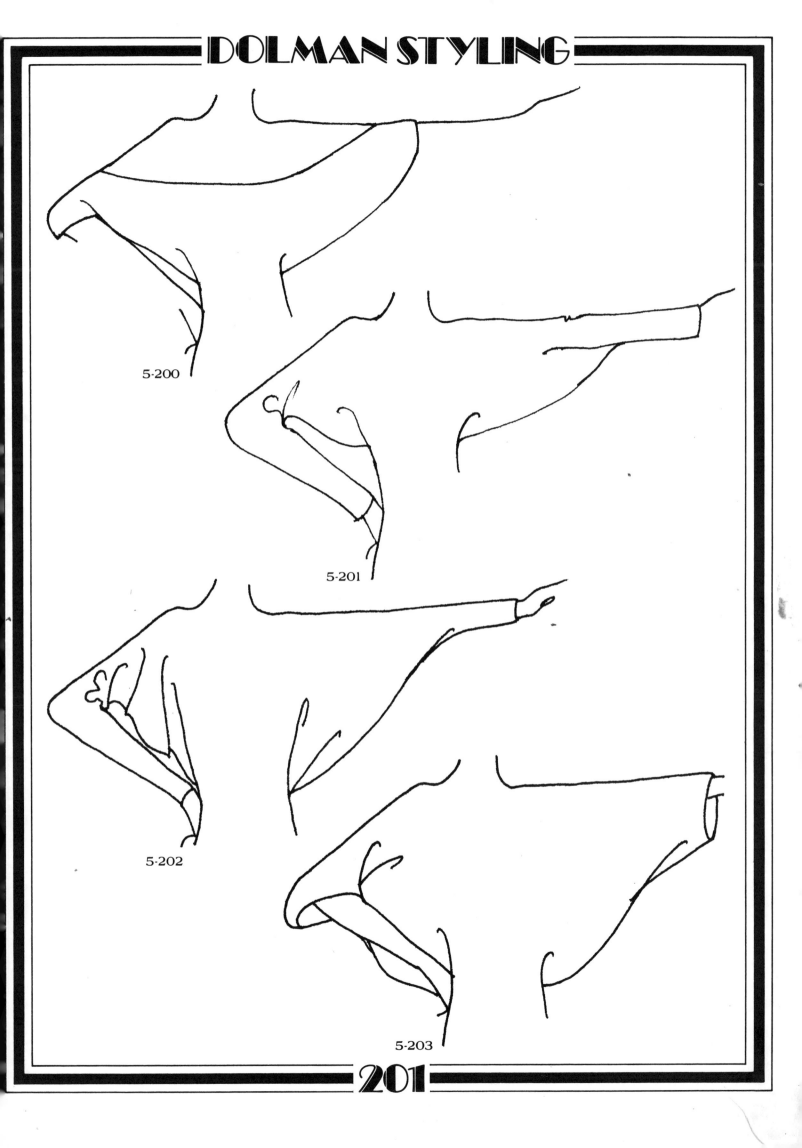

5-200

5-201

5-202

5-203

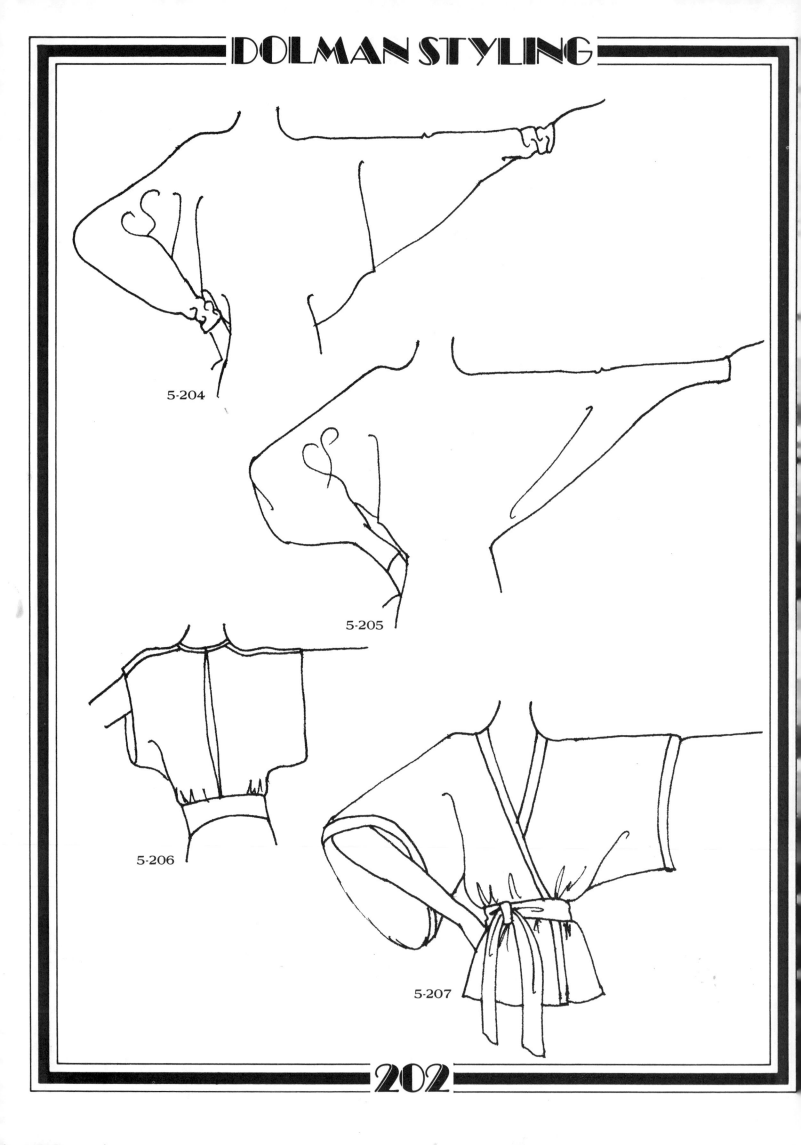

5-204

5-205

5-206

5-207

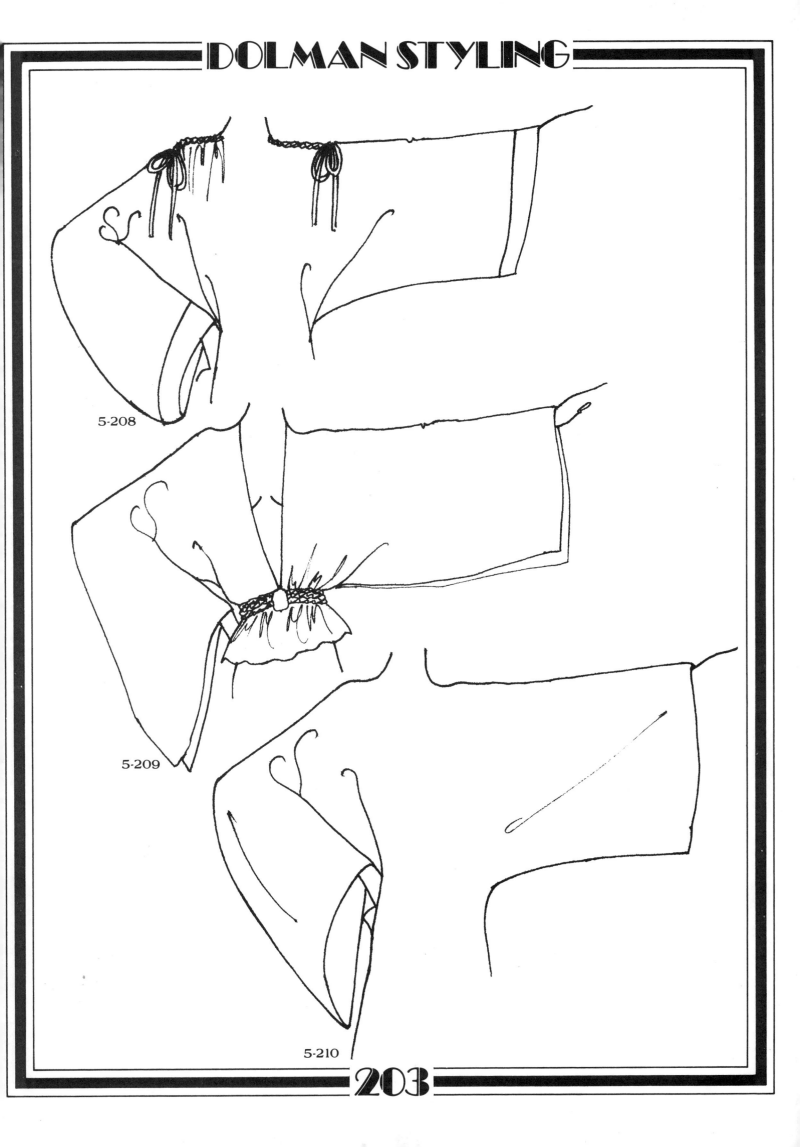

5-208

5-209

5-210

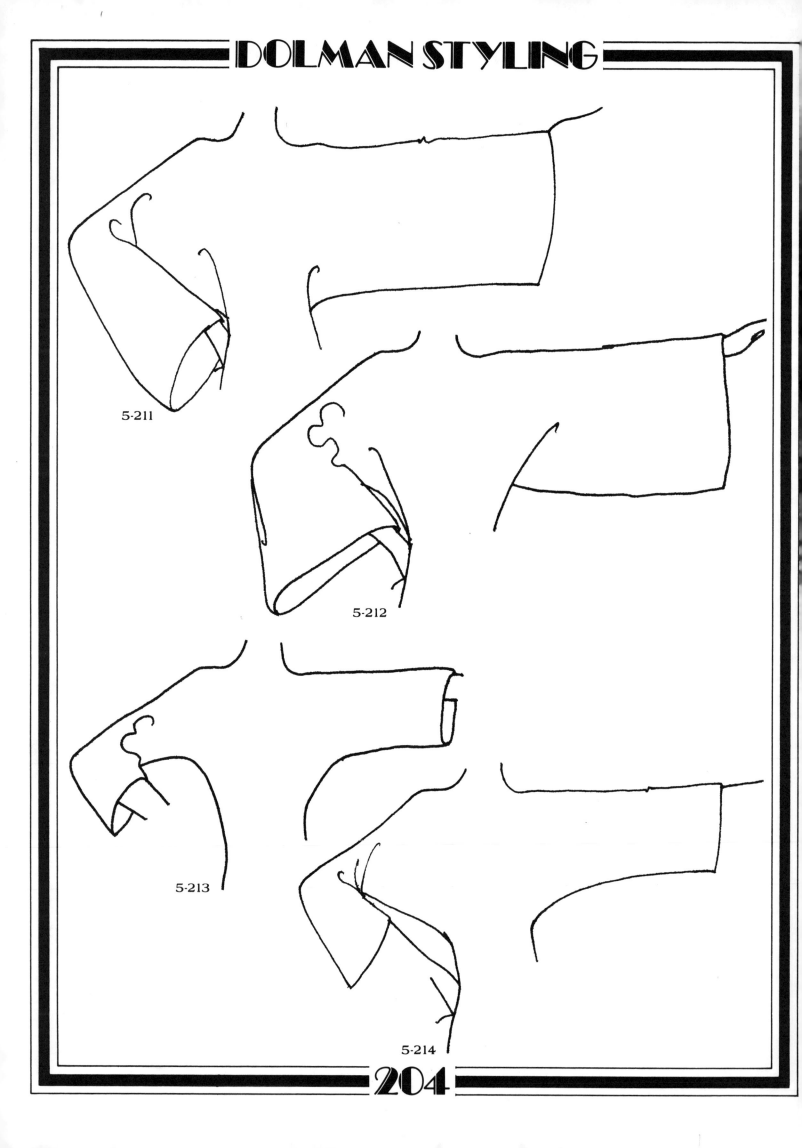

5-211

5-212

5-213

5-214

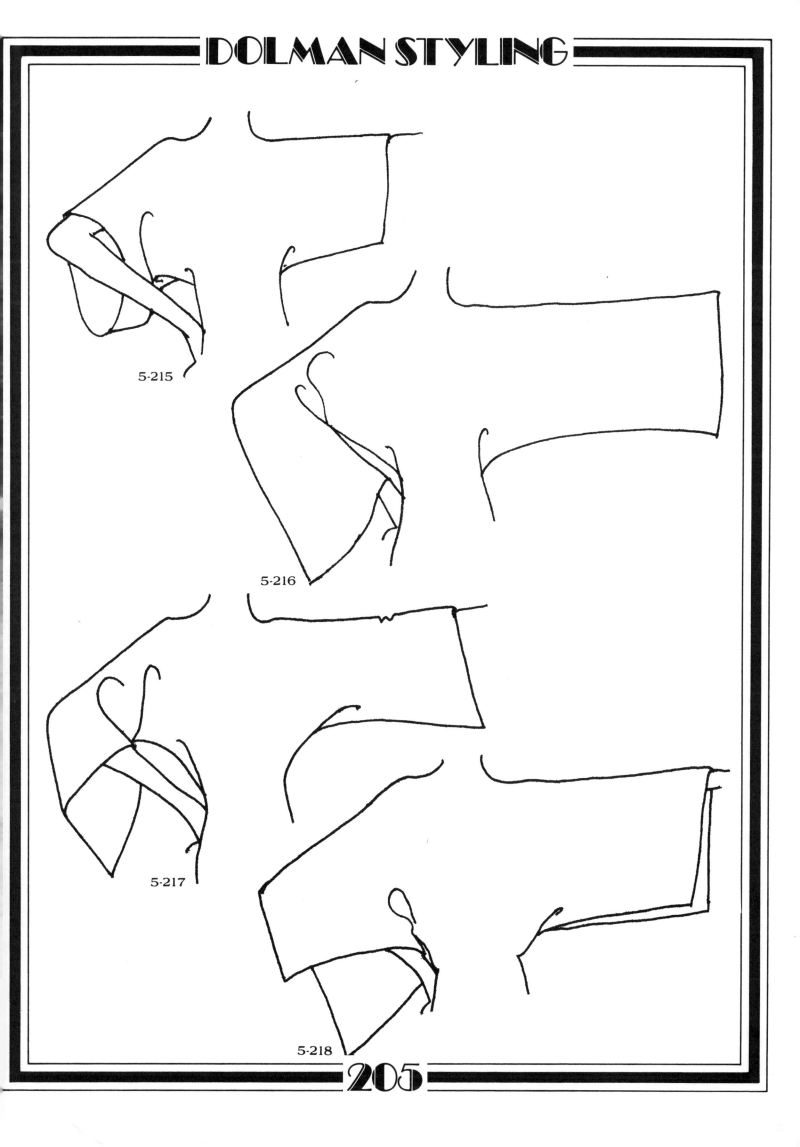

5-215

5-216

5-217

5-218

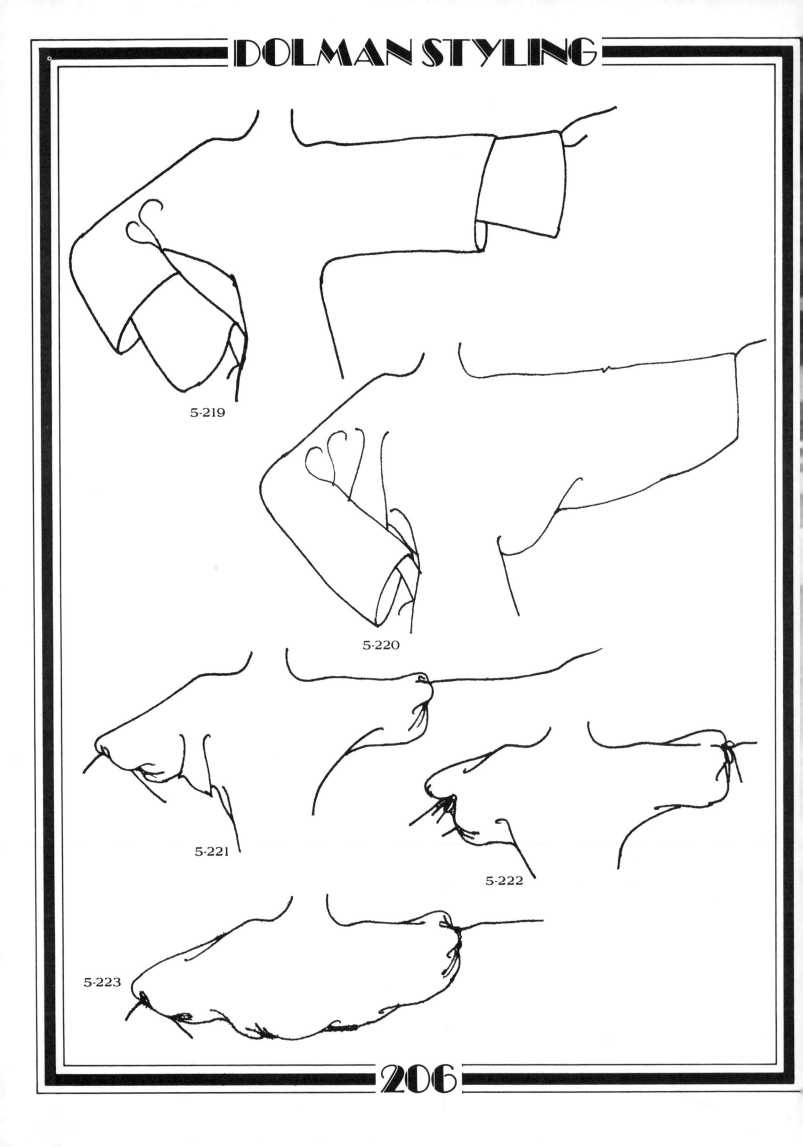

5-219

5-220

5-221

5-222

5-223

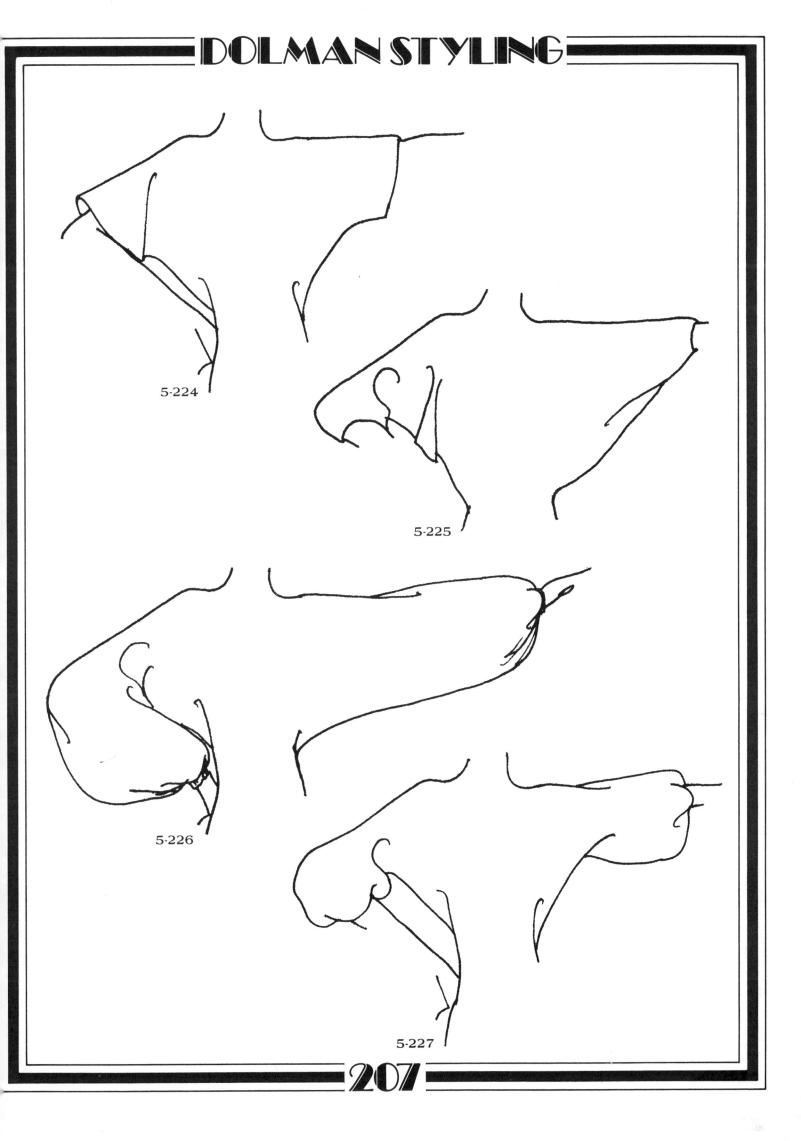

5-224

5-225

5-226

5-227

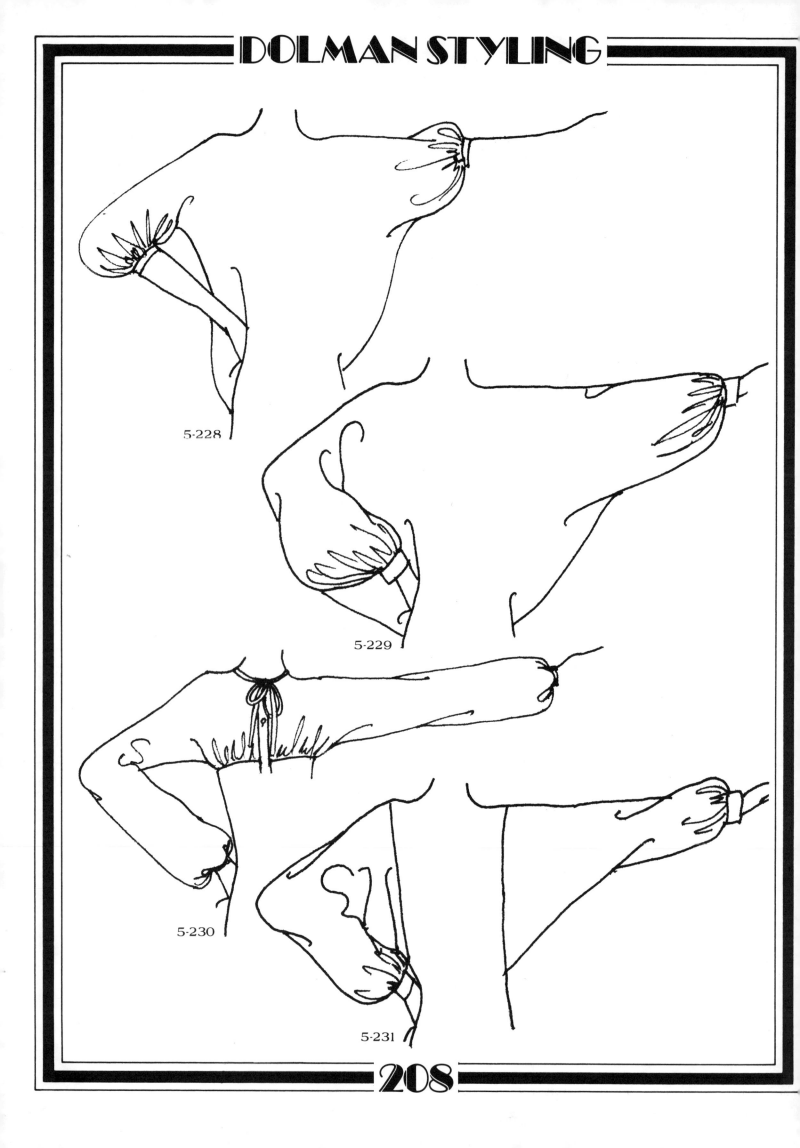

5-228

5-229

5-230

5-231

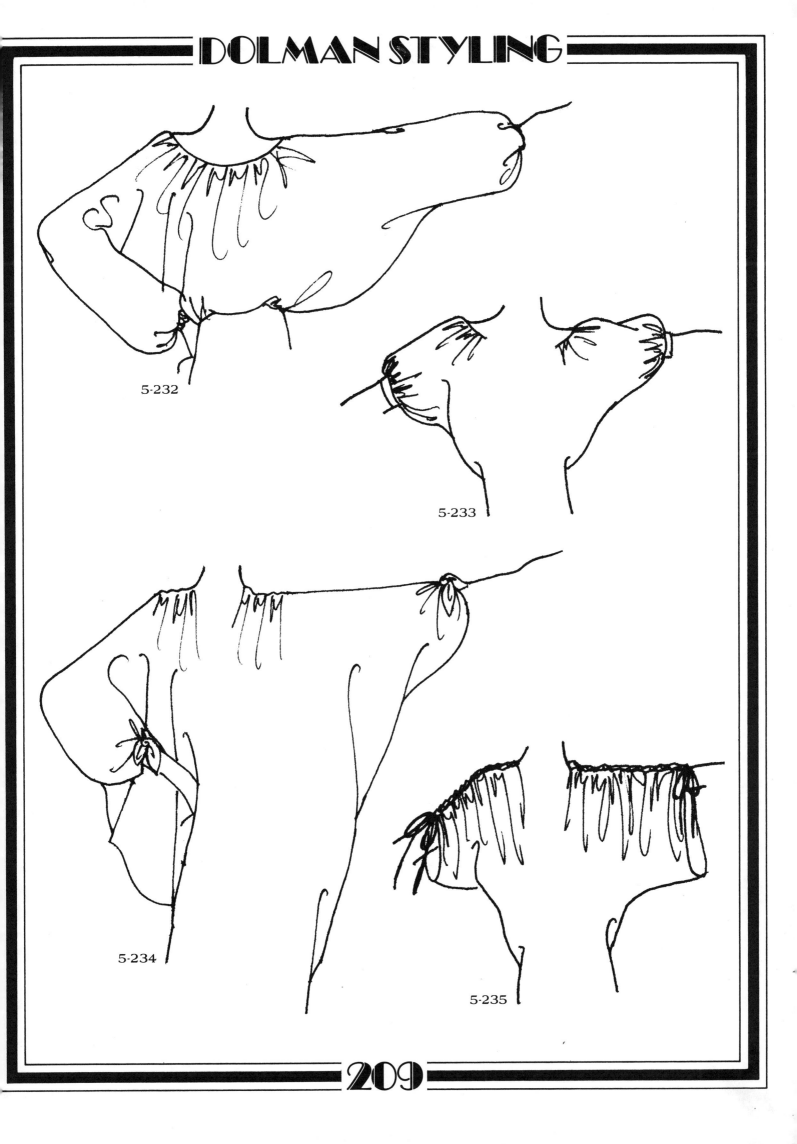

5-232

5-233

5-234

5-235

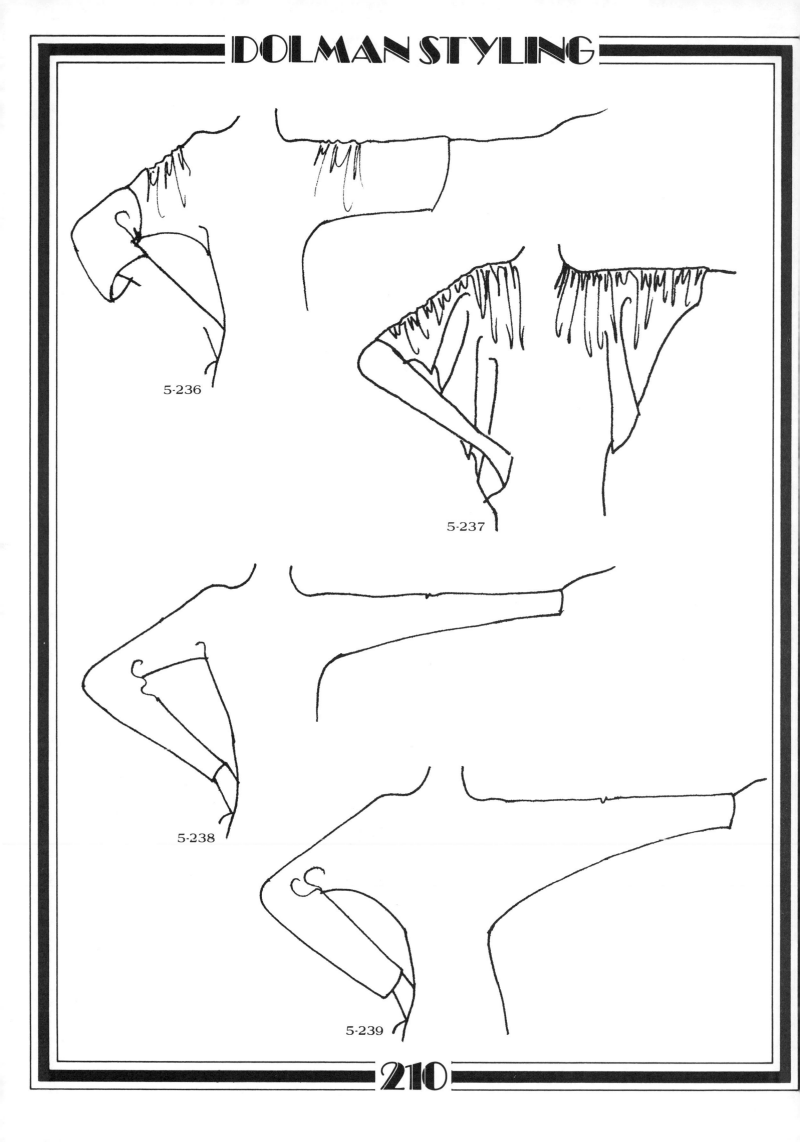

5-236

5-237

5-238

5-239

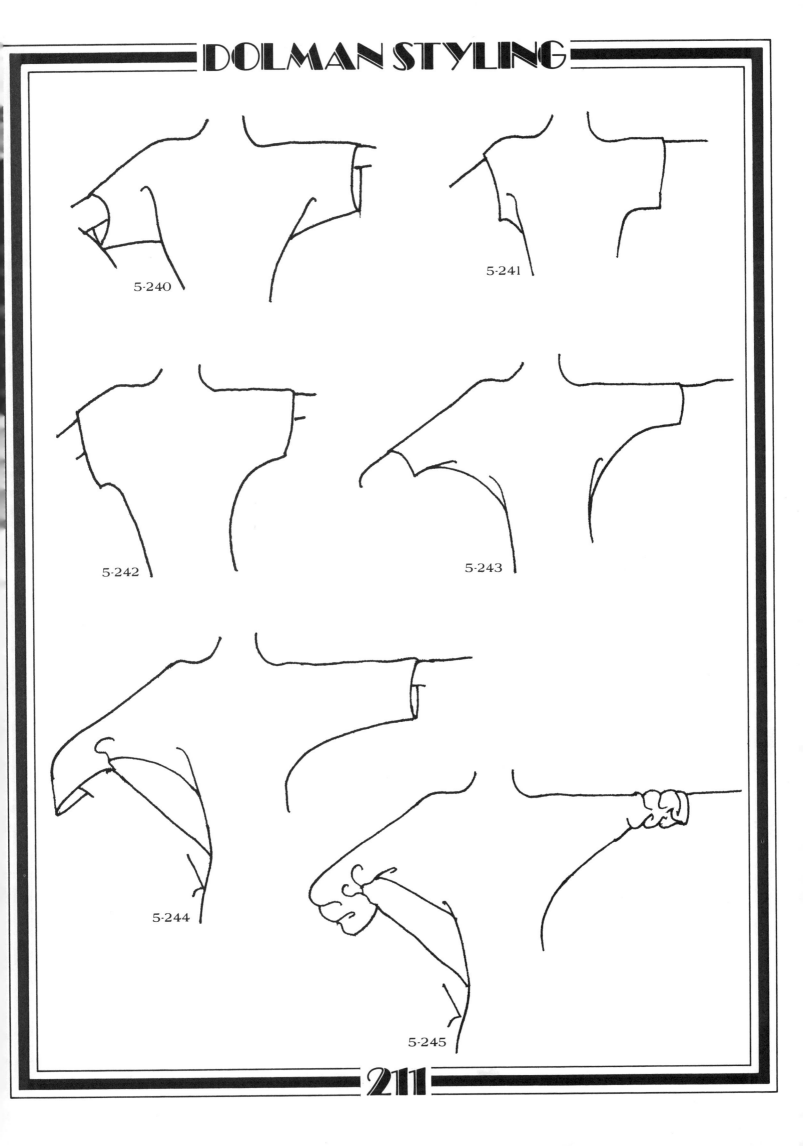

5-240

5-241

5-242

5-243

5-244

5-245

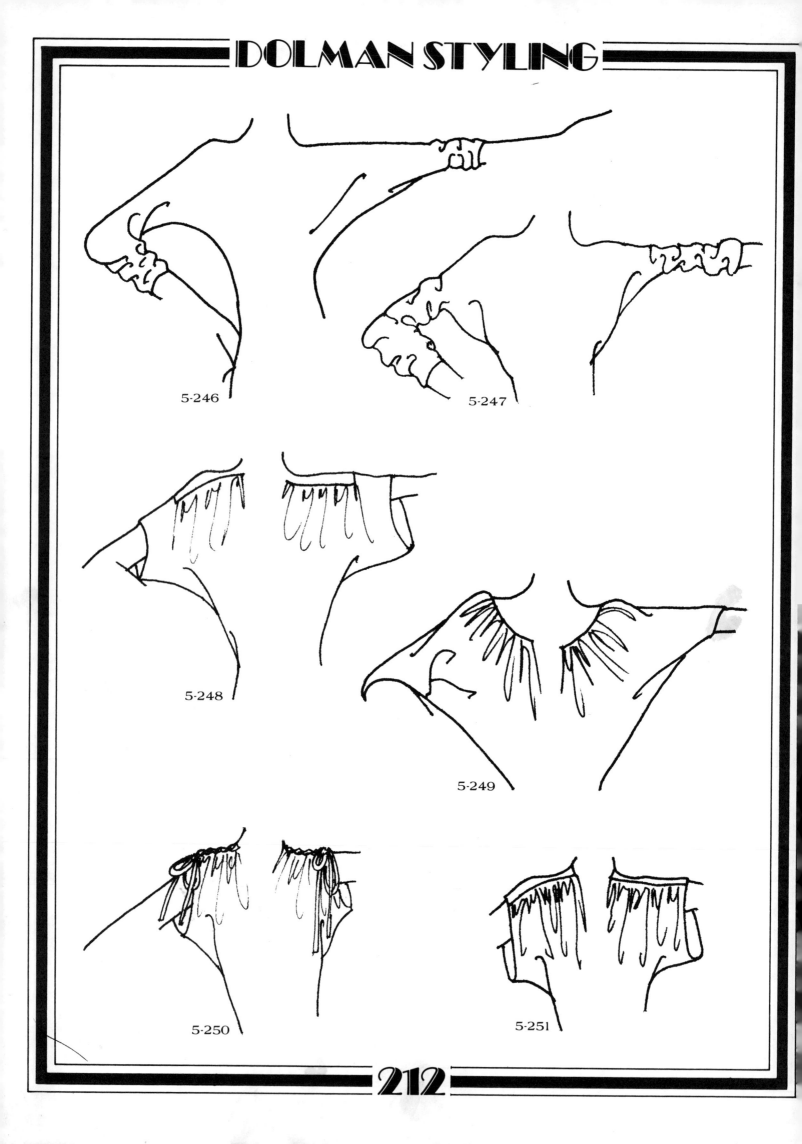

5-246

5-247

5-248

5-249

5-250

5-251

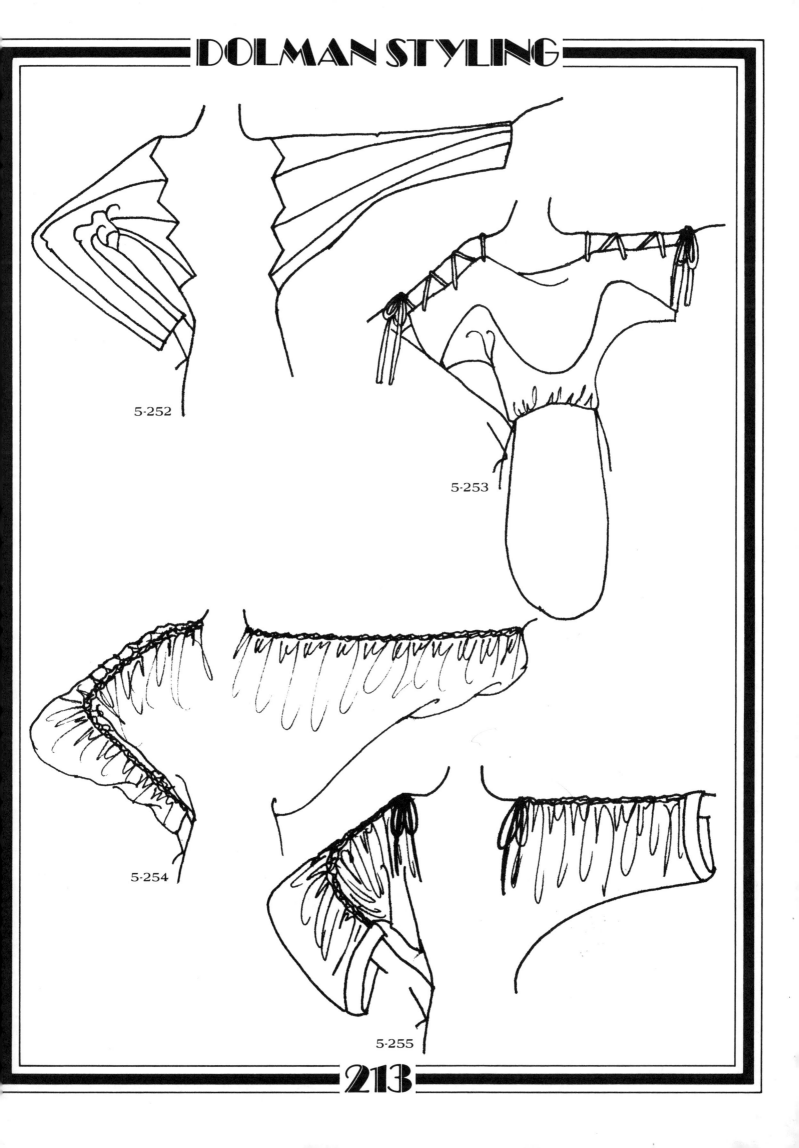

5-252

5-253

5-254

5-255

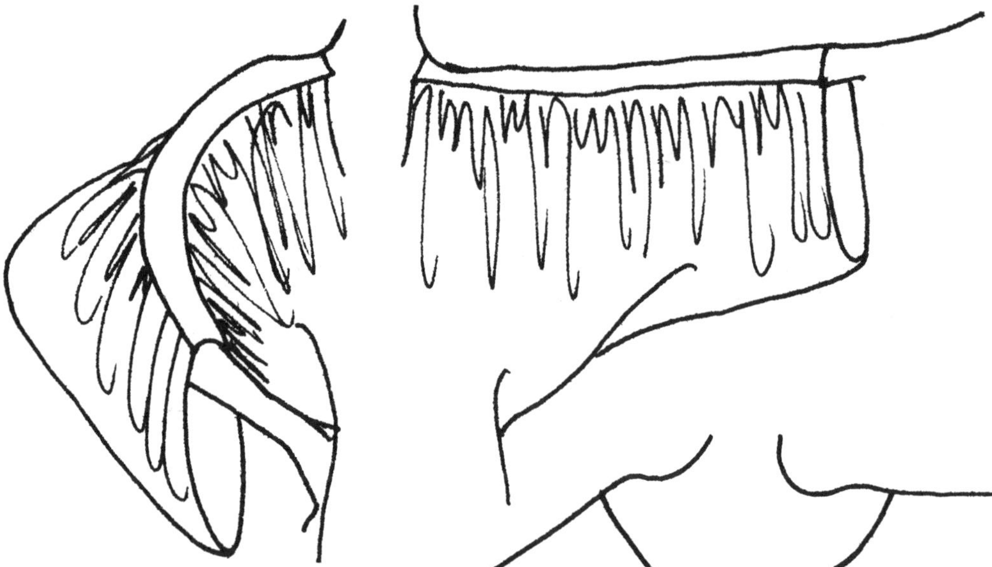

5-256

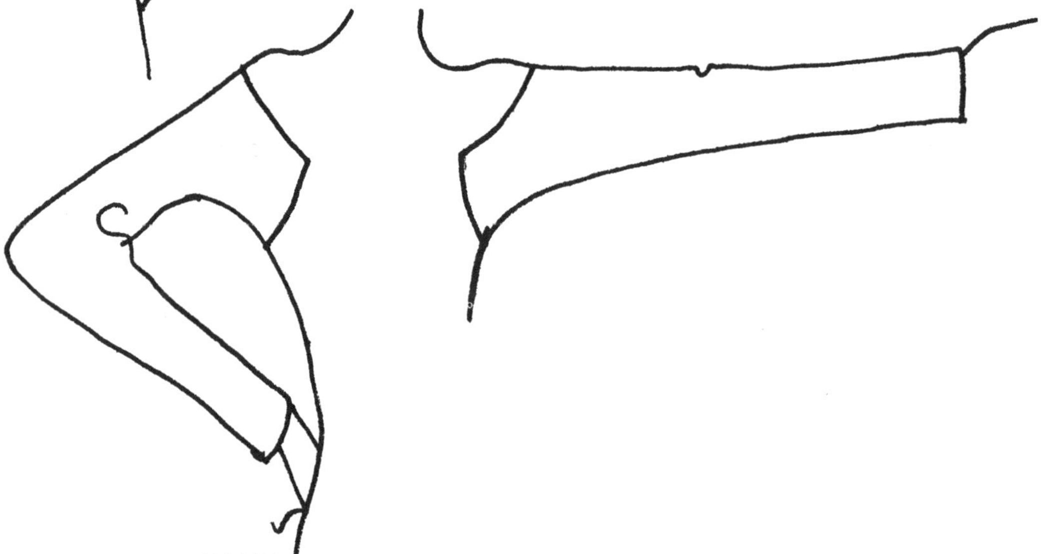

5-257

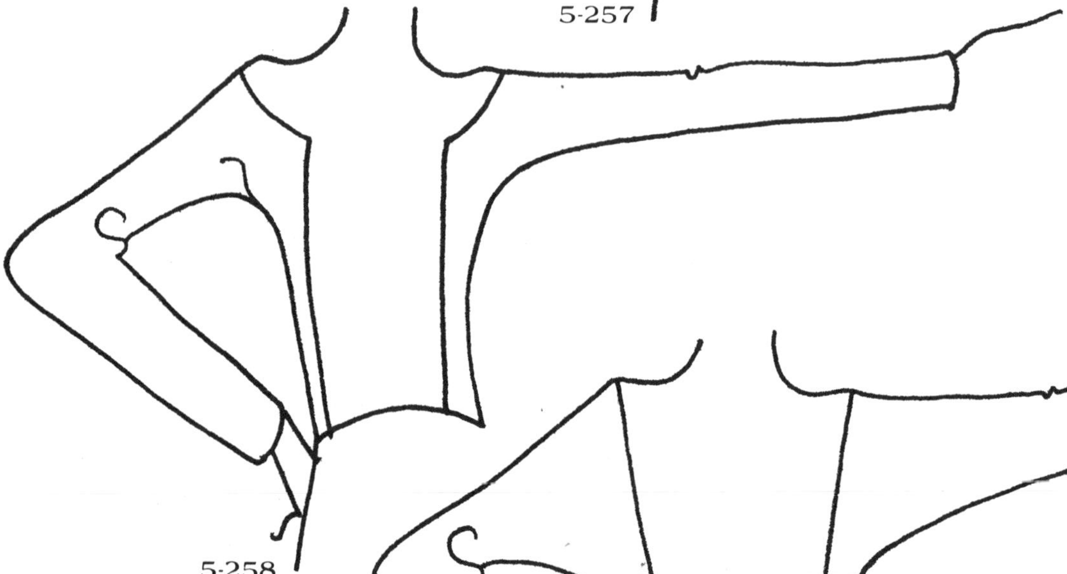

5-258

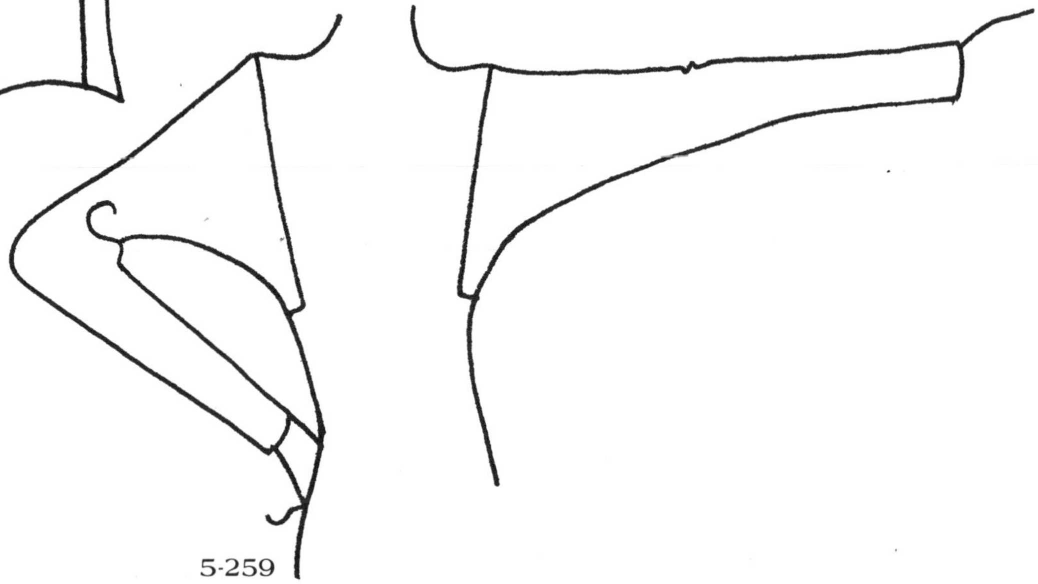

5-259

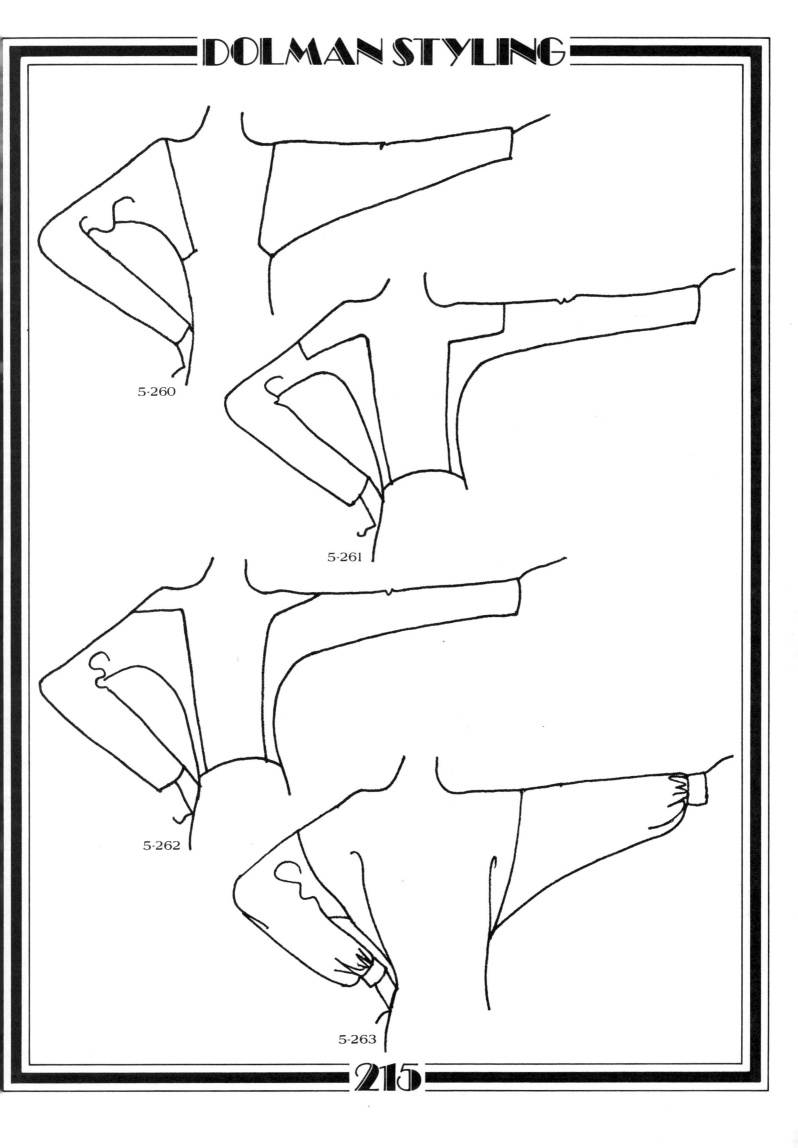

5-260

5-261

5-262

5-263

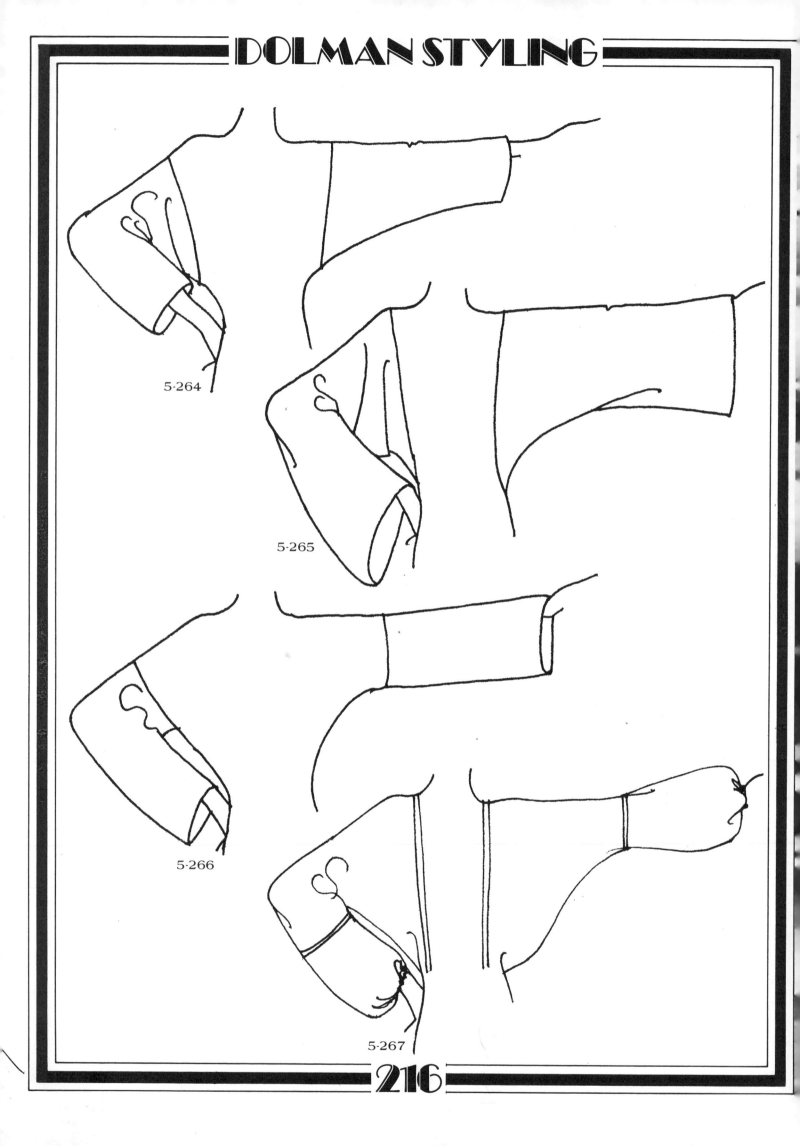

5-264

5-265

5-266

5-267

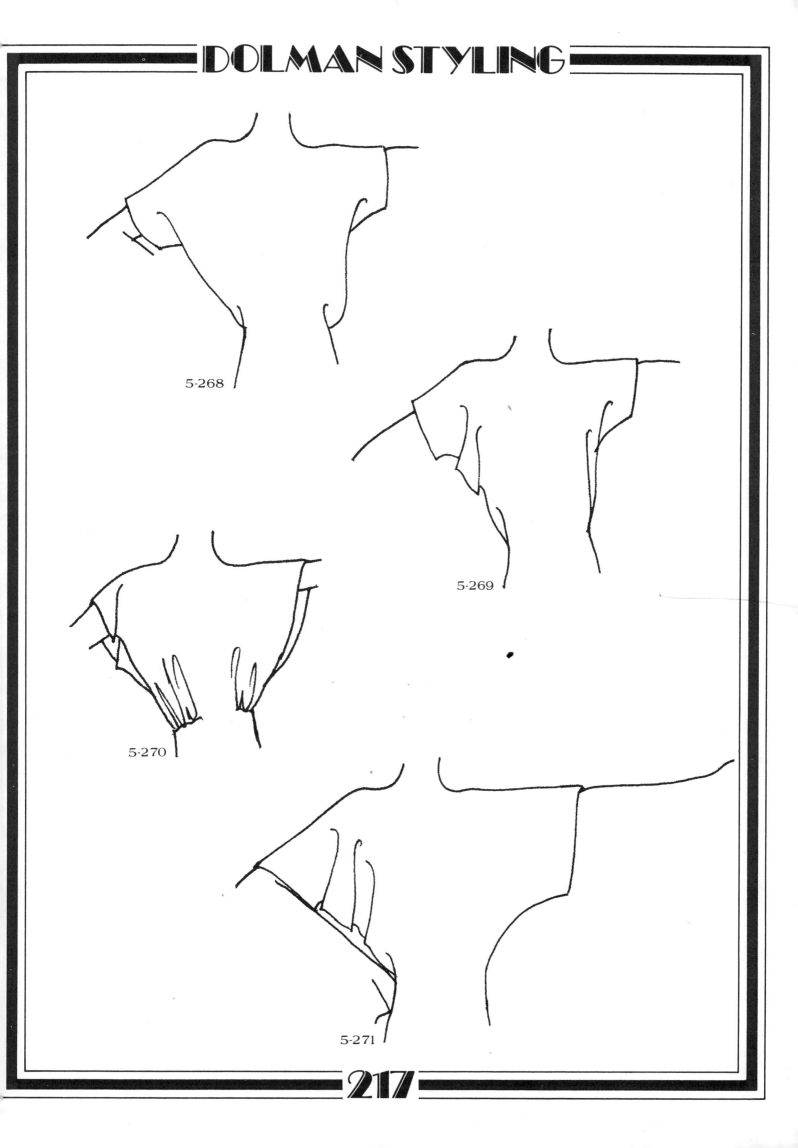

5·268

5·269

5·270

5·271

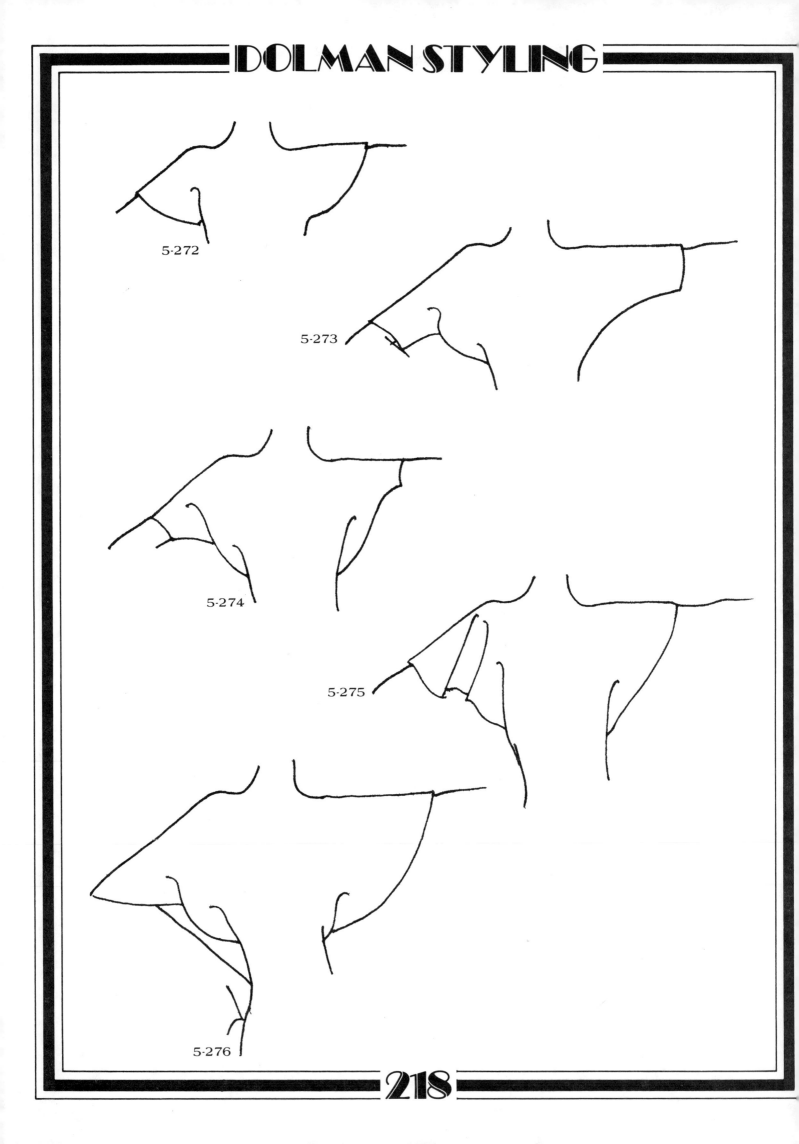

5·272

5·273

5·274

5·275

5·276

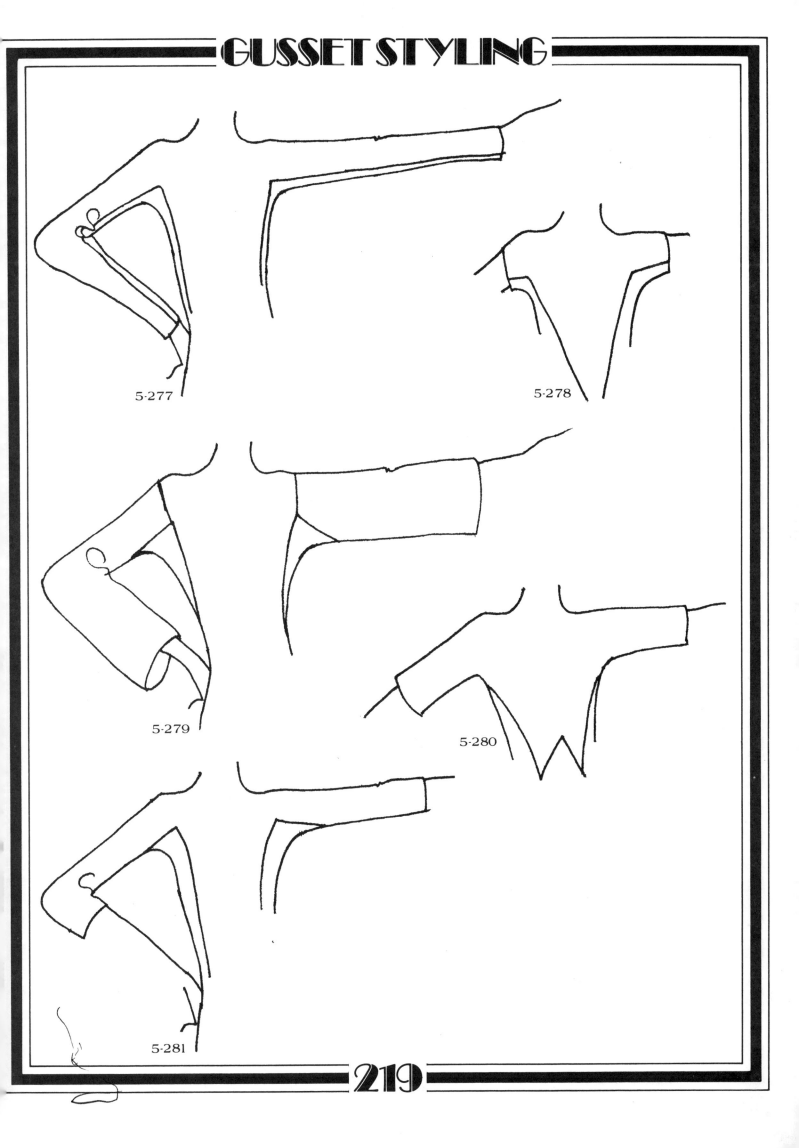

5-277

5-278

5-279

5-280

5-281

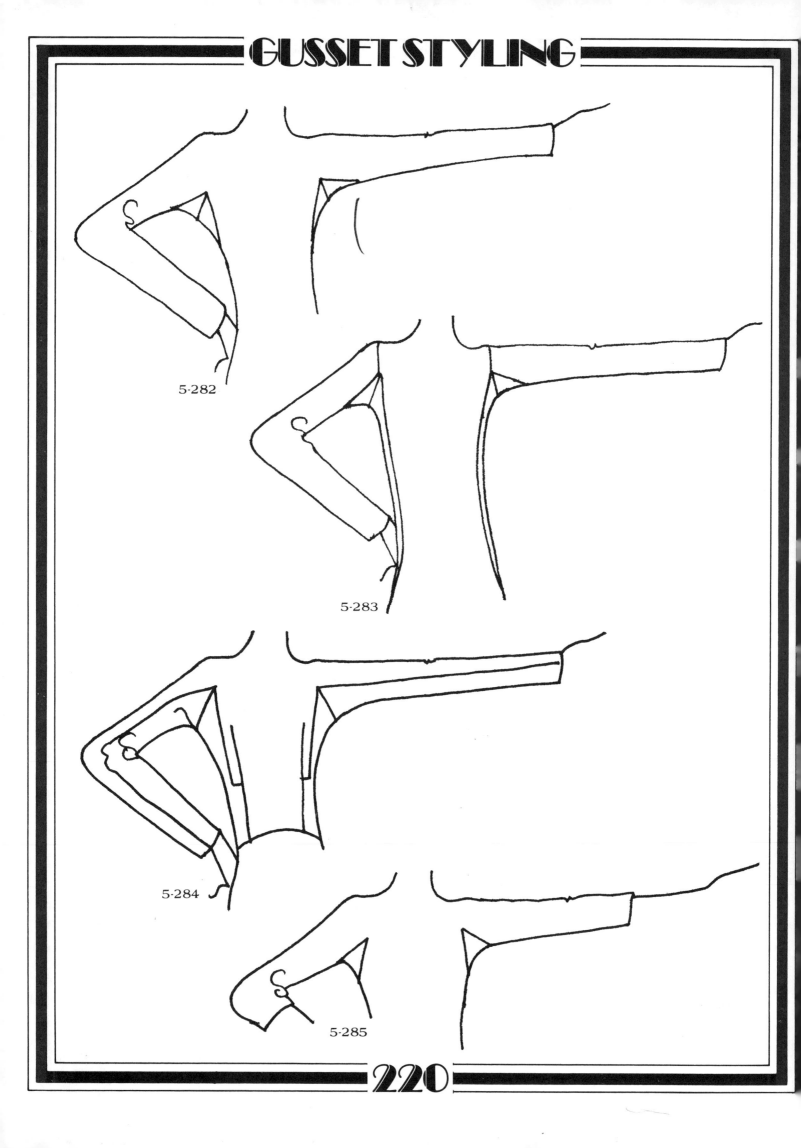

5·282

5·283

5·284

5·285

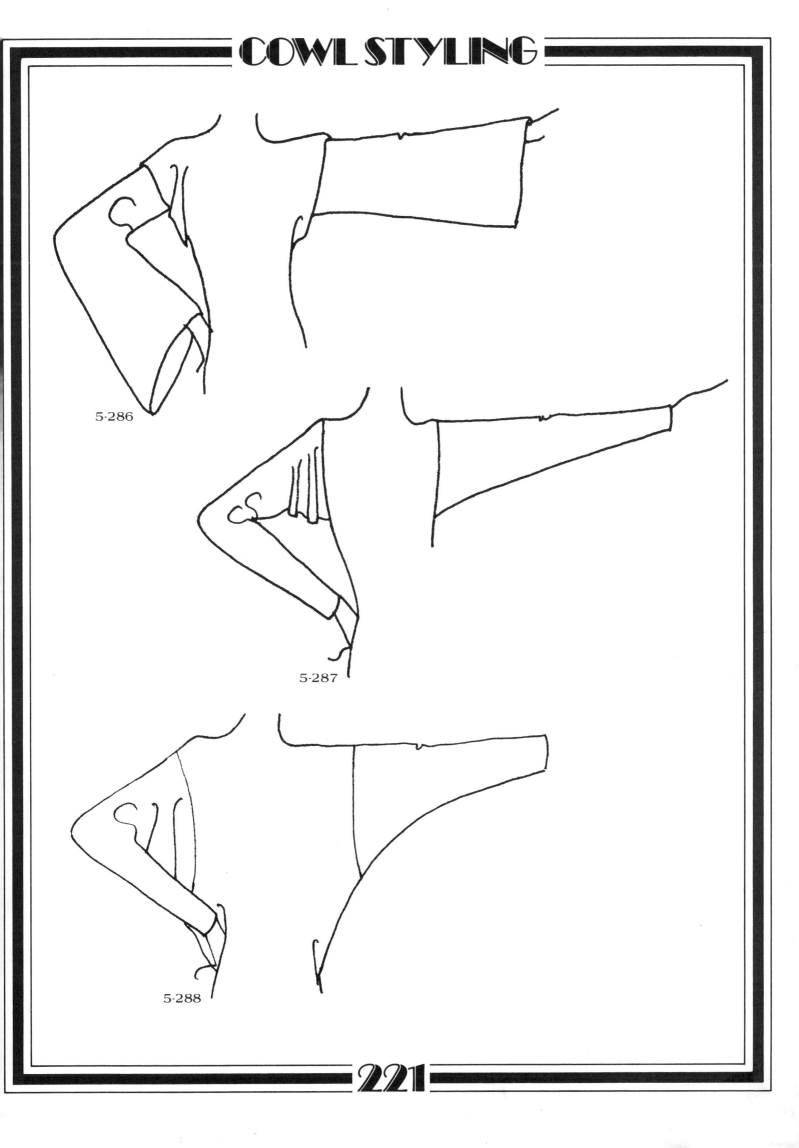

5-286

5-287

5-288

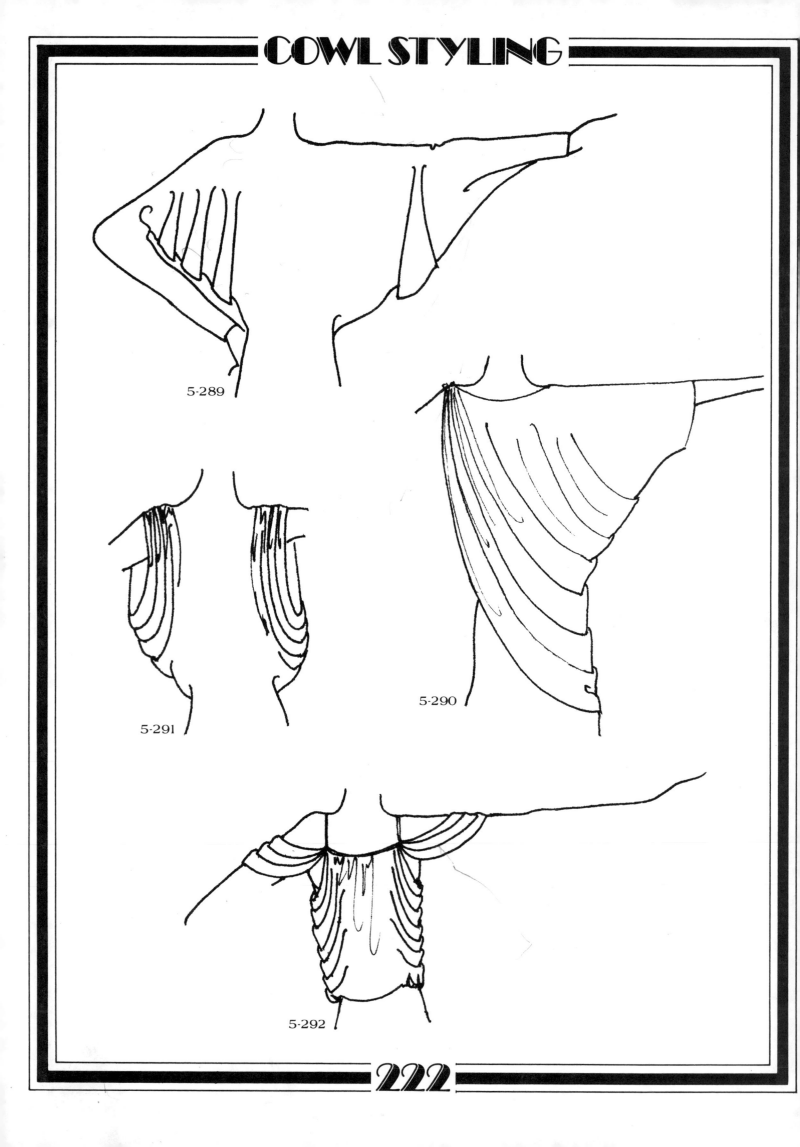

5-289

5-290

5-291

5-292

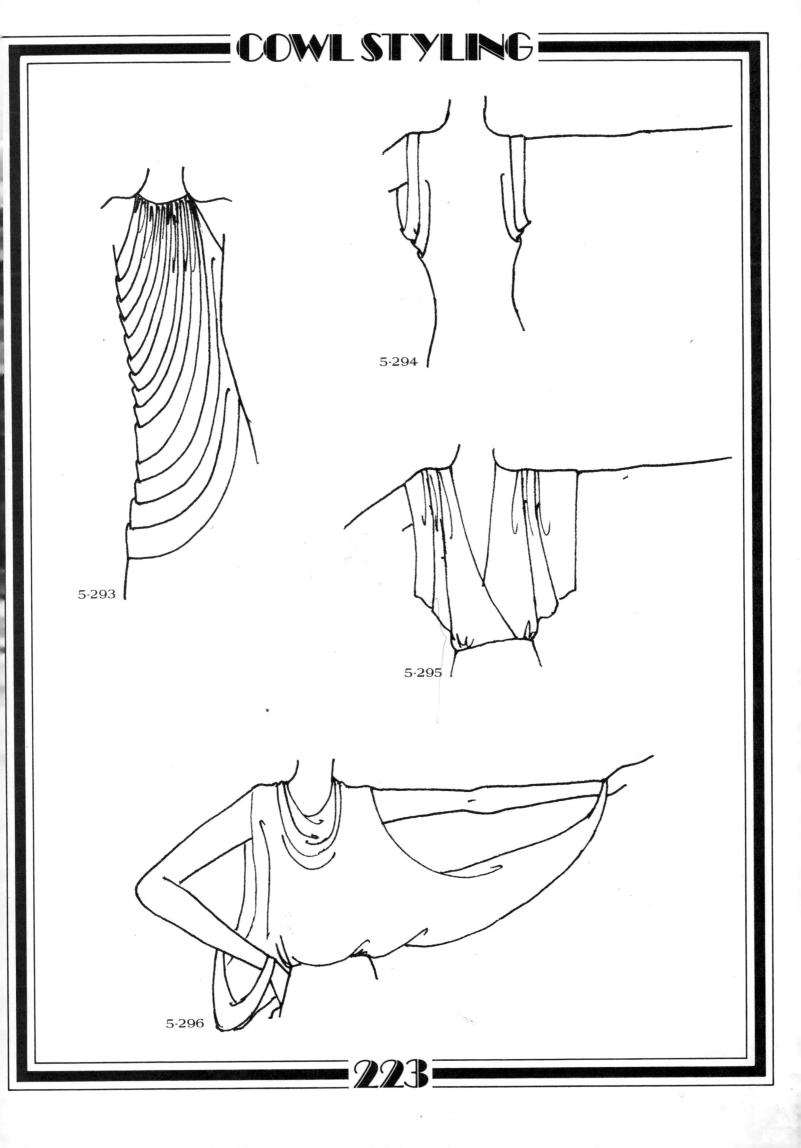

5-294

5-293

5-295

5-296

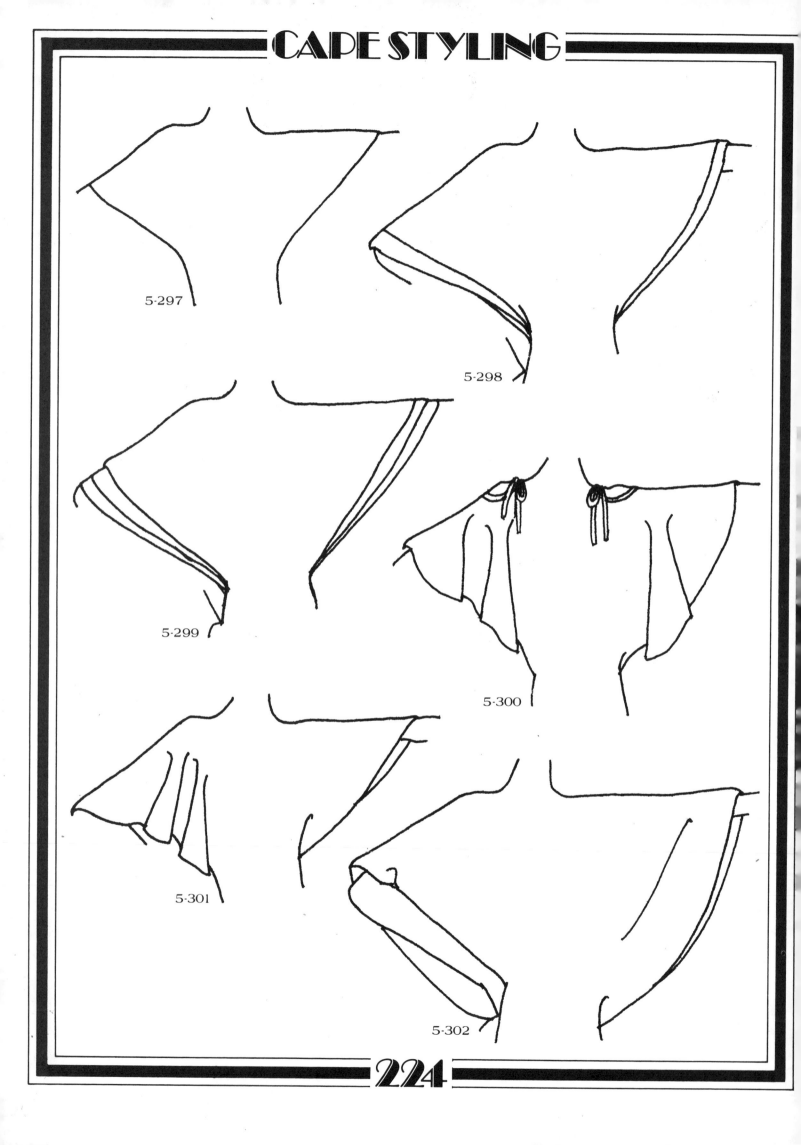

5-297

5-298

5-299

5-300

5-301

5-302

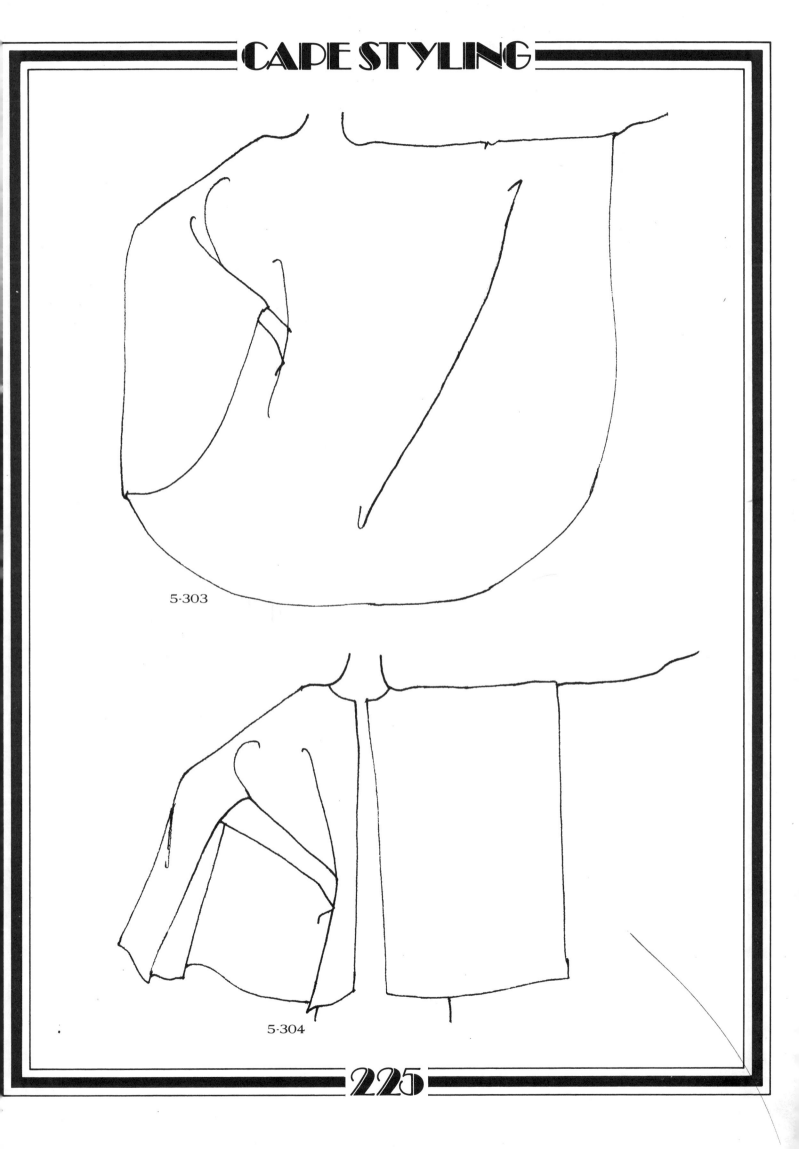

5-303

5-304

5-305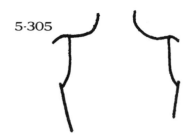

5-306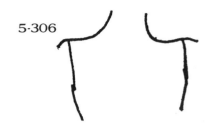

5-307

5-308

5-309

5-310

5-311

5-312

SIX·SLEEVE DETAILS

6-1

6-2

6-3

6-4

6-5

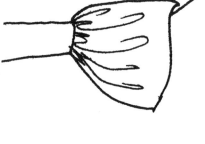

6-6

6-7

6-8

6-9

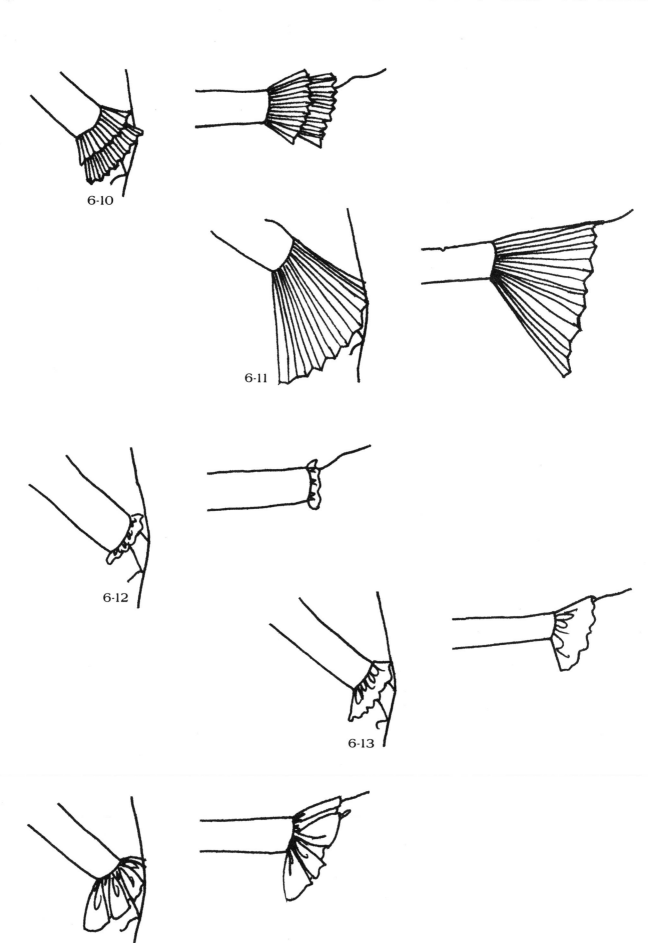

6-10

6-11

6-12

6-13

6-14

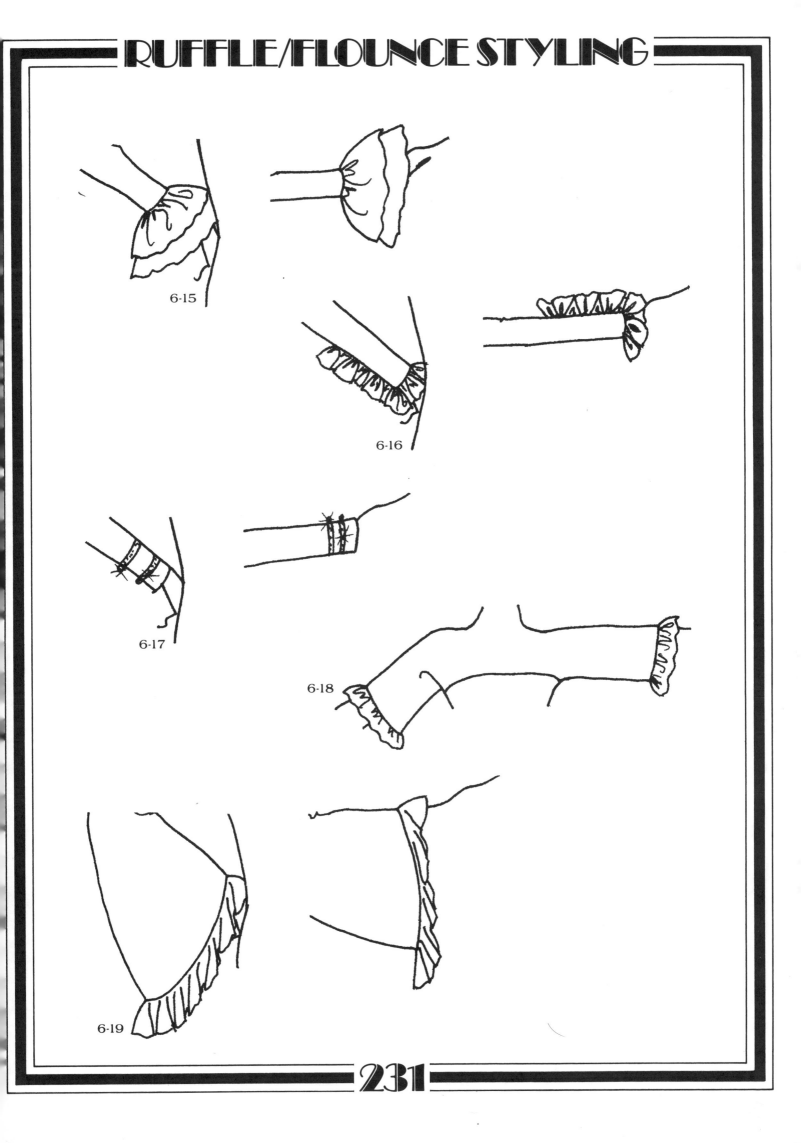

6-15

6-16

6-17

6-18

6-19

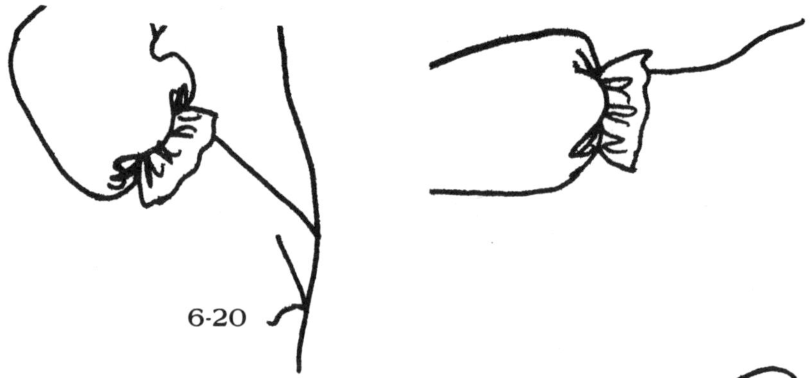

6-20

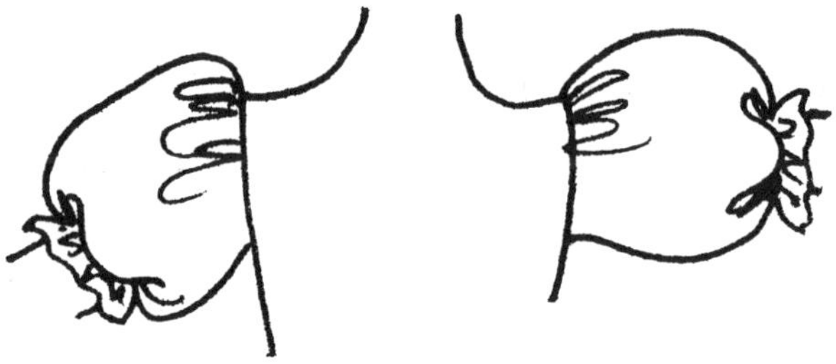

6-21

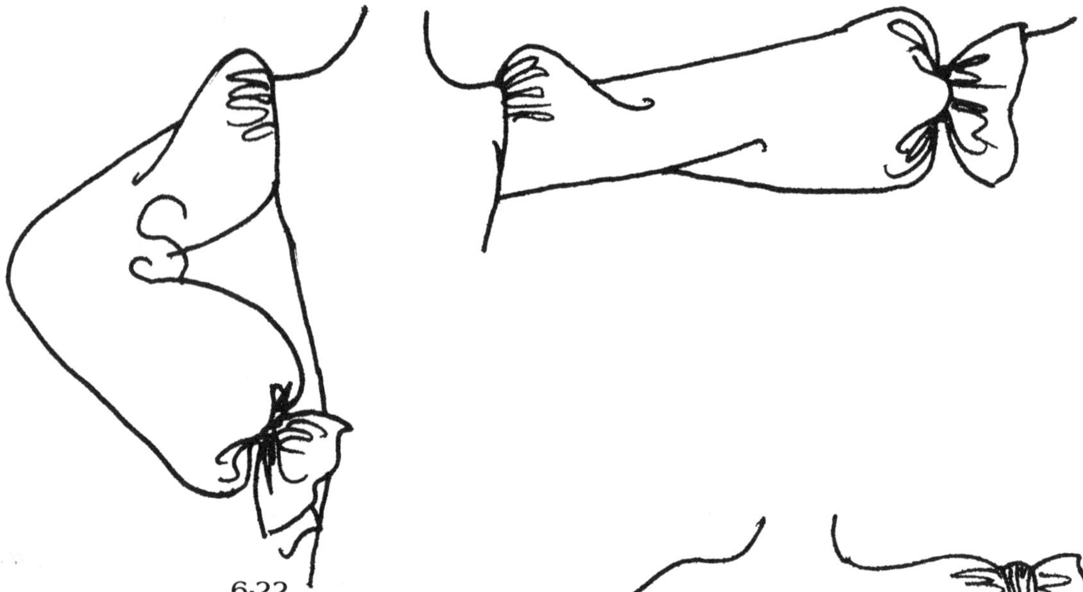

6-22

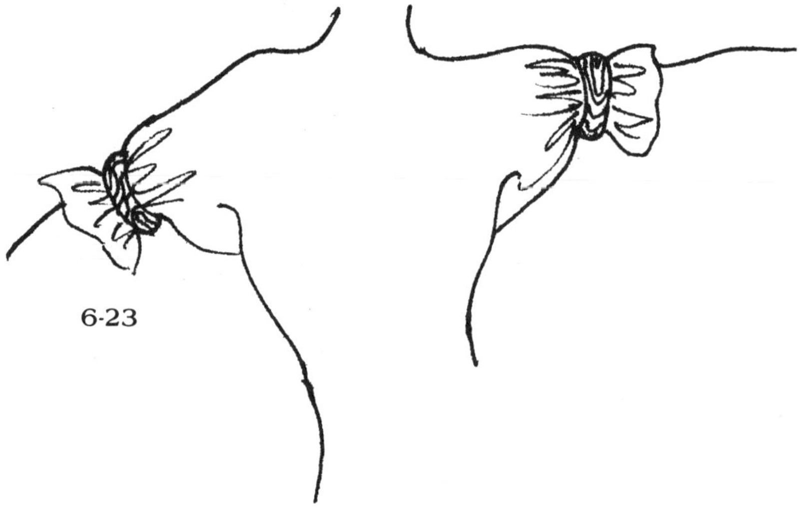

6-23

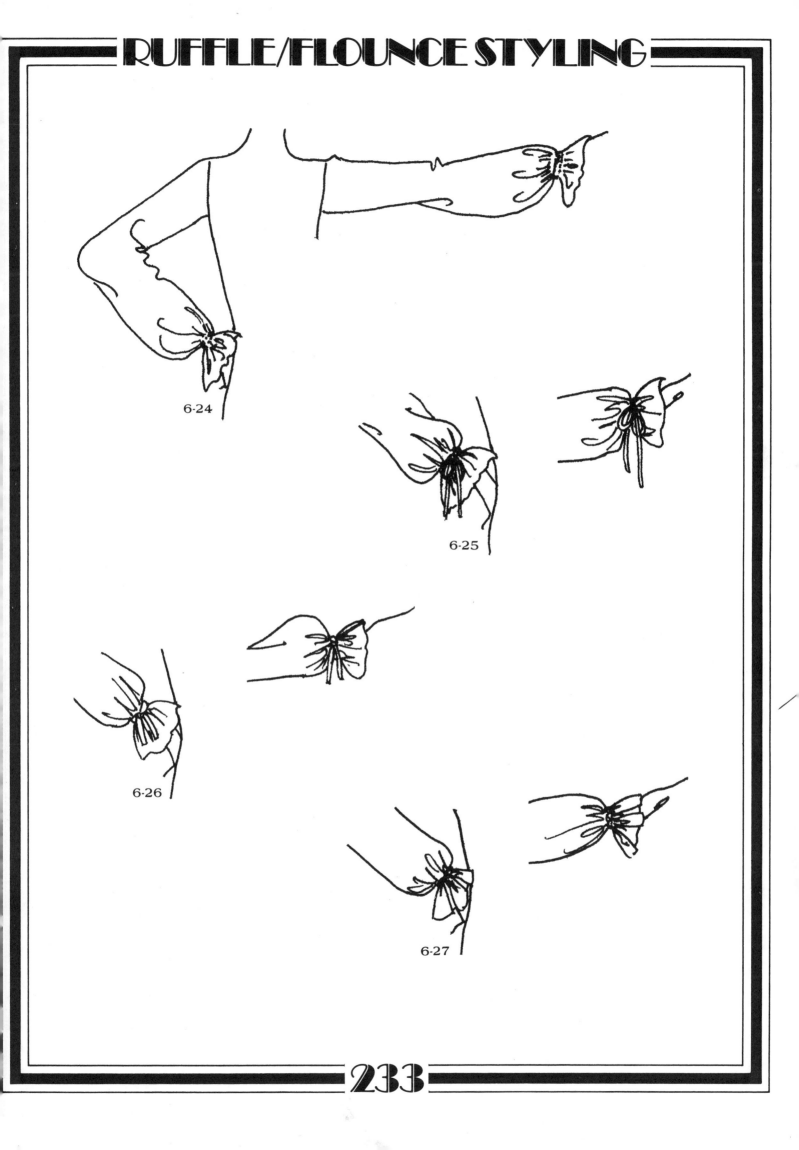

6-24

6-25

6-26

6-27

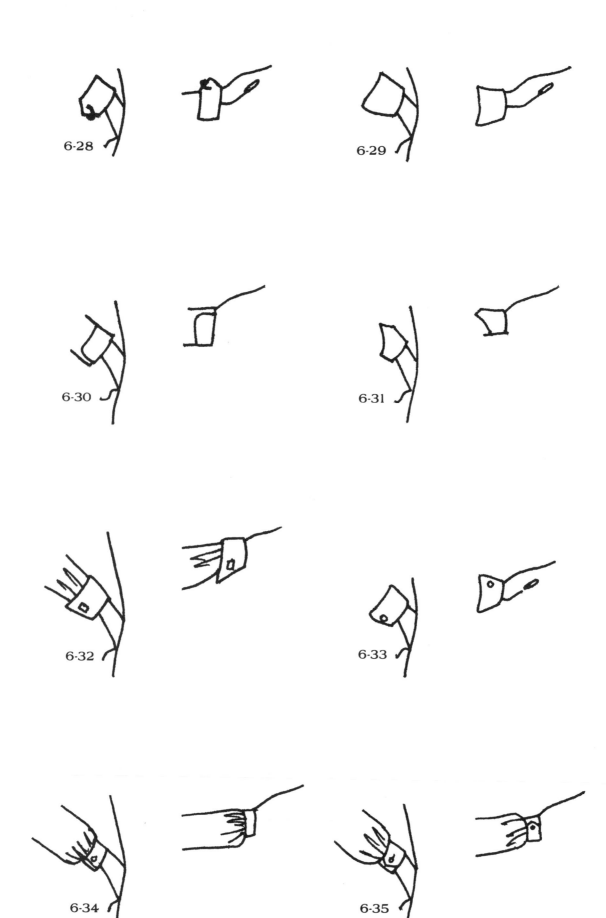

6-28

6-29

6-30

6-31

6-32

6-33

6-34

6-35

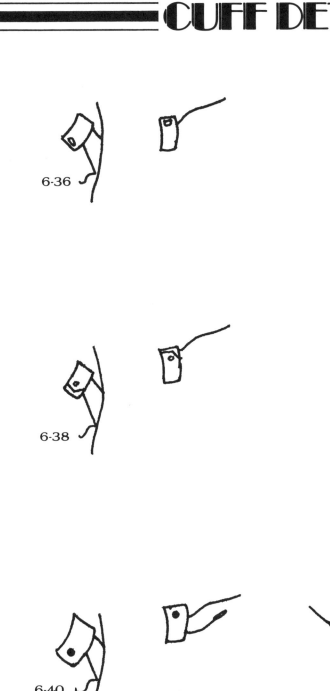

6-36

6-37

6-38

6-39

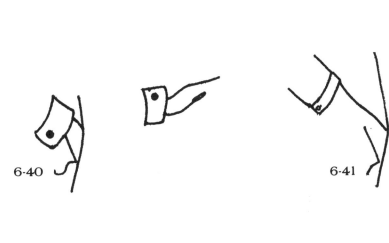

6-40

6-41

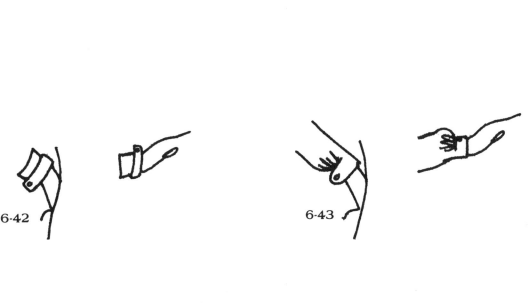

6-42

6-43

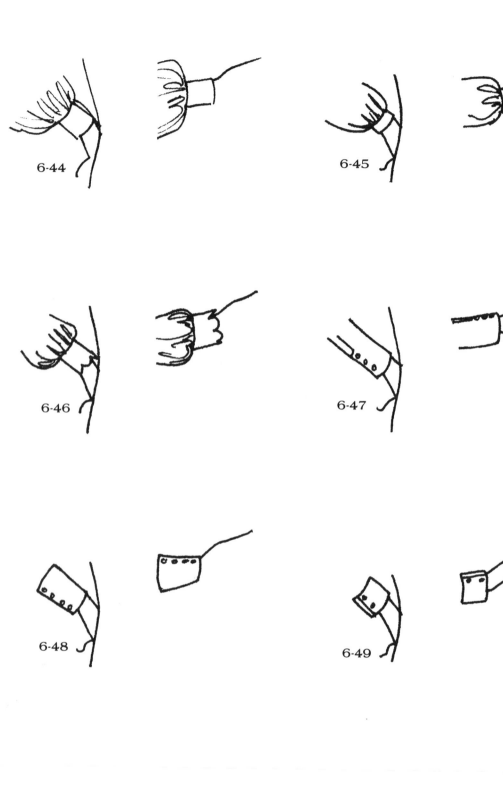

6-44

6-45

6-46

6-47

6-48

6-49

6-50

6-51

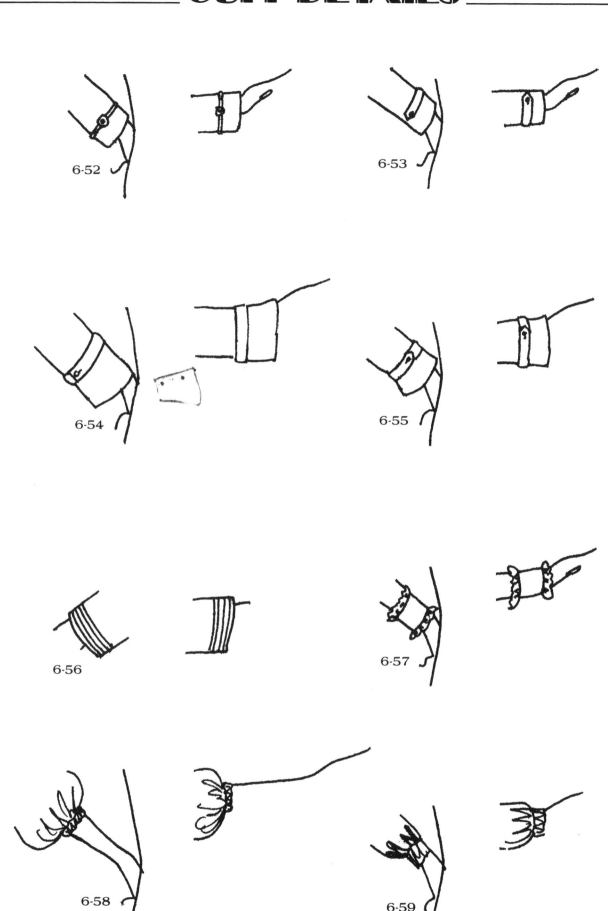

6-52

6-53

6-54

6-55

6-56

6-57

6-58

6-59

6-60

6-61

6-62

6-63

6-64

6-65

6-66

6-67

6-68

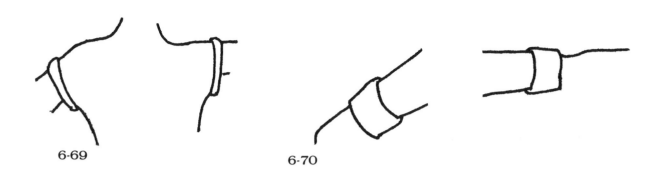

6-69   6-70

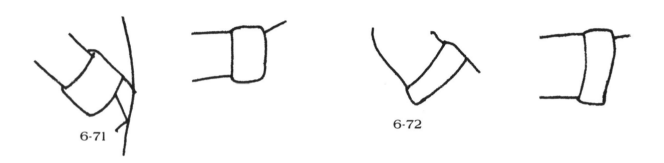

6-71   6-72

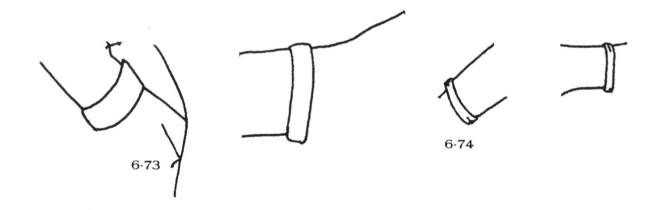

6-73   6-74

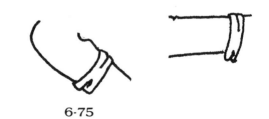

6-75

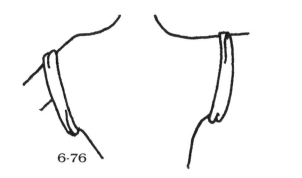

6-76

6-77

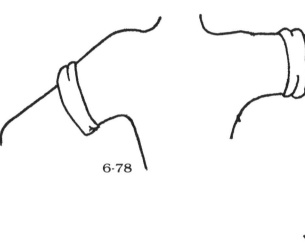

6-78

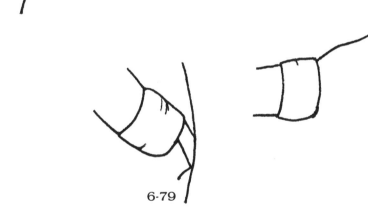

6-79

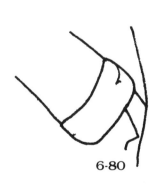

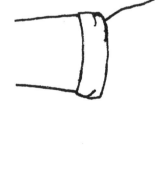

6-80

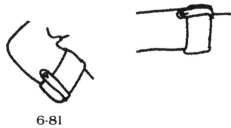

6-81

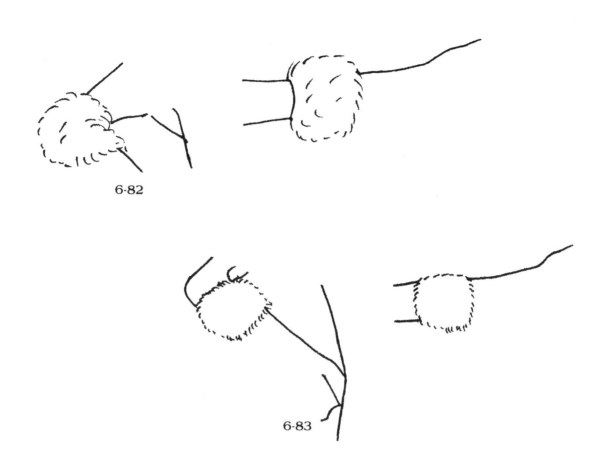

6-82

6-83

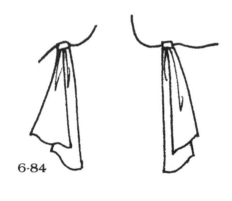

6-84

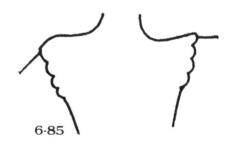

6-85

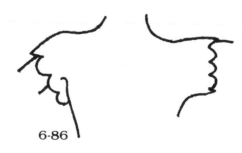

6-86

Shoulder/Bodice Yoke Styling   7-1 to 7-93

7-1   7-2   7-3

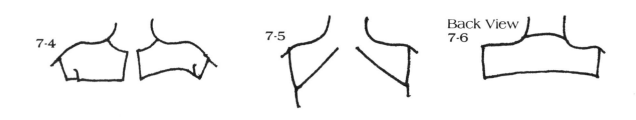

7-4   7-5   Back View 7-6

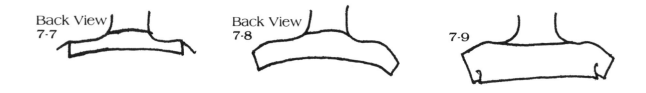

Back View 7-7   Back View 7-8   7-9

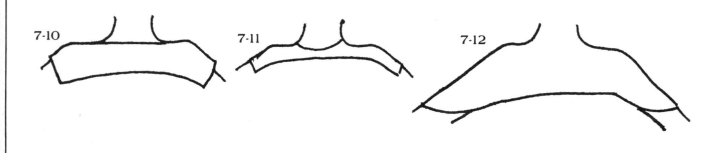

7-10   7-11   7-12

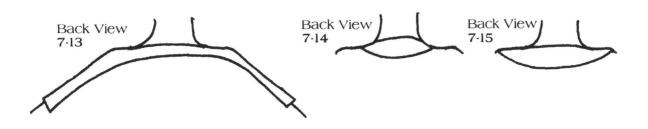

Back View
7-13

Back View
7-14

Back View
7-15

Back View
7-16

7-17

7-18

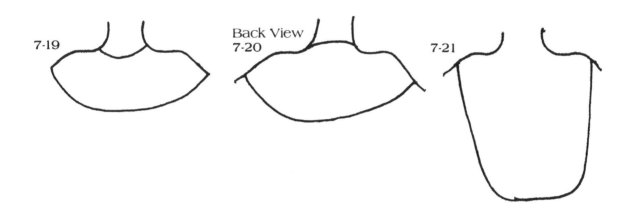

7-19

Back View
7-20

7-21

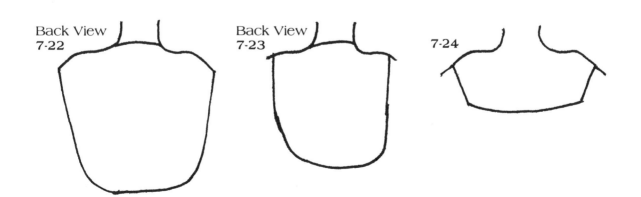

Back View
7-22

Back View
7-23

7-24

Back View
7-25
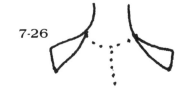

7-26
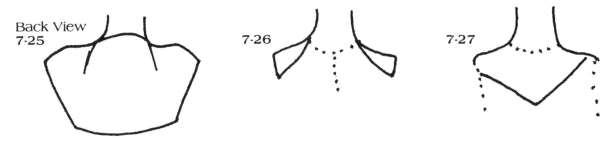

7-27
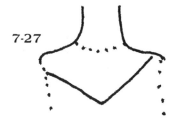

7-28
7-29
7-30
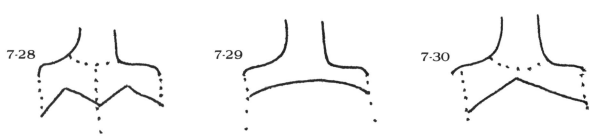
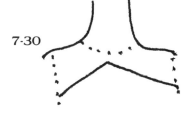

7-31
7-32
7-33
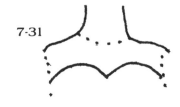
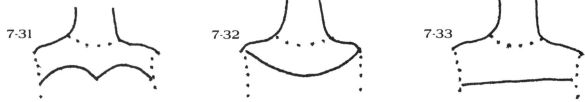

7-34
7-35
7-36
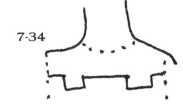
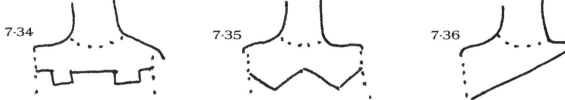
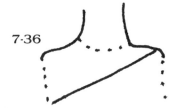

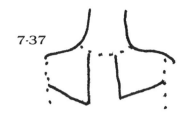

7-37

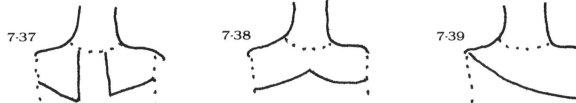

7-38

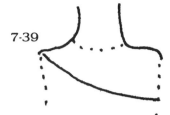

7-39

7-40

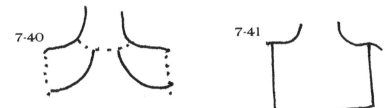

7-41

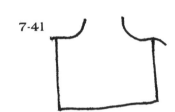

Back View
7-42

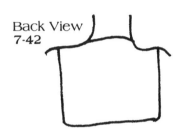

Back View
7-43

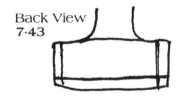

7-44

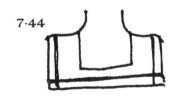

7-45

7-46

7-47

7-48

Back View
7-49

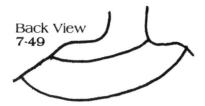

7-50

7-51

7-52

7-53

7-54

Back View
7-55

7-56

7-57

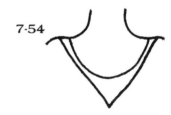

7-58

7-59

7-60

7-61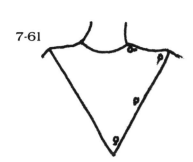

7-62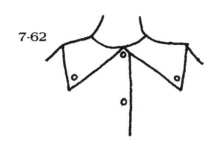

7-63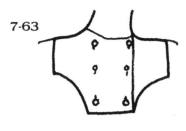

7-64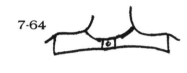

7-65

7-66

7-67

7-68

7-69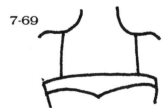

7-70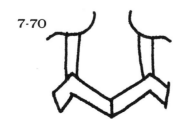

7-71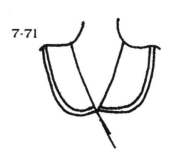

7-72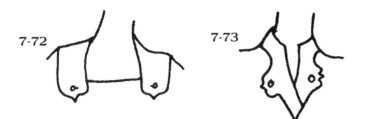

7-73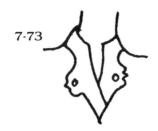

7-74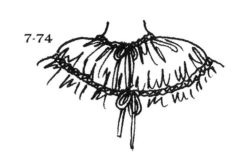

7-75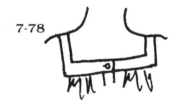

7-76

7-77

7-78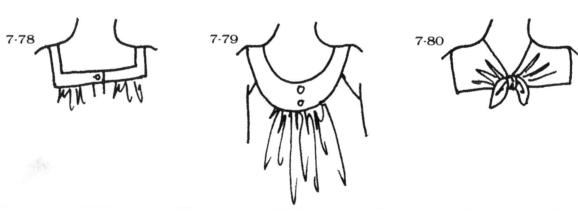

7-79

7-80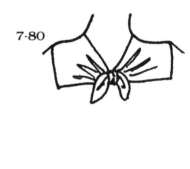

7-81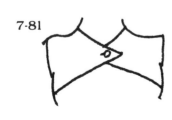

7-82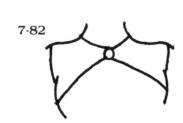

7-83

Back View
7-84

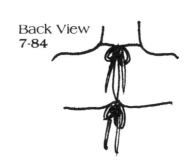

7-85

7-86

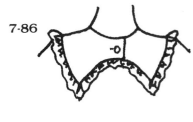

7-87

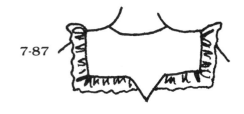

7-88

7-89

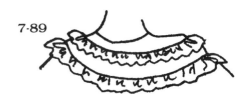

7-90

7-91

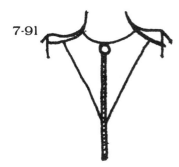

7-92

7-93

Midriff Styling   8-1 to 8-52

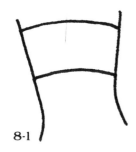

8-1

8-2

8-3

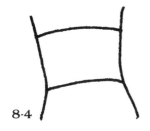

8-4

8-5

8-6

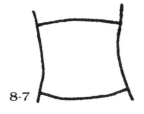

8-7

8-8

8-9

8-10

8-11

8-12

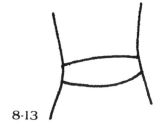

8-13

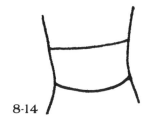

8-14

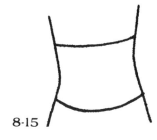

8-15

8-16

8-17

8-18

8-19

8-20

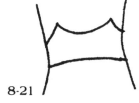

8-21

8-22

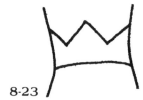

8-23

8-24

8-25

8-26

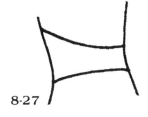

8-27

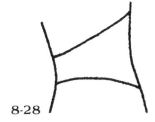

8-28

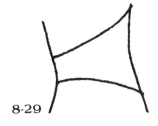

8-29

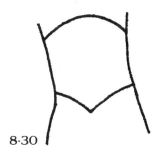

8-30

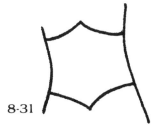

8-31

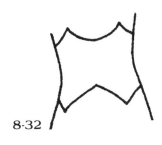

8-32

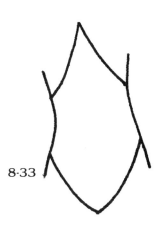

8-33

8-34

8-35

8-36

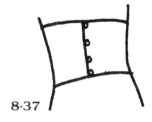

8-37

8-38

8-39

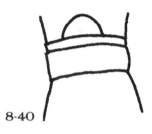

8-40

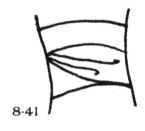

8-41

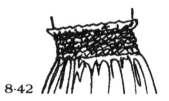

8-42

8-43

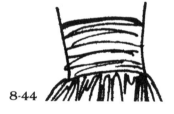

8-44

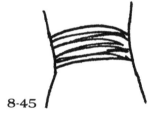

8-45

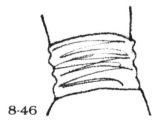

8-46

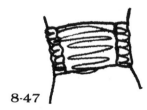

8-47

8-48

8-49

8-50

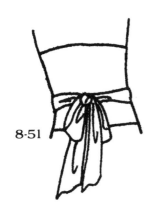

8-51

8-52

Waistline Styling   9-1 to 9-226

9-1

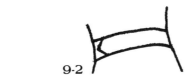

9-2

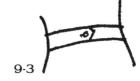

9-3

9-4

9-5

9-6

9-7

9-8

9-9

9-10

9-11

9-12

9-13

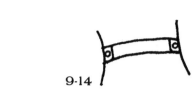

9-14

9-15

9-16

9-17

9-18

9-19

9-20

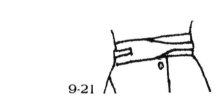

9-21

9-22

9-23

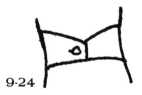

9-24

9-25

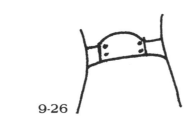
9-26

9-27

9-28

9-29

9-30

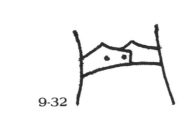
9-31

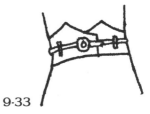
9-32

9-33

9-34

9-35

9-36

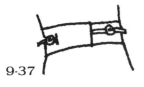

9-37

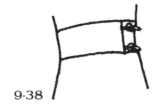

9-38

9-39

9-40

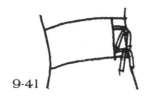

9-41

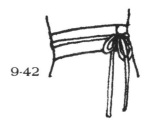

9-42

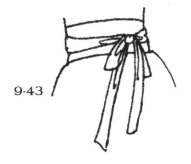

9-43

9-44

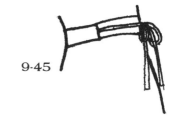

9-45

9-46

9-47

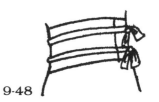

9-48

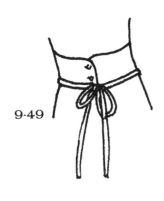

9-49

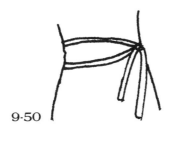

9-50

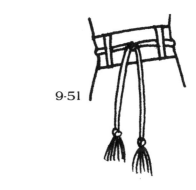

9-51

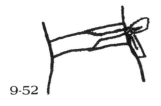

9-52

9-53

9-54

9-55

9-56

9-57

9-58

9-59

9-60

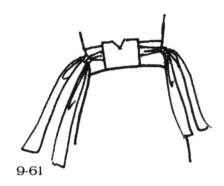

9-61

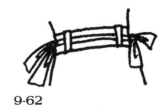

9-62

9-63

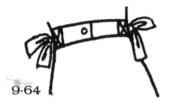

9-64

9-65

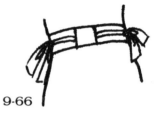

9-66

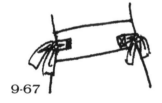

9-67

9-68

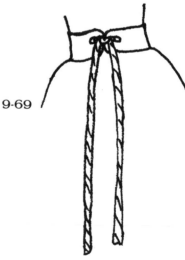

9-69

9-70

9-71

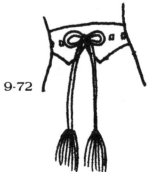

9-72

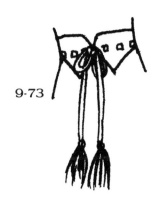

9-73

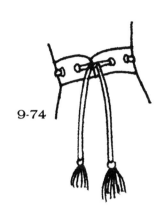

9-74

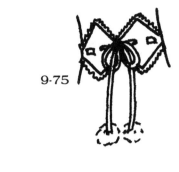

9-75

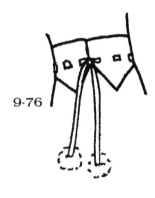

9-76

9-77

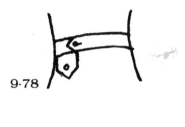

9-78

9-79

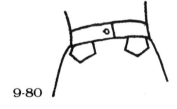

9-80

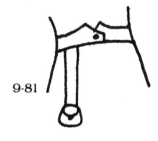

9-81

9-82

9-83

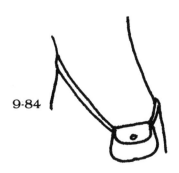

9-84

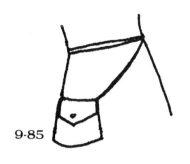

9-85

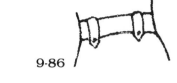

9-86

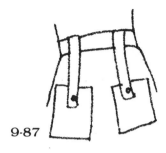

9-87

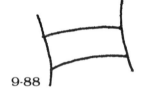

9-88

9-89

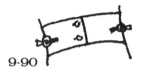

9-90

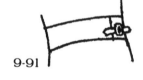

9-91

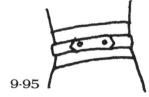

9-92

9-93

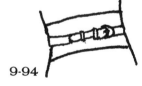

9-94

9-95

9-96

9-97

9-98

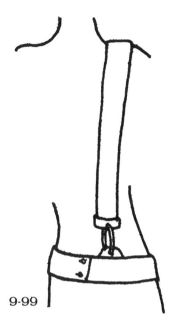

9-99

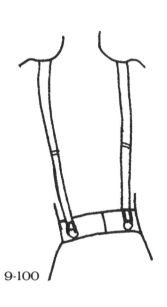

9-100

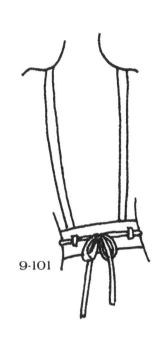

9-101

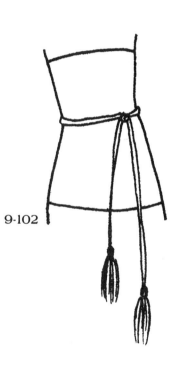

9-102

9-103

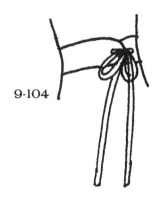

9-104

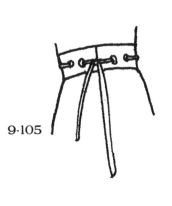

9-105

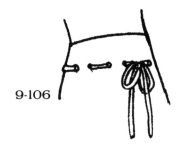

9-106

9-107

9-108

9-109

9-110

9-111

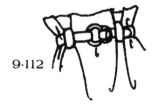

9-112

9-113

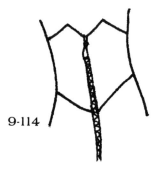

9-114

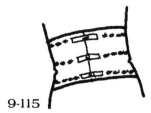

9-115

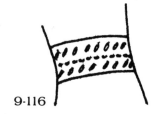

9-116

9-117

9-118

9-119

9-120

9-121

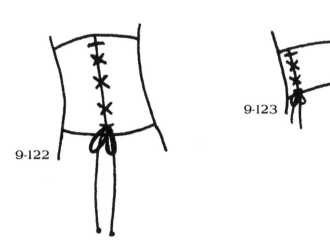

9-122

9-123

9-124

9-125

9-126

9-127

9-128

9-129

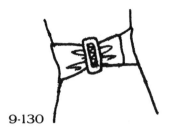

9-130

9-131

9-132

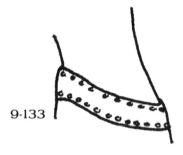

9-133

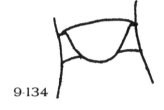

9-134

9-135

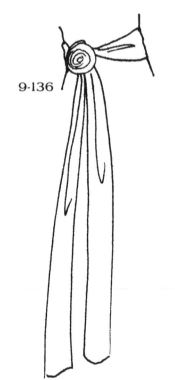

9-136

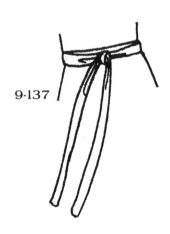

9-137

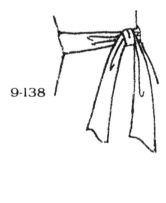

9-138

9-139

9-140

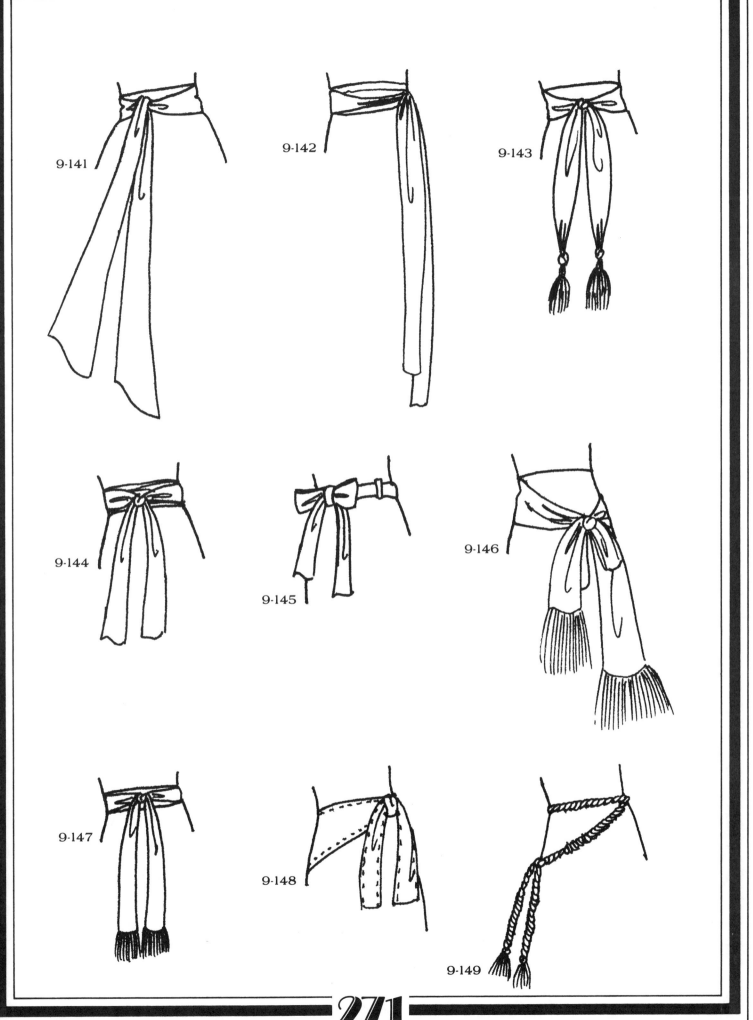

9-141

9-142

9-143

9-144

9-145

9-146

9-147

9-148

9-149

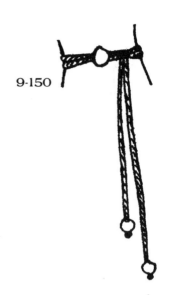

9·150

9·151

9·152

9·153

9·154

9·155

9·156

9·157

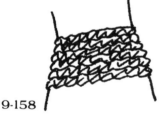

9·158

9·159

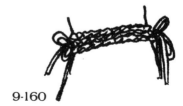

9·160

9·161

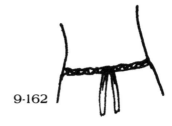

9-162

9-163

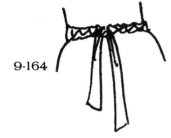

9-164

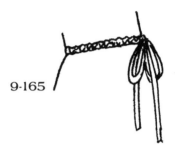

9-165

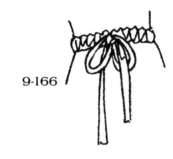

9-166

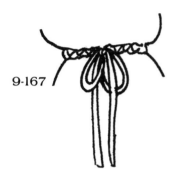

9-167

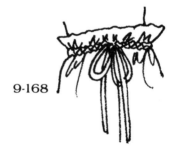

9-168

9-169

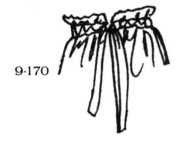

9-170

9-171

9-172

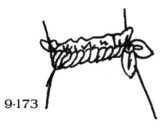

9-173

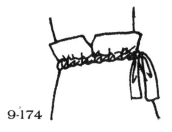

9-174

9-175

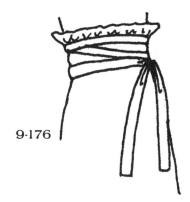

9-176

9-177

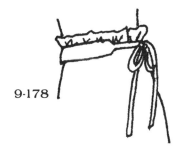

9-178

9-179

9-180

9-181

9-182

9-183

9-184

9-185

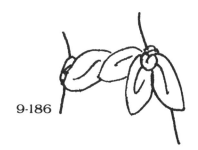

9-186

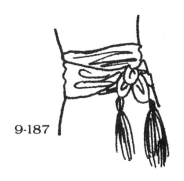

9-187

9-188

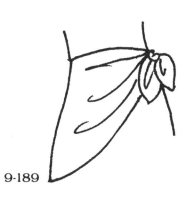

9-189

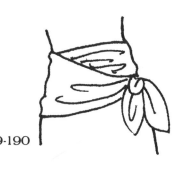

9-190

9-191

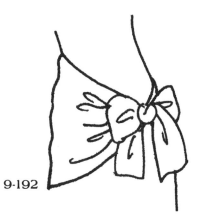

9-192

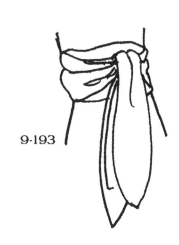

9-193

9-194

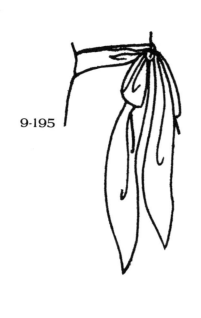

9-195

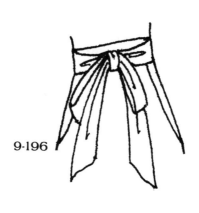

9-196

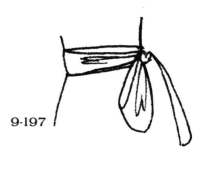

9-197

9-198

9-199

9-200

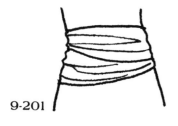

9-201

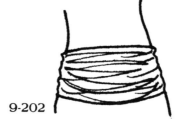

9-202

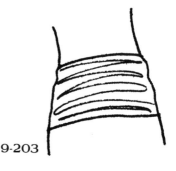

9-203

9-204

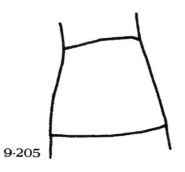

9-205

9-206

9-207

9-208

9-209

9-210

9-211

9-212

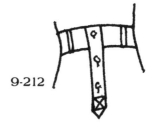

9-213

9-214

9-215

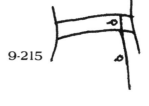

9-216

9-217

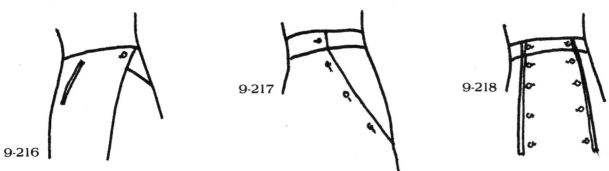

9-218

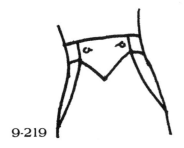

9-219

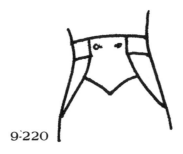

9-220

9-221

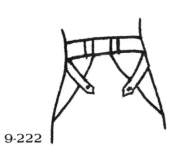

9-222

9-223

9-224

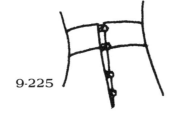

9-225

9-226

Hip Yoke Styling   10-1 to 10-109

10-1

10-2

10-3

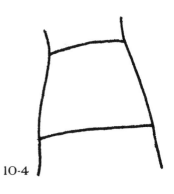

10-4

10-5

10-6

10-7

10-8

10-9

10-10

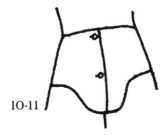

10-11

10-12

10-13

10-14

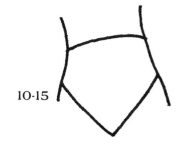

10-15

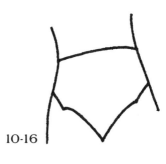

10-16

10-17

10-18

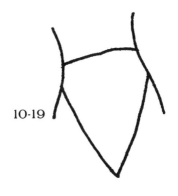

10-19

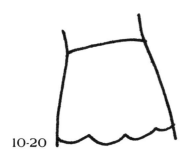

10-20

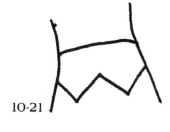

10-21

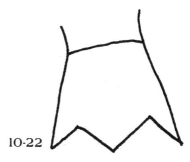

10-22

10-23

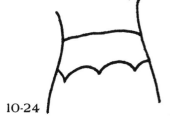

10-24

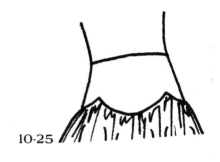

10-25

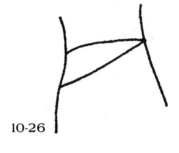

10-26

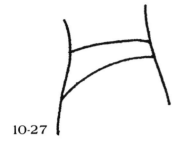

10-27

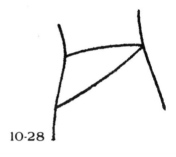

10-28

10-29

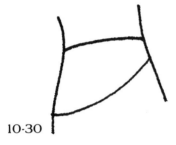

10-30

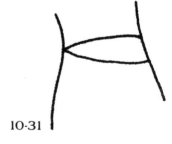

10-31

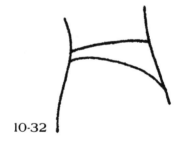

10-32

10-33

10-34

10-35

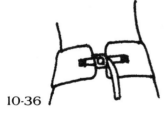

10-36

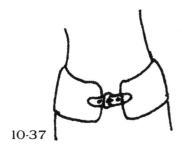

10-37

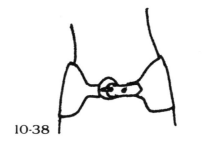

10-38

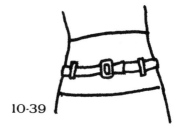

10-39

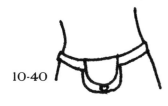

10-40

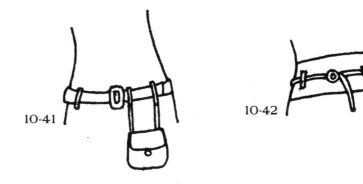

10-41

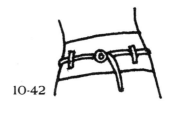

10-42

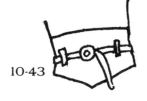

10-43

10-44

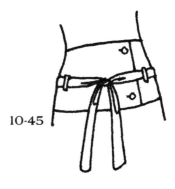

10-45

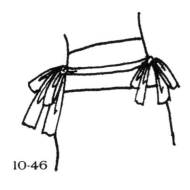

10-46

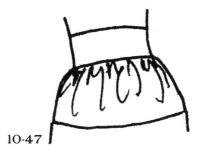

10-47

10-48

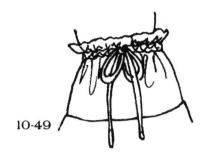

10-49

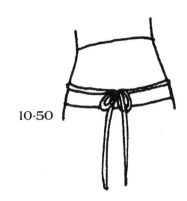

10-50

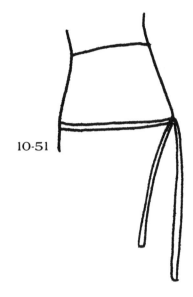

10-51

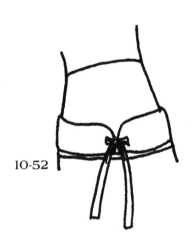

10-52

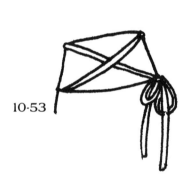

10-53

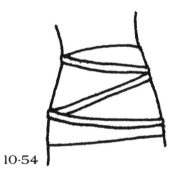

10-54

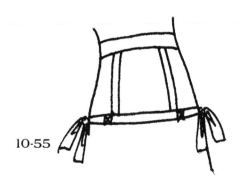

10-55

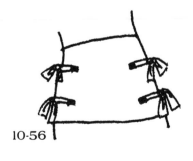

10-56

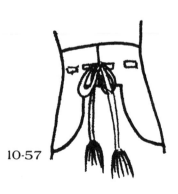

10-57

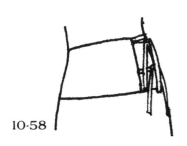

10-58

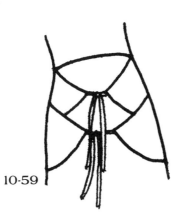

10-59

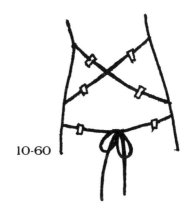

10-60

10-61

10-62

10-63

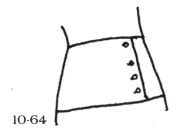

10-64

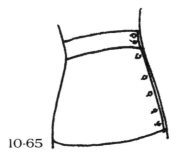

10-65

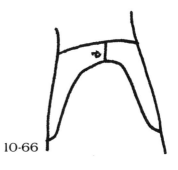

10-66

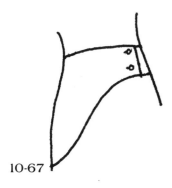

10-67

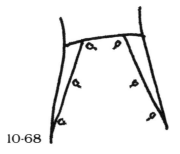

10-68

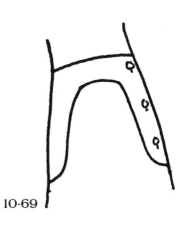

10-69

10-70

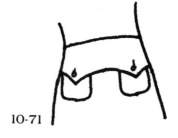

10-71

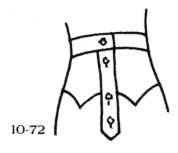

10-72

10-73

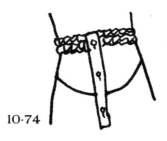

10-74

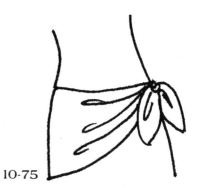

10-75

10-76

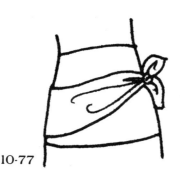

10-77

10-78

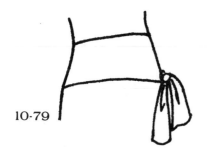

10-79

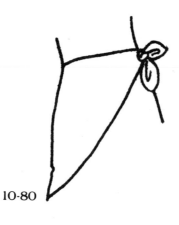

10-80

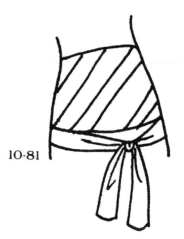

10-81

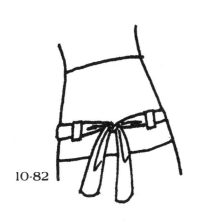

10-82

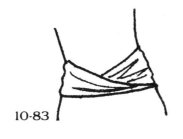

10-83

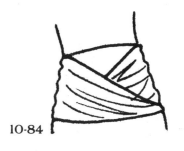

10-84

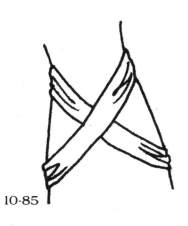

10-85

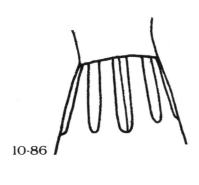

10-86

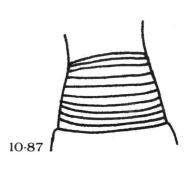

10-87

10-88

10-89

10-90

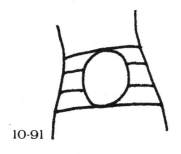

10-91

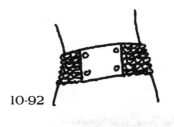

10-92

10-93

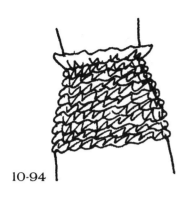

10-94

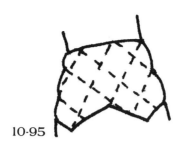

10-95

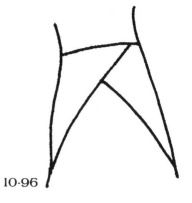

10-96

10-97

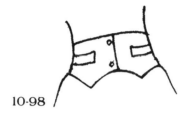

10-98

10-99

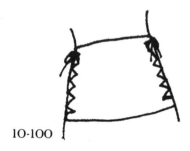

10-100

10-101

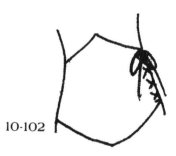

10-102

10-103

10-104

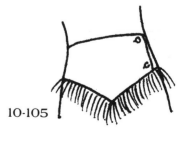

10-105

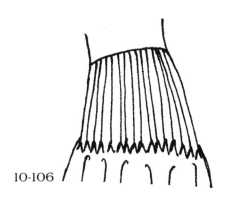

10-106

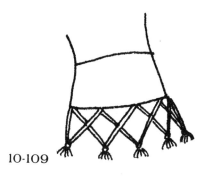

10-107

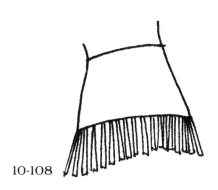

10-108

10-109

Peplum Styling   11-1 to 11-23

11-1

11-2

11-3

11-4

11-5

11-6

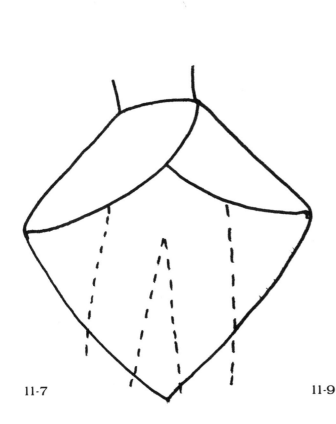

11-7

11-8

11-9

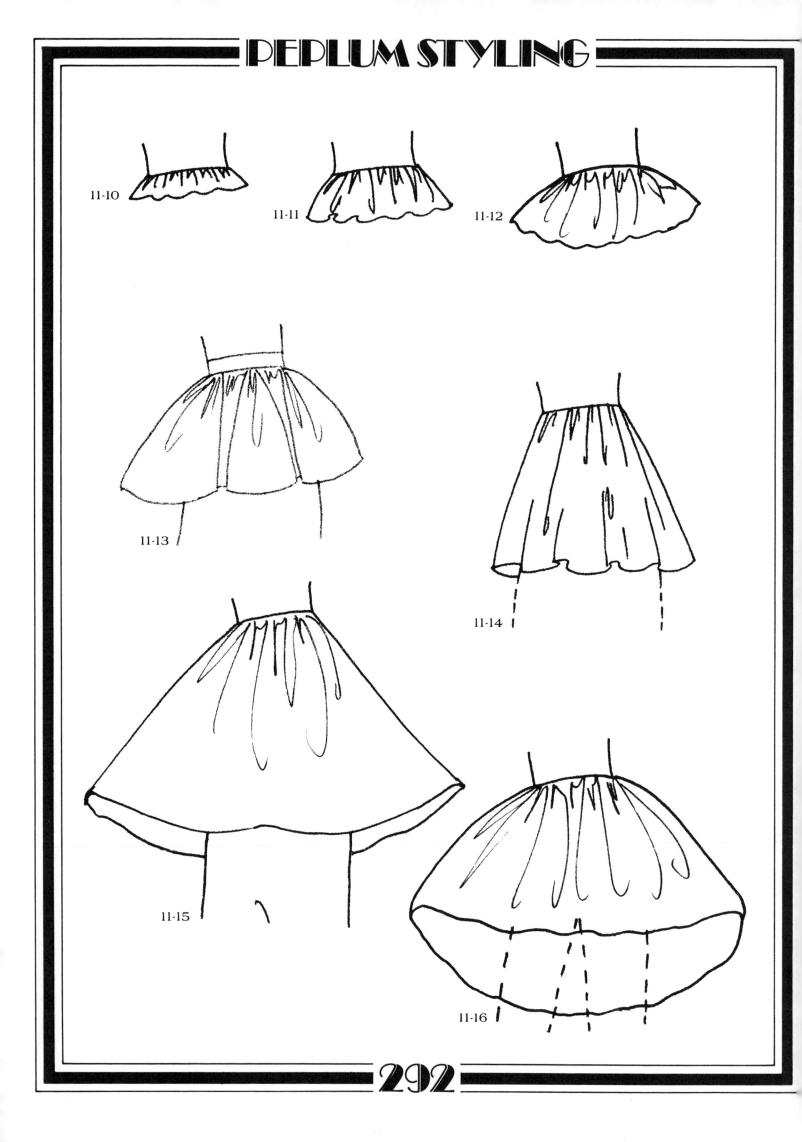

11-10

11-11

11-12

11-13

11-14

11-15

11-16

11-17

11-18

11-19

11-20

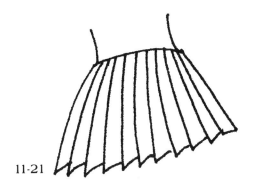

11-21

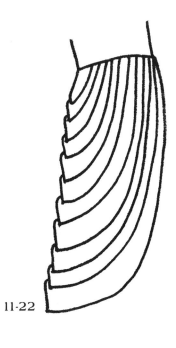

11-22

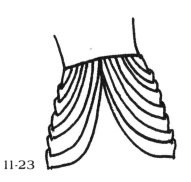

11-23

Vest Styling   12-1 to 12-61

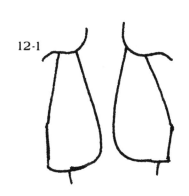

12-1

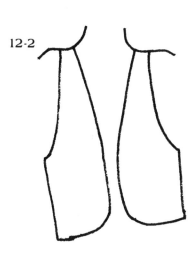

12-2

12-3

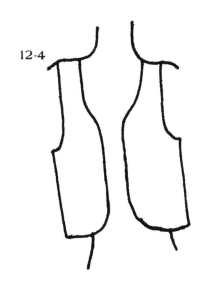

12-4

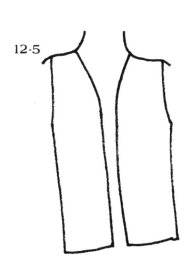

12-5

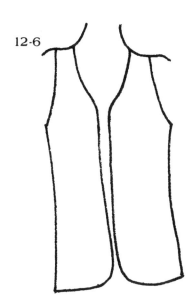

12-6

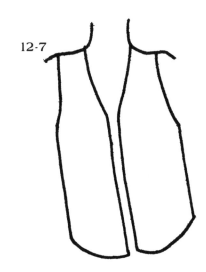

12-7

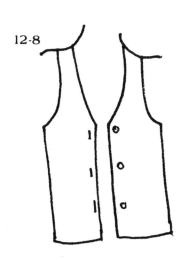

12-8

12-9

12·10

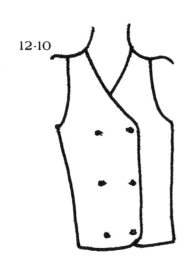

12·11

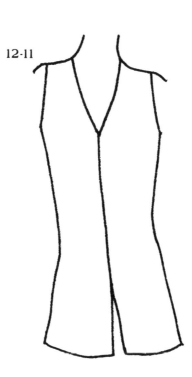

12·12

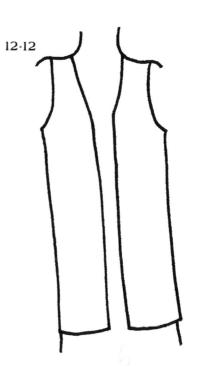

12·13

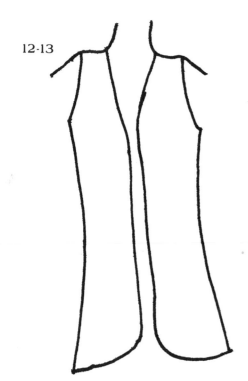

12·14

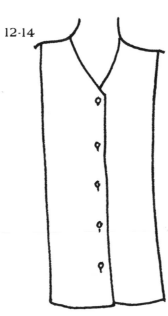

12·15

12-16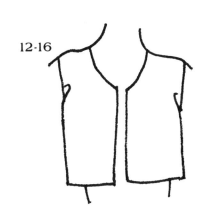

12-17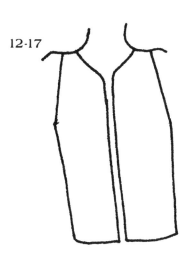

12-18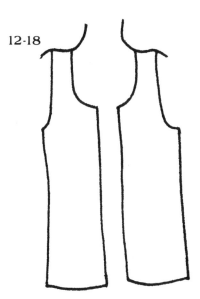

12-19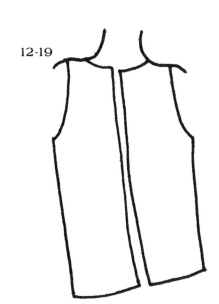

12-20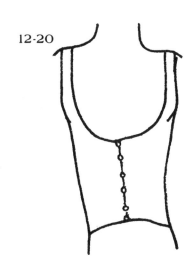

12-21

12-22

12-23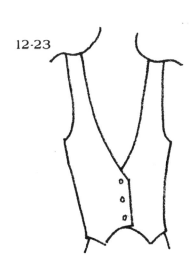

12-24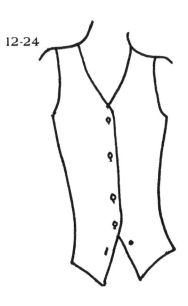

12-25

12-26

12-27

12-28
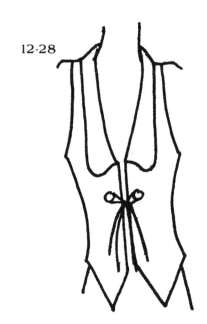

12-29

12-30

12-31
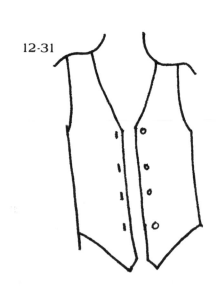

12-32

12-33

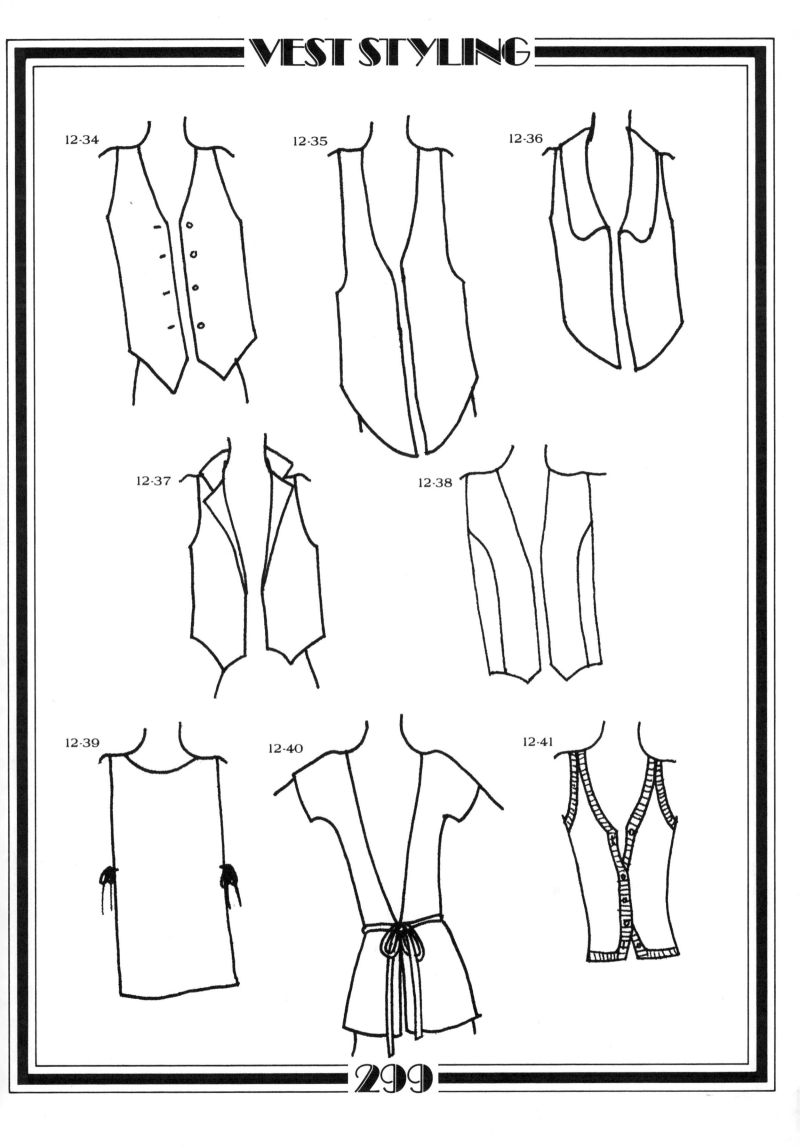

12-34

12-35

12-36

12-37

12-38

12-39

12-40

12-41

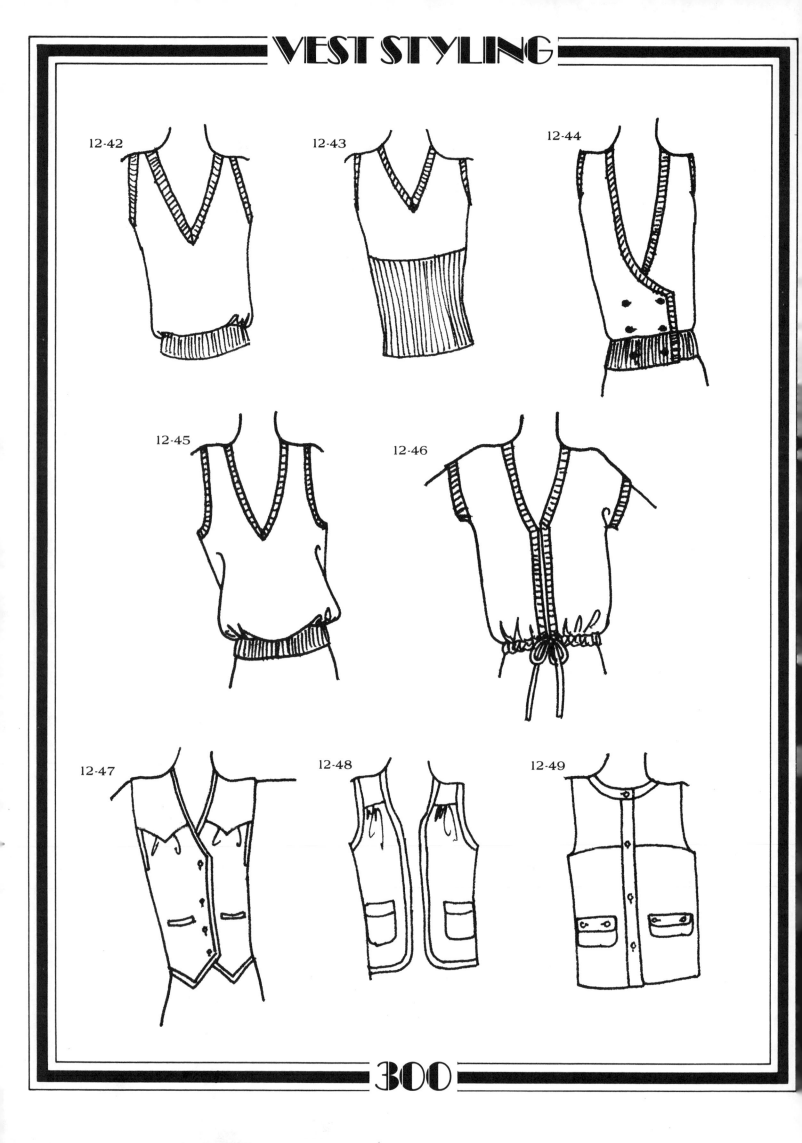

12-42

12-43

12-44

12-45

12-46

12-47

12-48

12-49

12-50

12-51

12-52

Back View
12-53

12-54

12-55

12-56

12-57

12-58

12-59

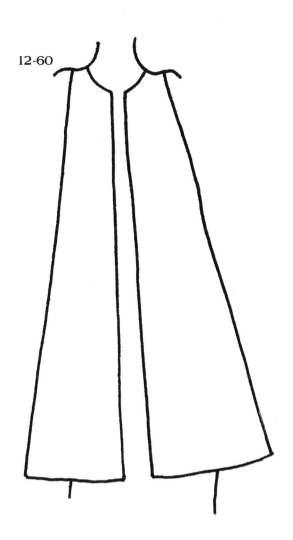

12-60

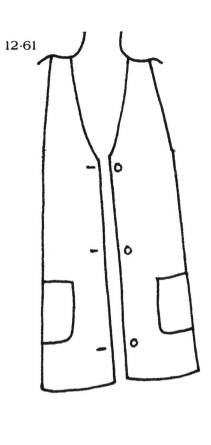

12-61

THIRTEEN·JACKETS

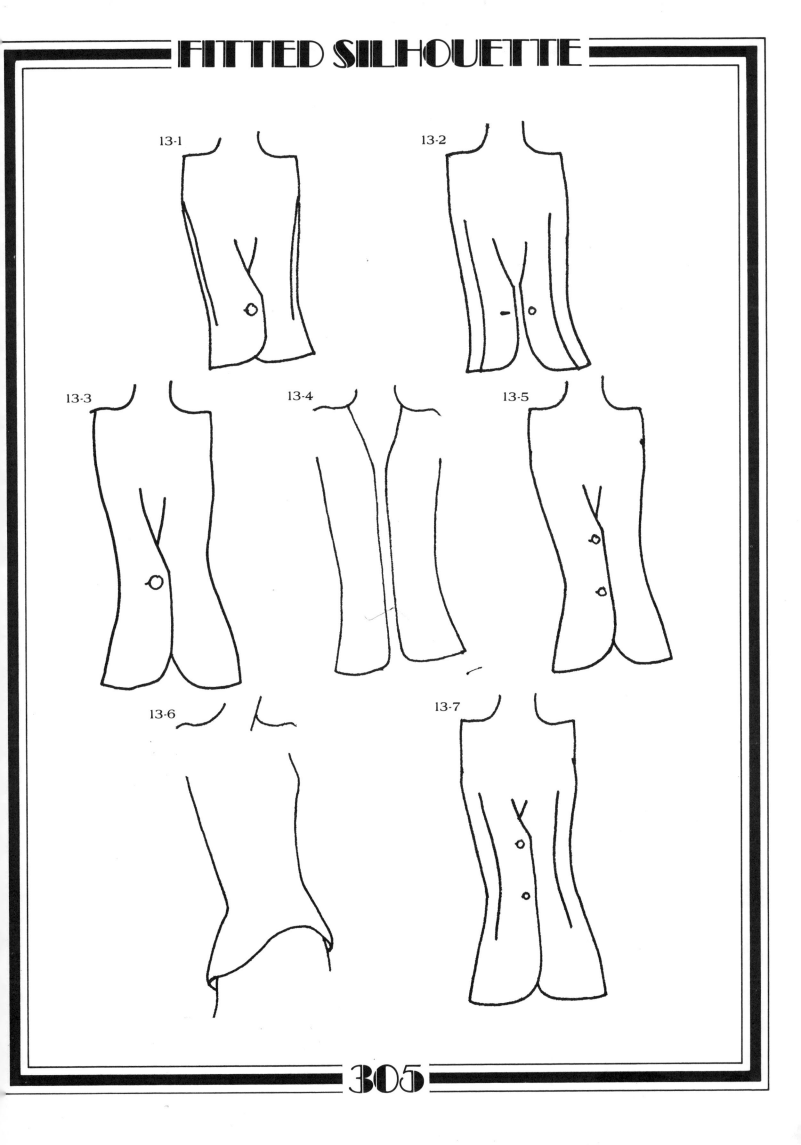

13-1

13-2

13-3

13-4

13-5

13-6

13-7

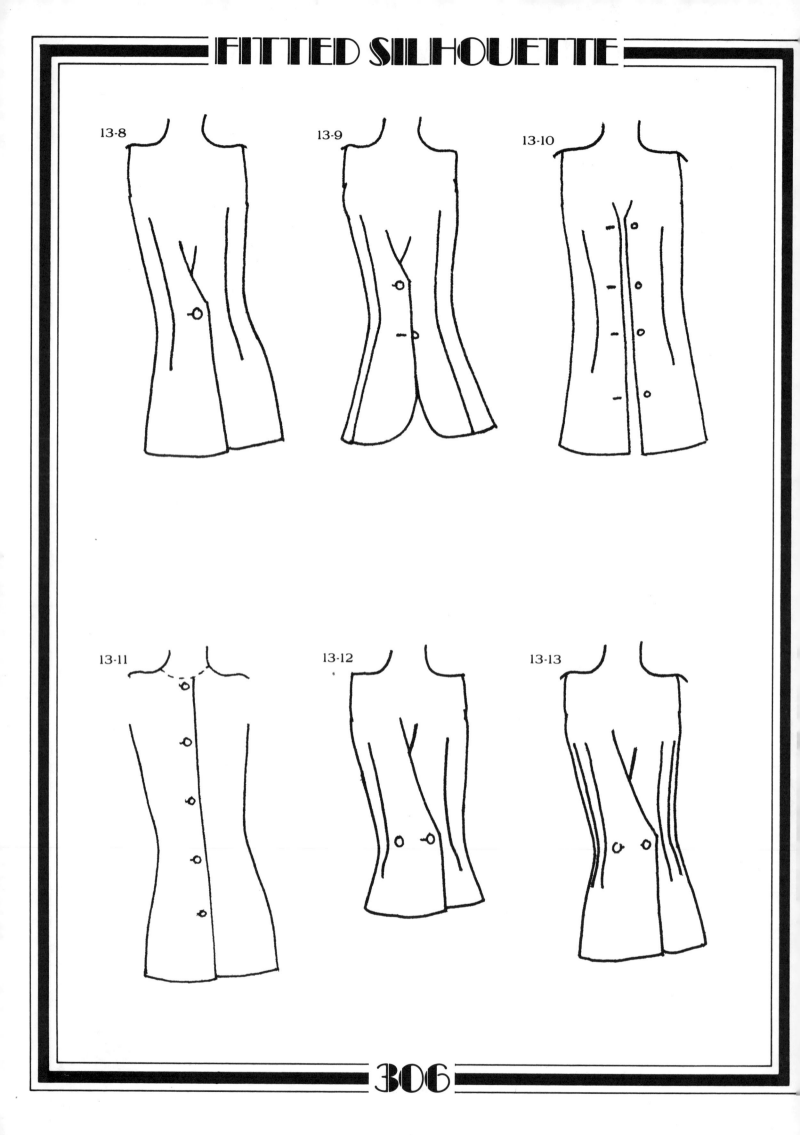

13-8

13-9

13-10

13-11

13-12

13-13

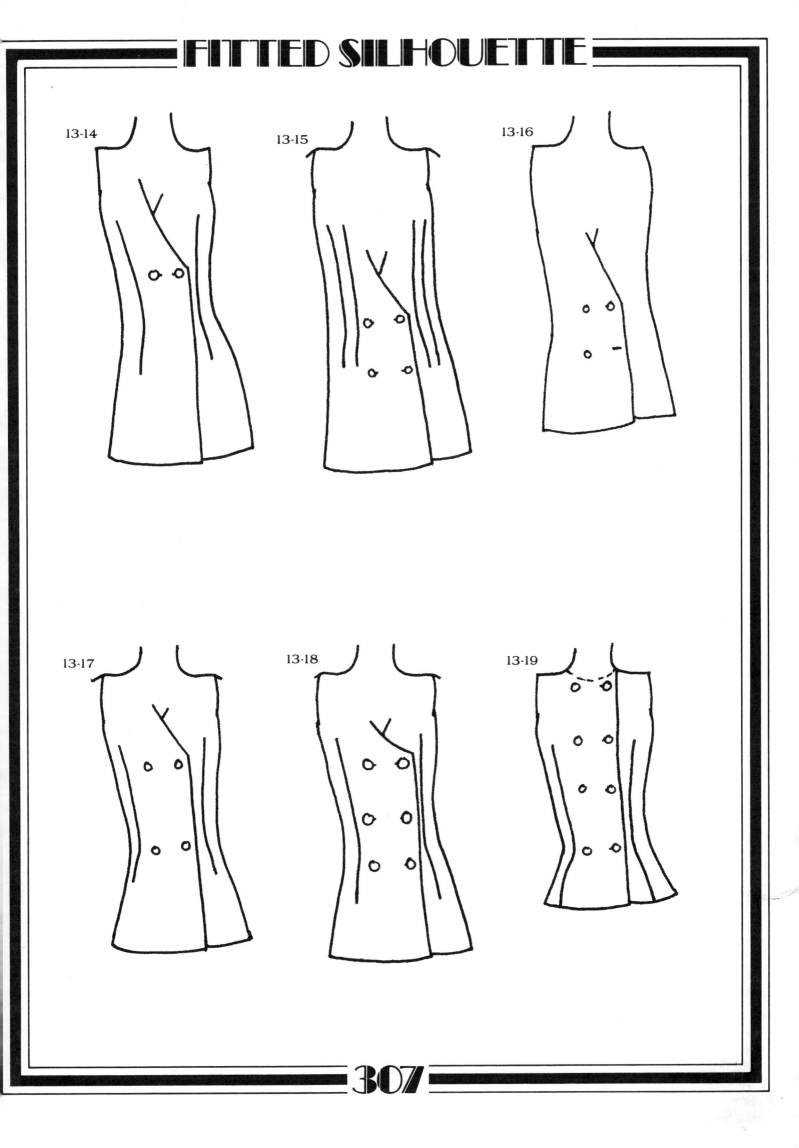

13-14

13-15

13-16

13-17

13-18

13-19

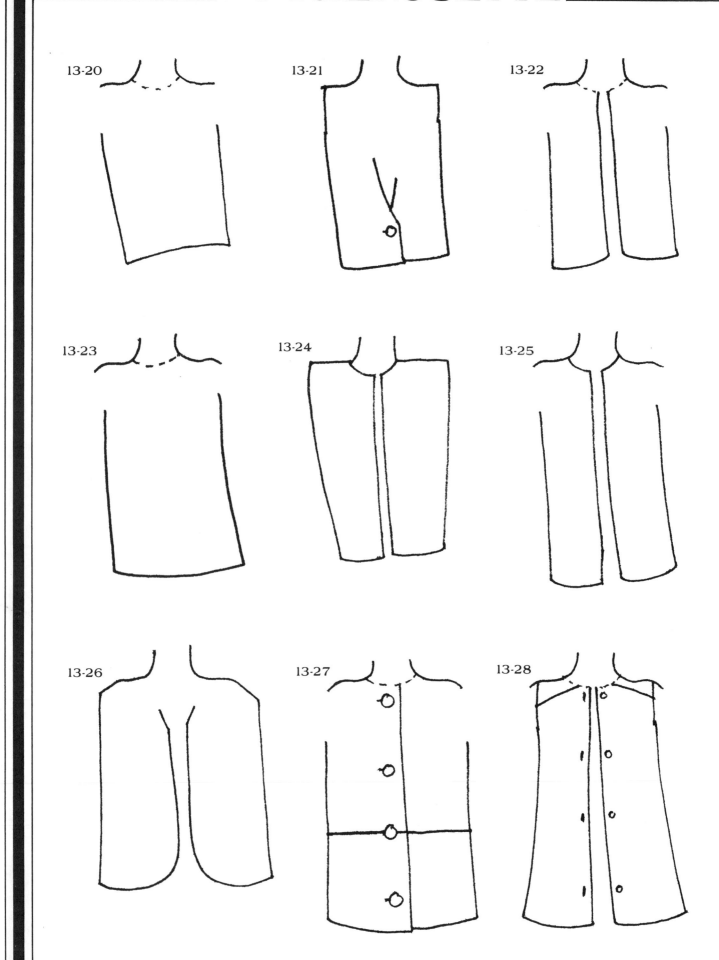

13-20

13-21

13-22

13-23

13-24

13-25

13-26

13-27

13-28

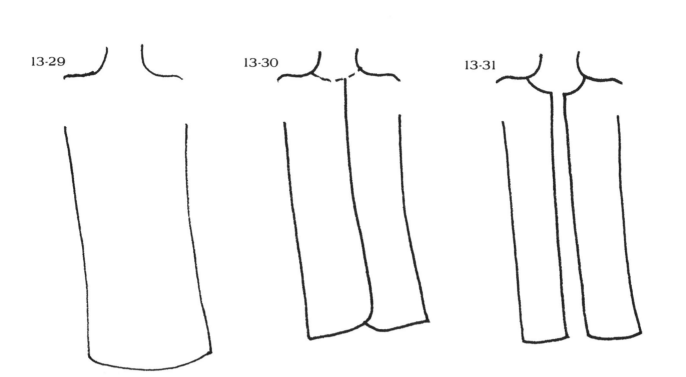

13-29   13-30   13-31

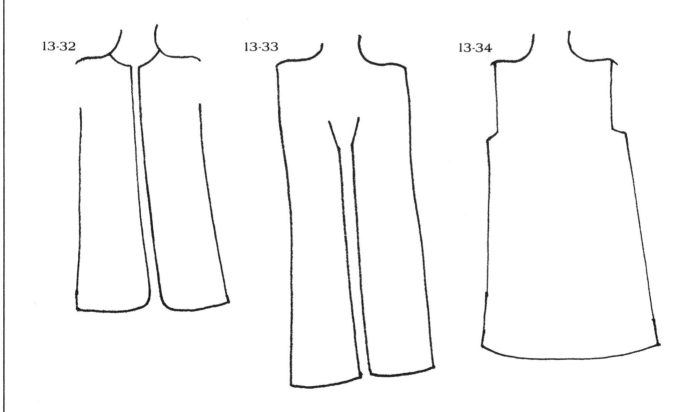

13-32   13-33   13-34

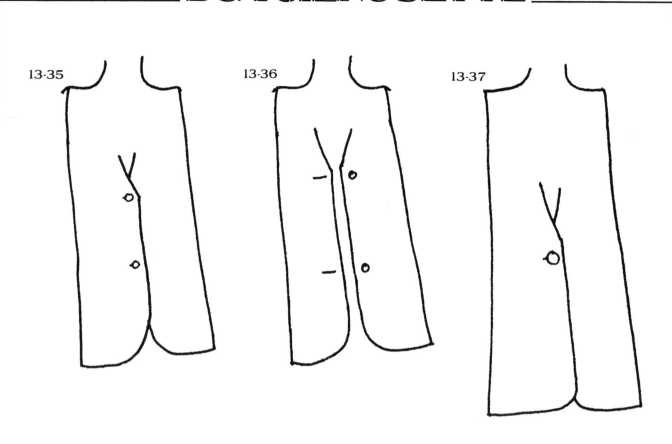

13-35

13-36

13-37

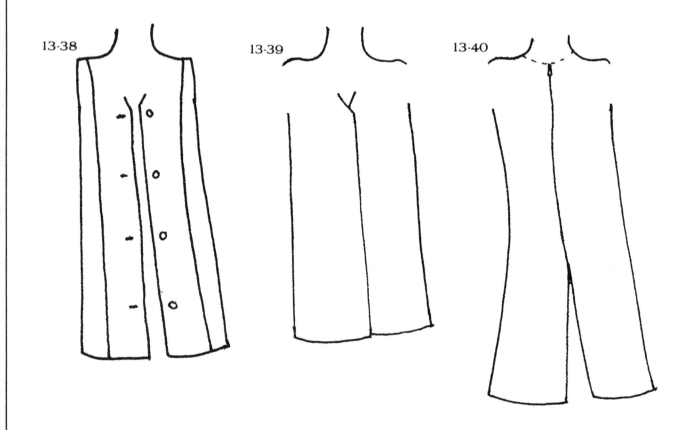

13-38

13-39

13-40

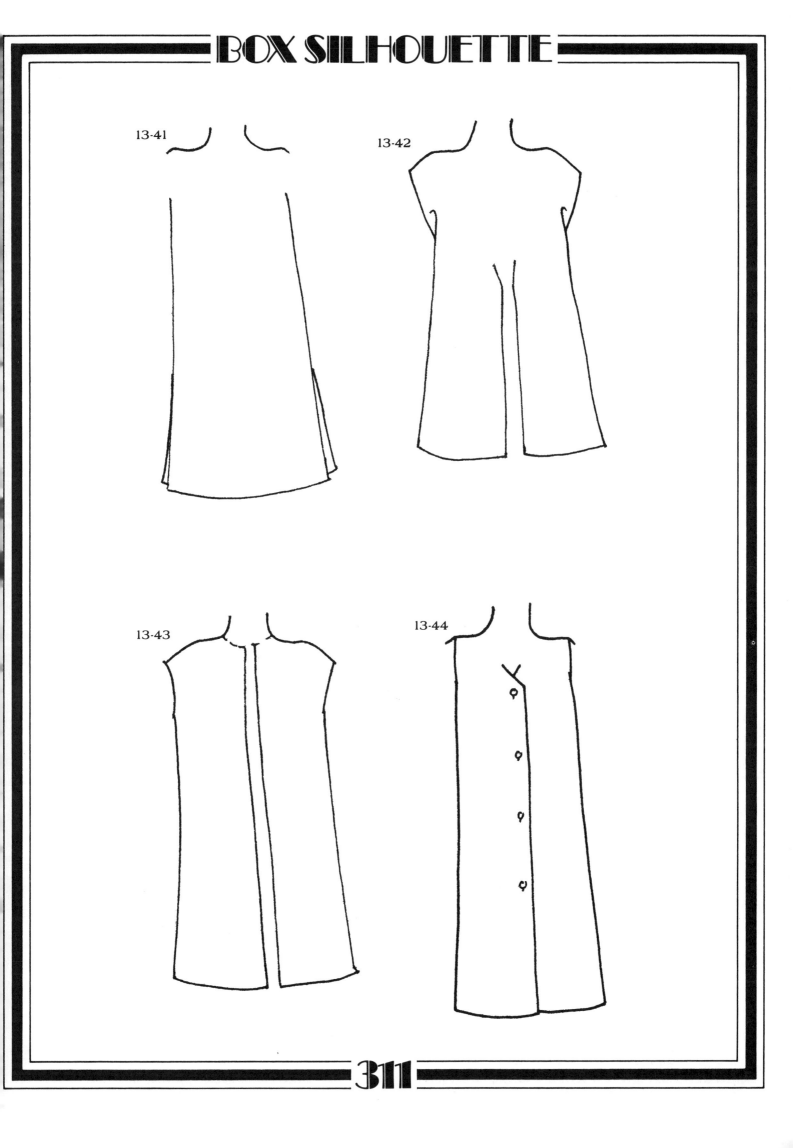

13-41

13-42

13-43

13-44

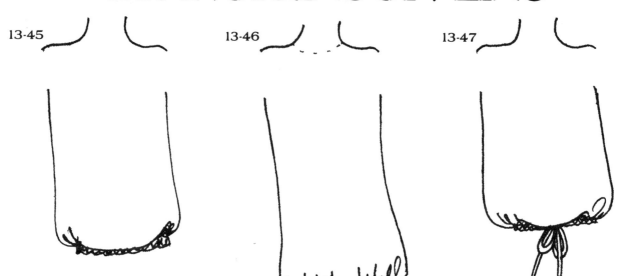

13-45

13-46

13-47

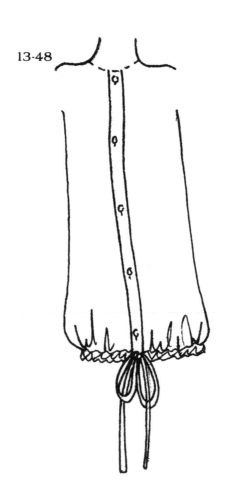

13-48

13-49

BLOUSON SILHOUETTE/
KNITTED BAND STYLING

13-50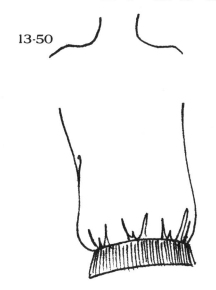

13-51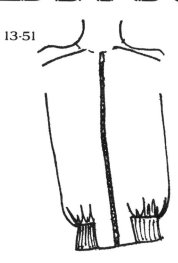

13-52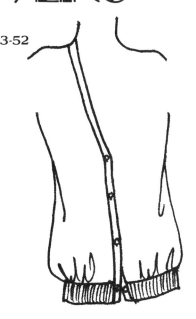

BLOUSON SILHOUETTE/
BAND STYLING

13-53

13-54

13-55

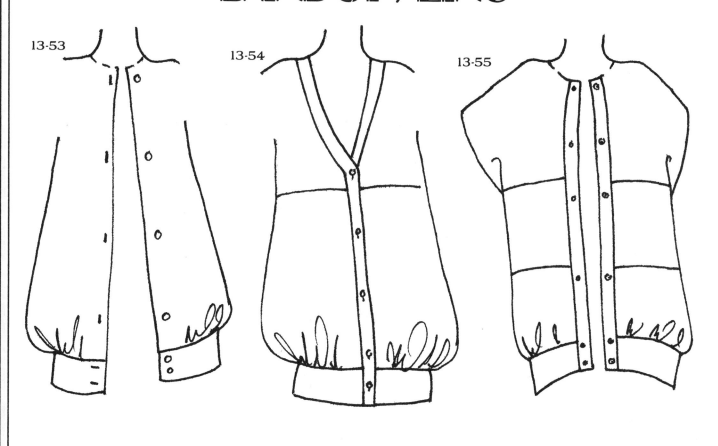

FULL SILHOUETTE/SHIRRING/ GATHERING STYLING

13-56

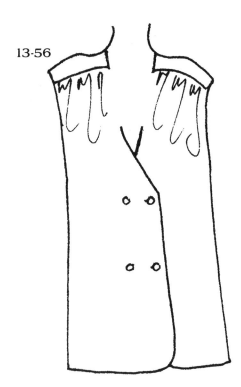

13-57

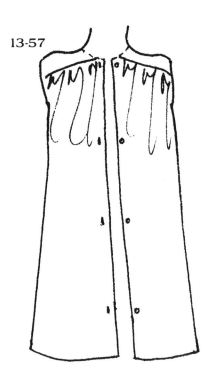

Back View
13-58

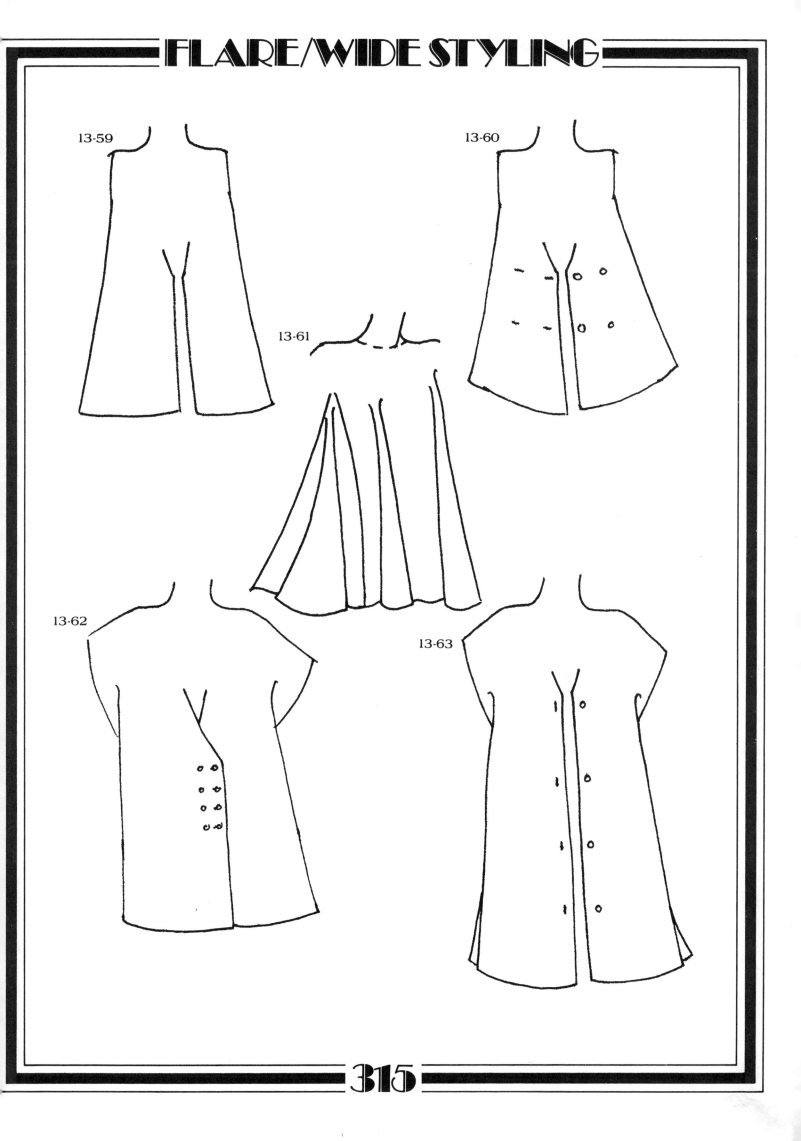

13-59

13-60

13-61

13-62

13-63

13-64

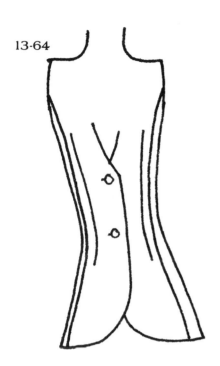

13-65

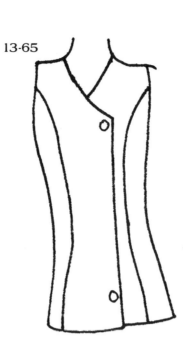

13-66

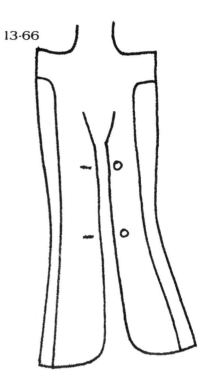

13-67

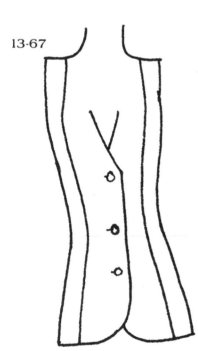

13-68

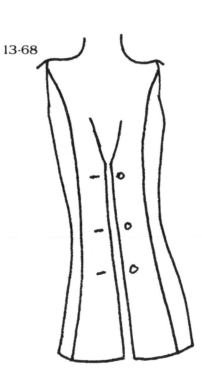

13-69

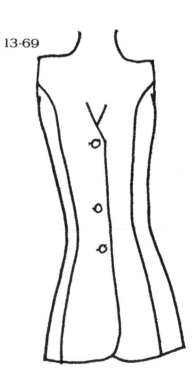

13-70

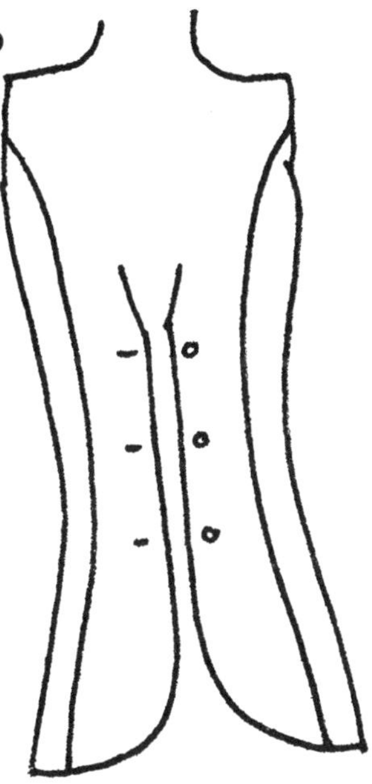

13-71

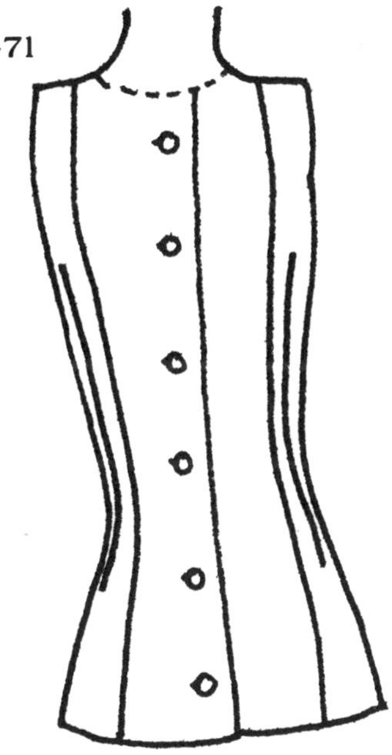

13-72

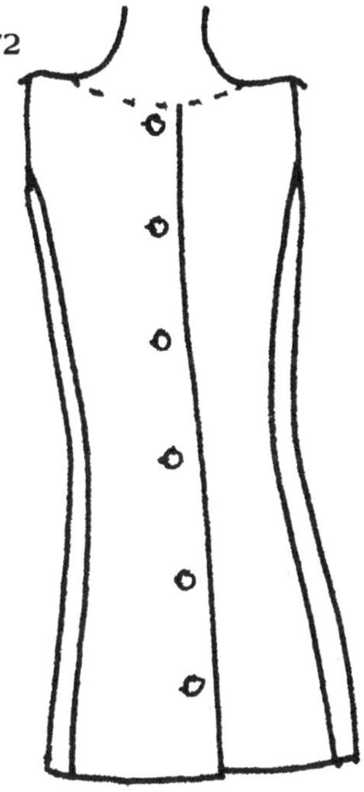

13-73

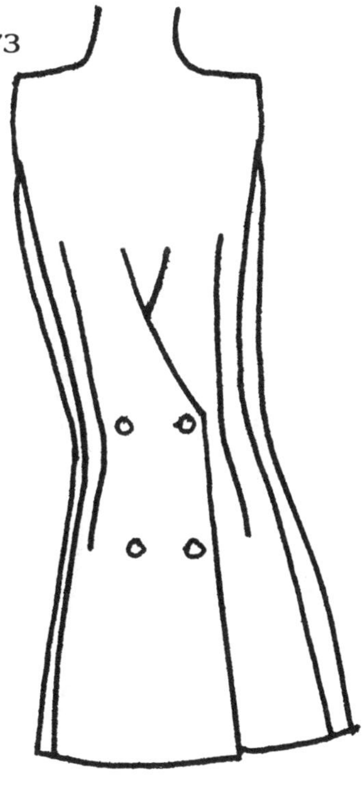

13-74

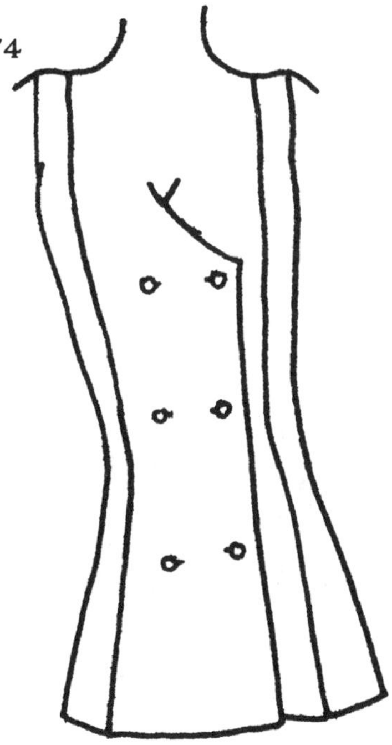

13-75

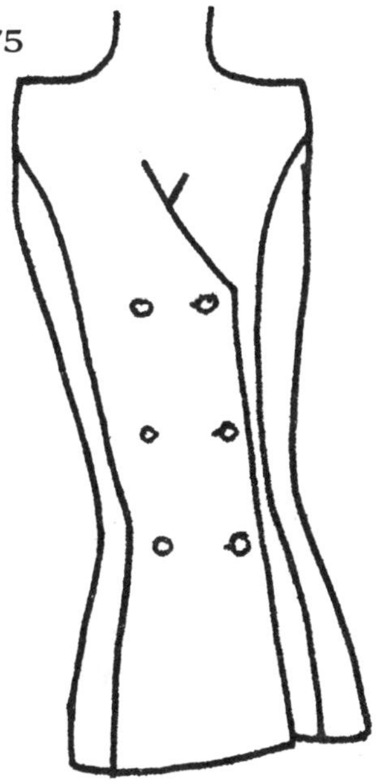

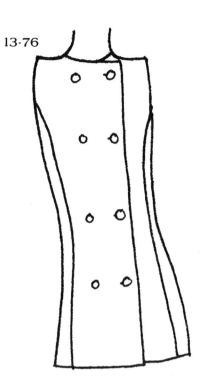

13-76

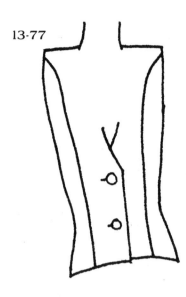

13-77

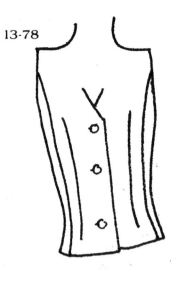

13-78

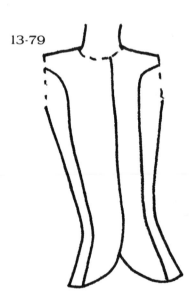

13-79

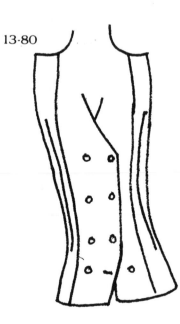

13-80

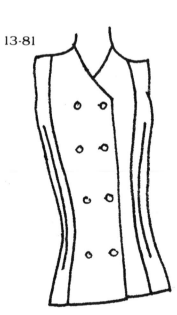

13-81

13-82
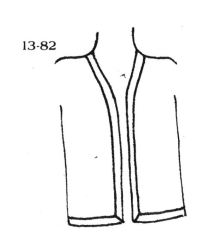

13-83
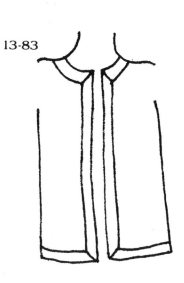

13-84
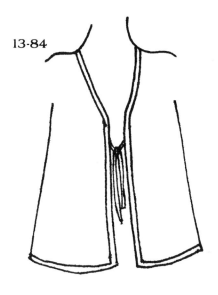

13-85
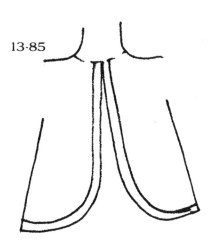

13-86
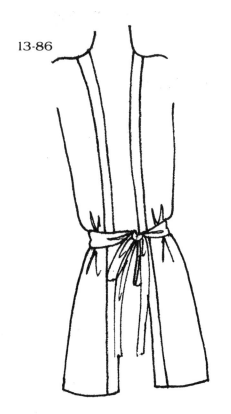

13-87

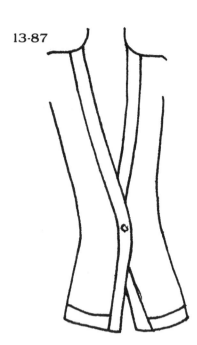

13-88

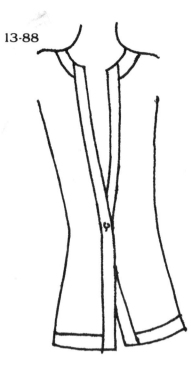

13-89

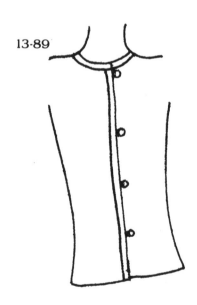

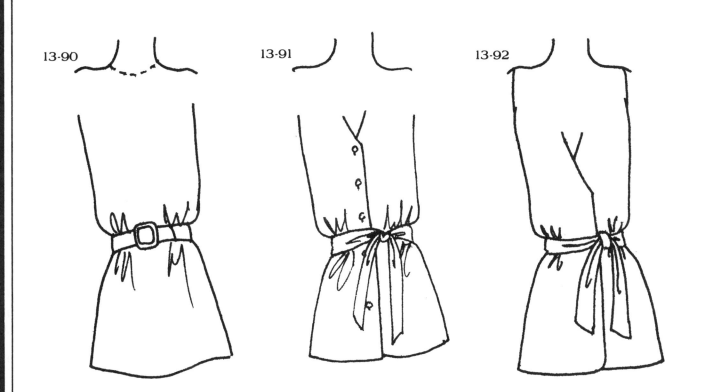

13-90

13-91

13-92

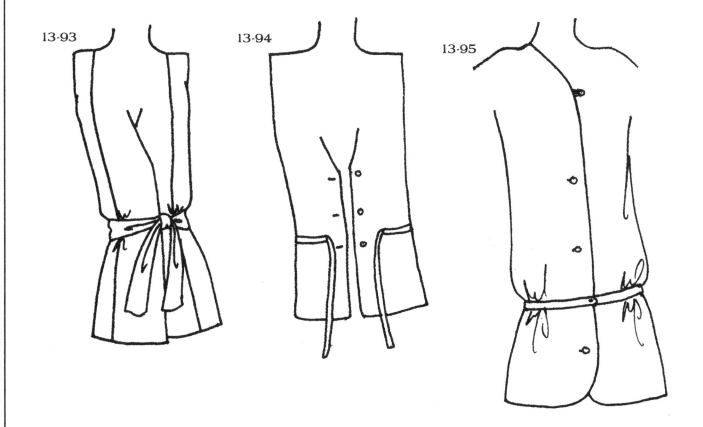

13-93

13-94

13-95

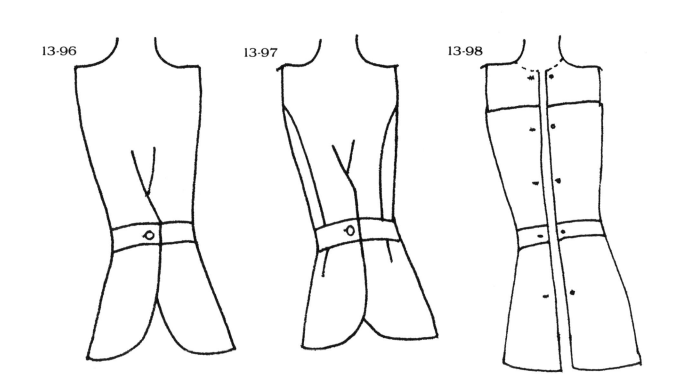

13-96   13-97   13-98

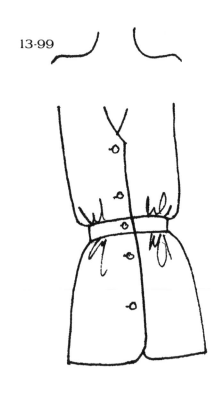

13-99

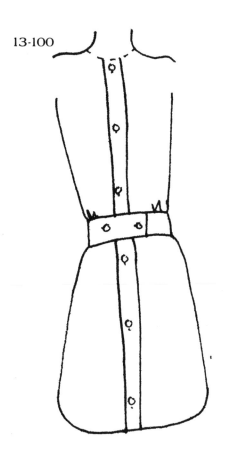

13-100

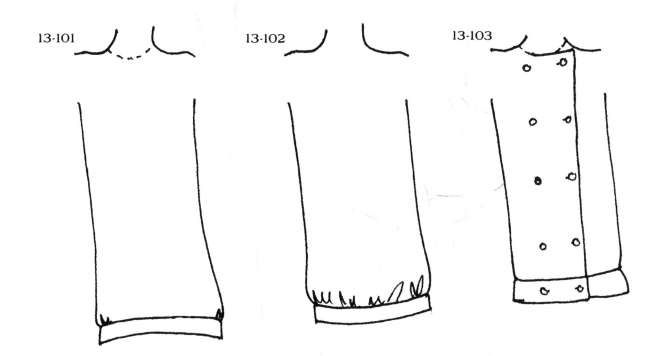

13-101   13-102   13-103

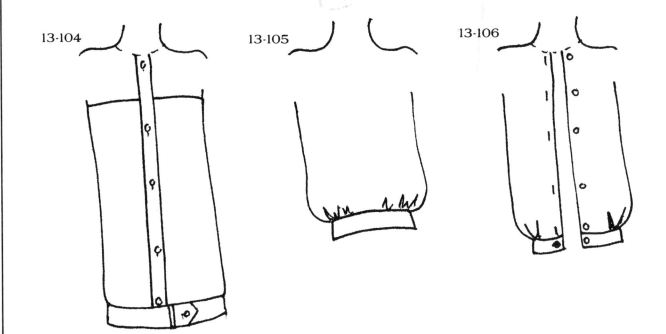

13-104   13-105   13-106

13-107

13-108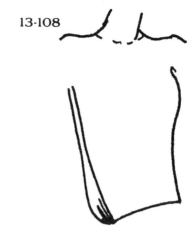

13-109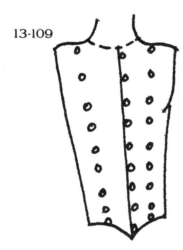

13-110

13-111

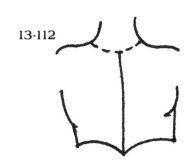

13-112

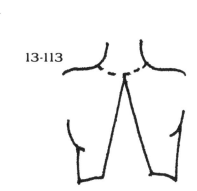

13-113

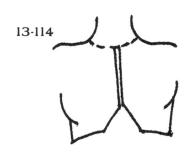

13-114

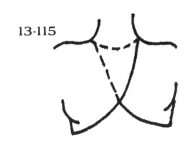

13-115

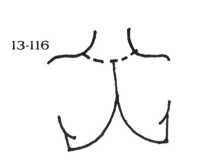

13-116

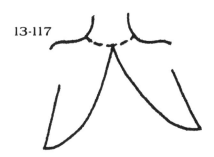

13-117

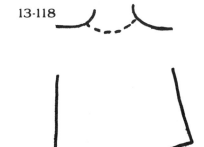

13-118

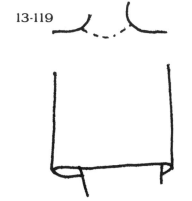

13-119

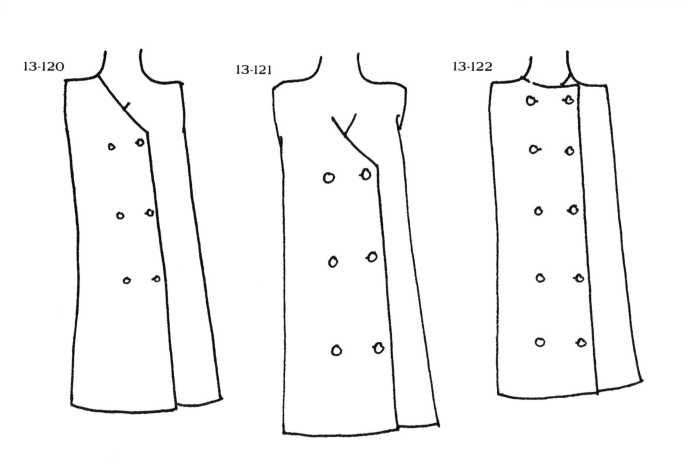

13-120 13-121 13-122

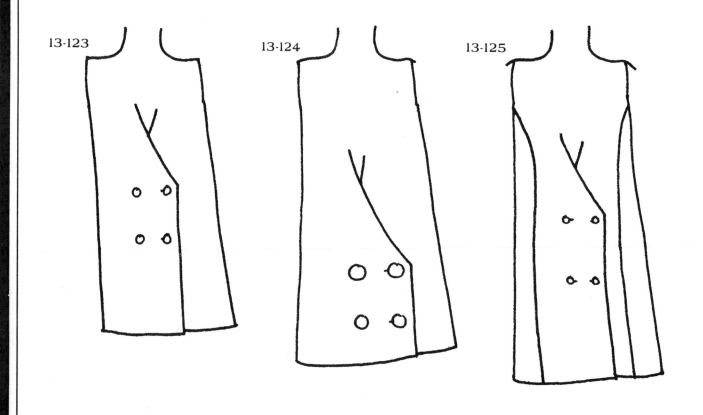

13-123 13-124 13-125

13-126

13-128

13-127

13-129

13-130

13-131

13-132

FOURTEEN·CLOSURES

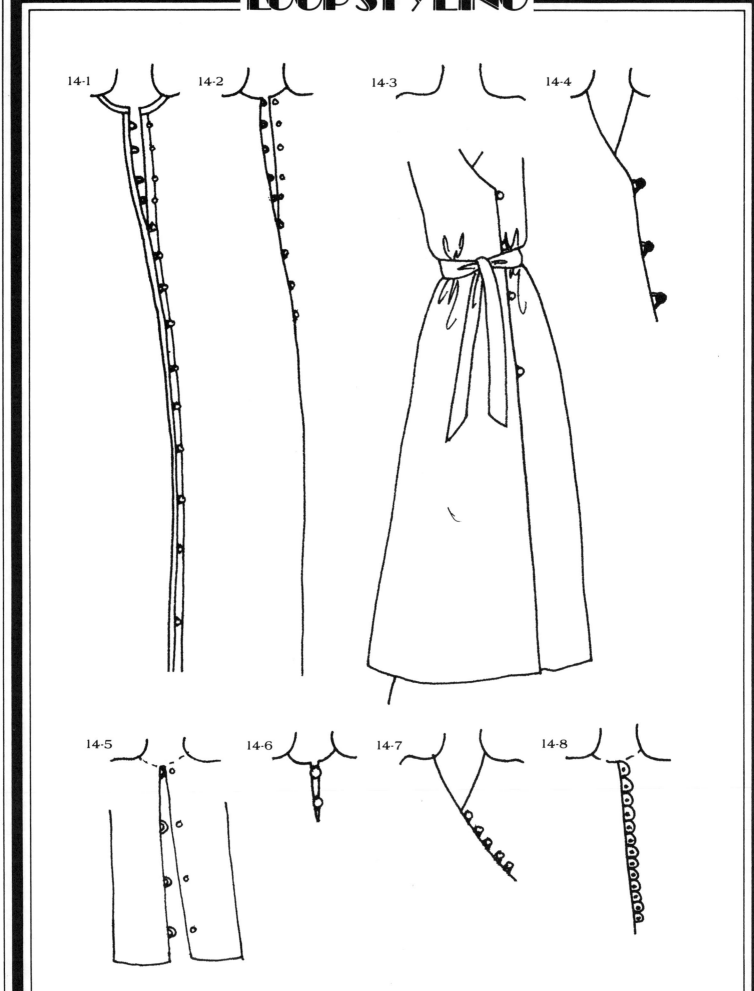

14-1 14-2 14-3 14-4

14-5 14-6 14-7 14-8

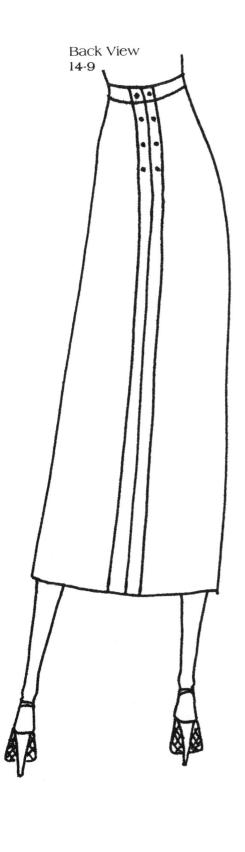

Back View
14-9

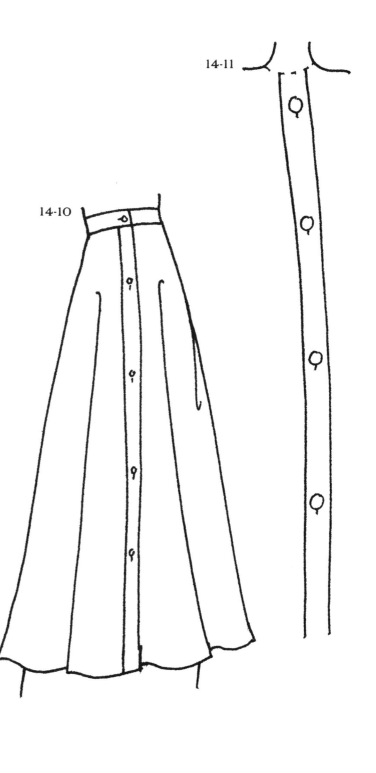

14-10

14-11

14-12
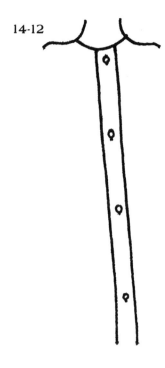

14-13
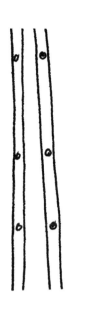

14-14

14-15
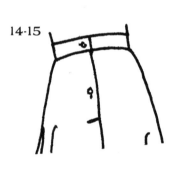

14-16
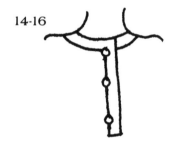

14-17
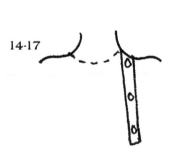

14-18

14-19

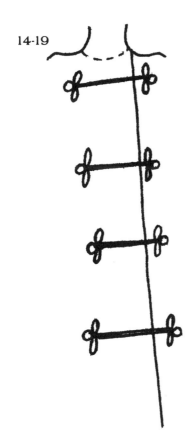

14-20

14-21

14-22

14-23

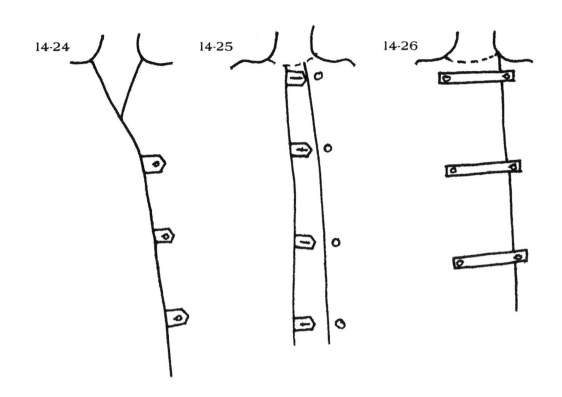

14-24 14-25 14-26

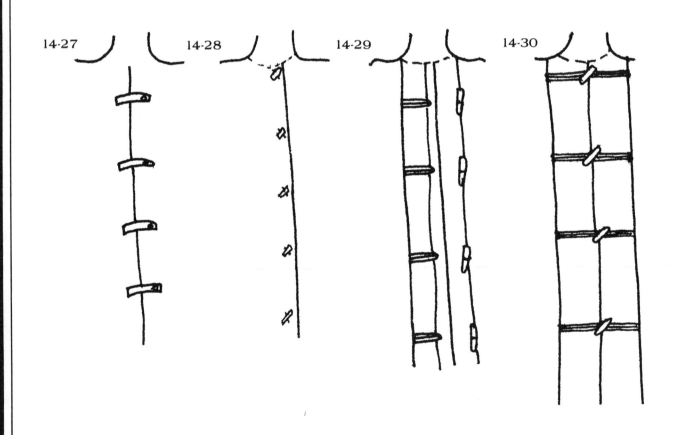

14-27 14-28 14-29 14-30

14-32

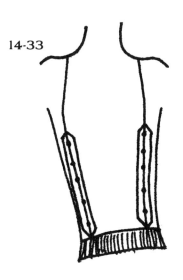

14-33

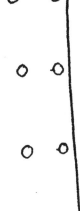

14-31

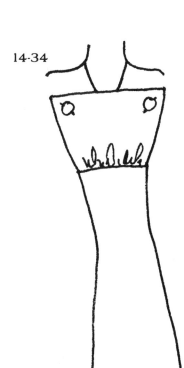

14-34

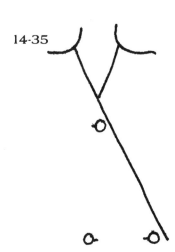

14-35

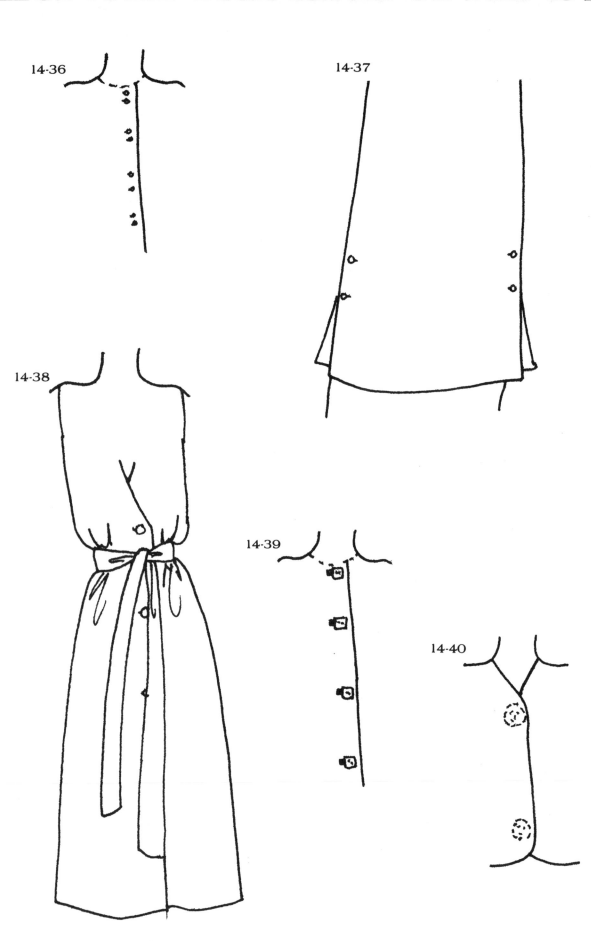

14-36

14-37

14-38

14-39

14-40

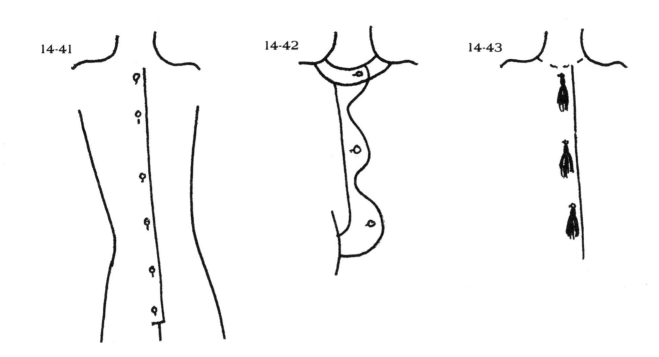

ASYMMETRICAL STYLING

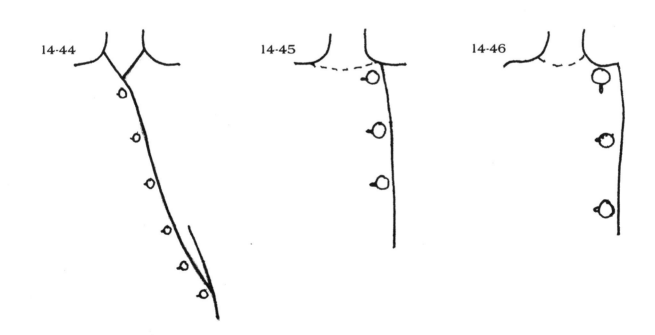

14-47

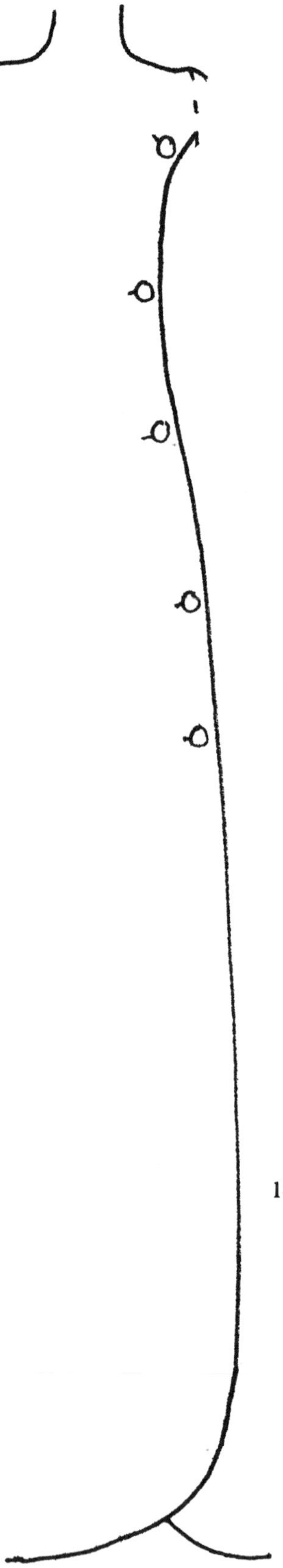

14-48

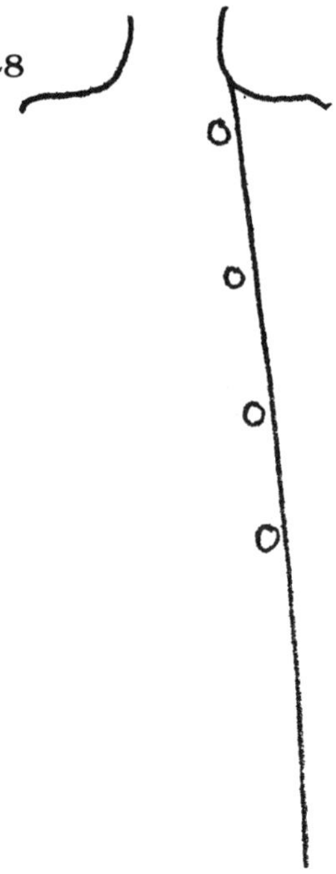

14-49

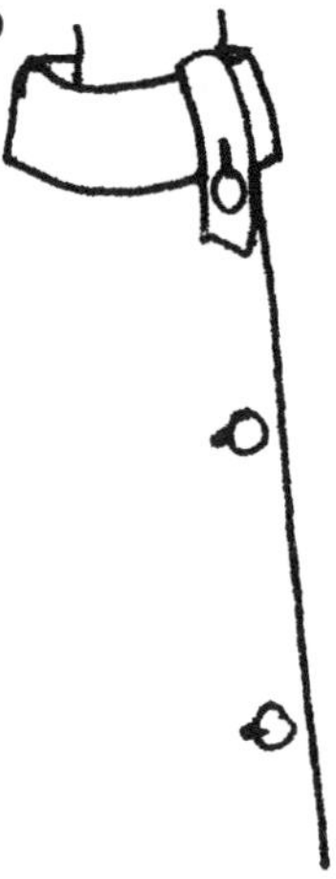

14-50

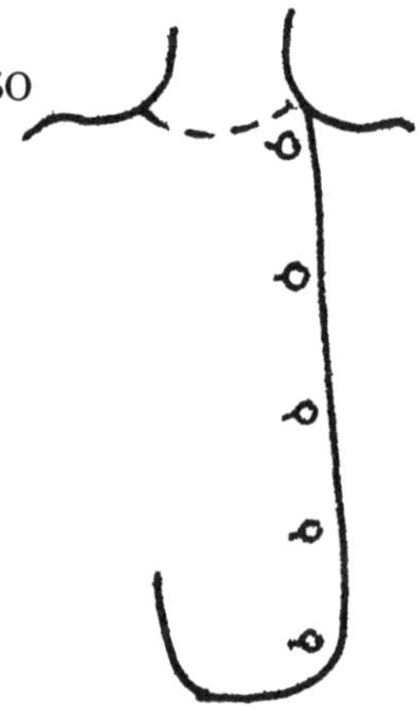

14-51

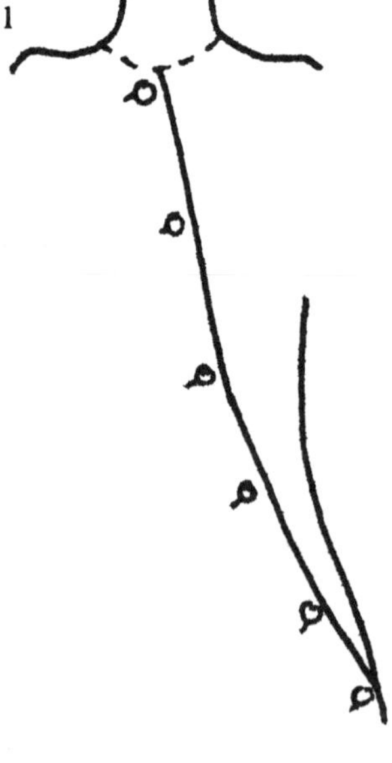

14-52

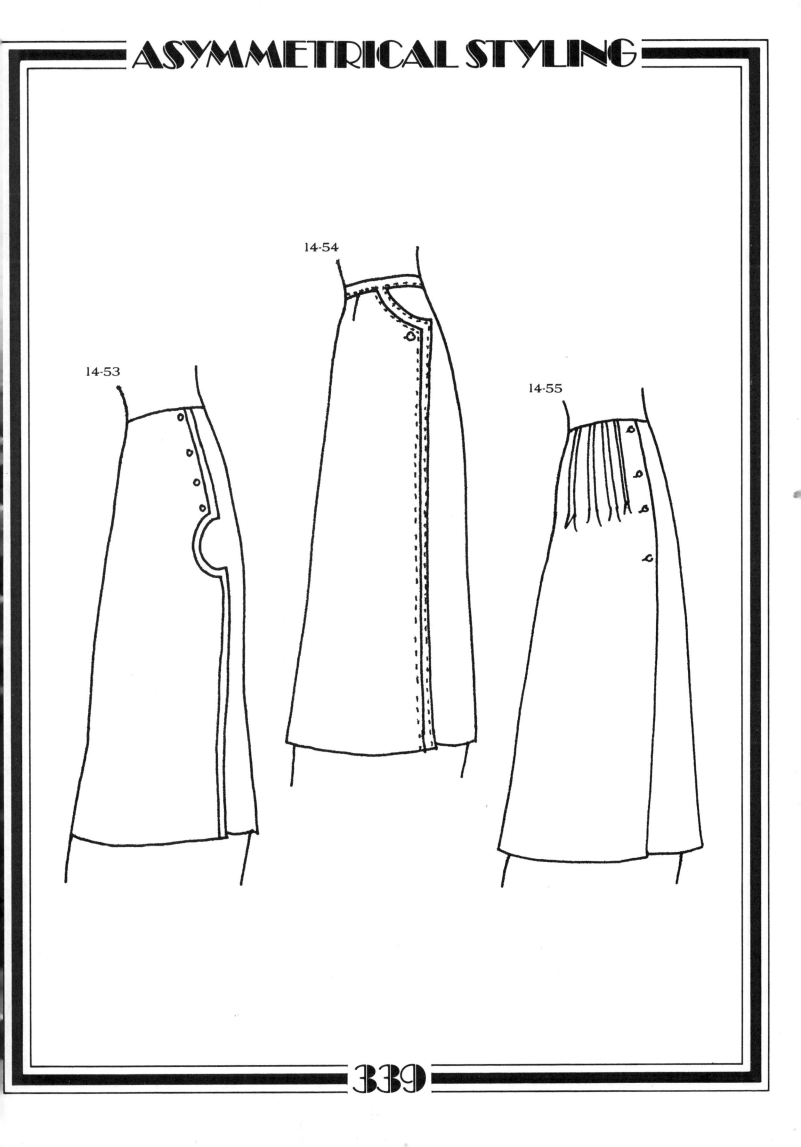

14-54

14-53

14-55

14-56

14-57

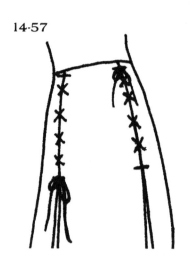

14-58

STRAP STYLING

14-59

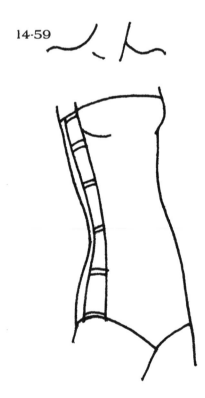

Back View
14-60

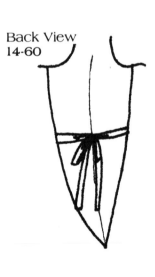

14-61

14-62

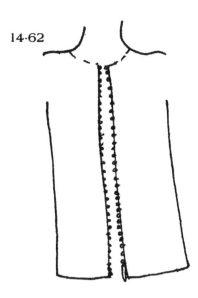

14-63

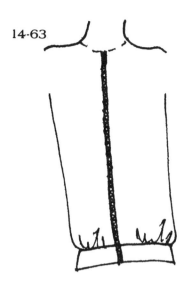

14-64

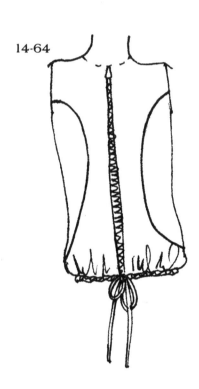

14-66

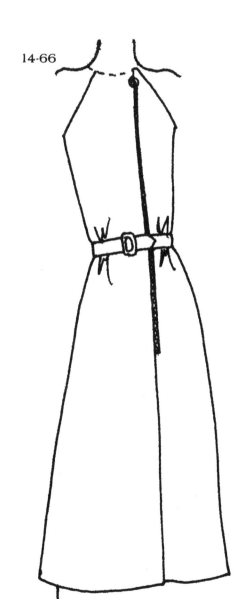

14-65

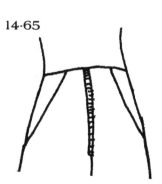

14-67

14-68

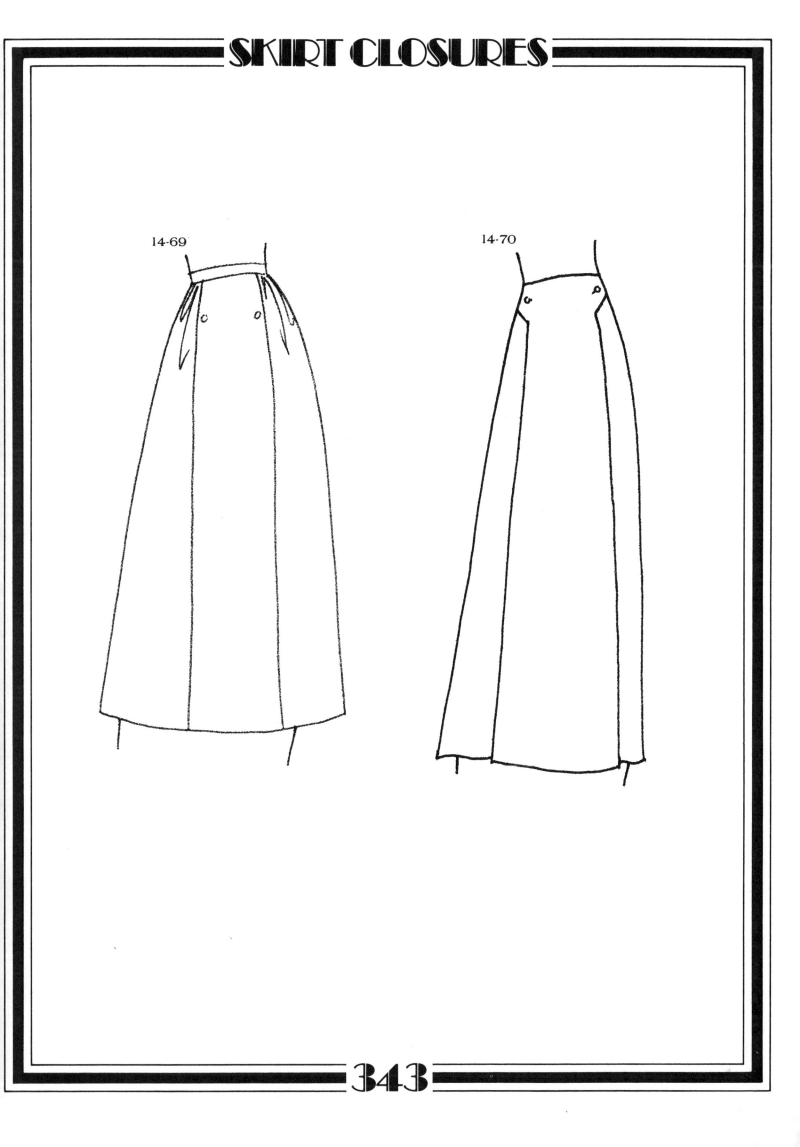

14-69

14-70

14-71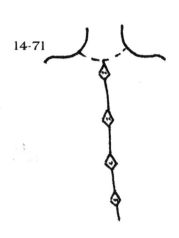

14-72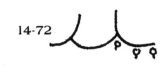

14-73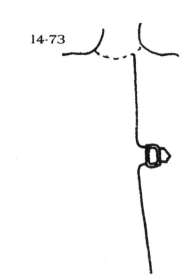

14-74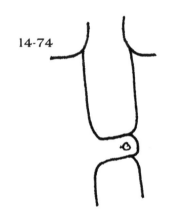

14-75

14-76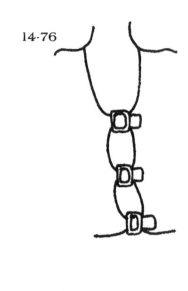

14-77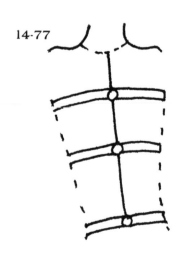

14-78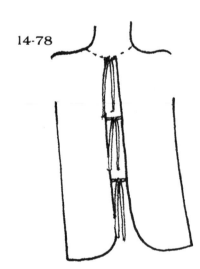

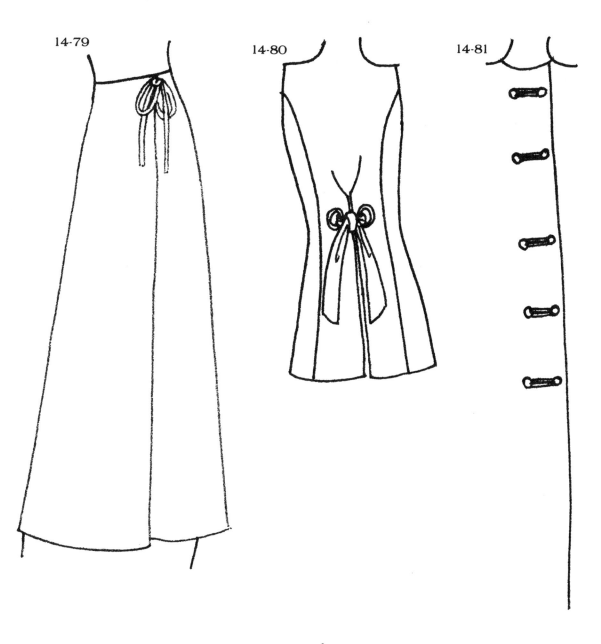

14-79

14-80

14-81

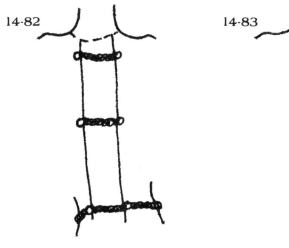

14-82

14-83

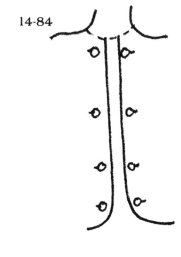

14-84

FIFTEEN·POCKETS

Proportions for Upper Torso

Patch Pocket Styling 15-1 to 15-99
Flap Pocket Styling 15-100 to 15-108
Flap & Patch Pocket Styling 15-109 to 15-122
Bound/Tailored Pocket Styling 15-123 to 15-138
Welt Pocket Styling 15-139 to 15-154
Insert & Patch Pocket Styling 15-155 to 15-166
Insert Pocket Styling 15-167 to 15-174

Proportions for Lower Torso

Patch Pocket Styling 15-175 to 15-220
Flap & Patch Pocket Styling 15-221 to 15-242
Bound & Welt Pocket Styling 15-243 to 15-254
Welt & Flap Pocket Styling 15-255 to 15-269
Insert & Flap Pocket Styling 15-270 to 15-282

15-1

15-2

15-3

15-4

15-5

15-6

15-7

15-8

15-9

15-10

15-11

15-12

15-13

15-14

15-15

15-16

15-17

15-18

15-19

15-20

15-21

15-22

15-23

15-24

15-25

15-26

15-27

15-28

15-29

15-30

15-31

15-32

15-33

15-34

15-35

15-36

15-37

15-38

15-39

15-40

15-41

15-42

15-43

15-44

15-45

15-46

15-47

15-48

15-49

15-50

15-51

15-52

15-53

15-54

15-55

15-56

15-57

15-58

15-59

15-60

15-61

15-62

15-63

15-64

15-65

15-66

15-67

15-68

15-69

15-70

15-71

15-72

15-73

15-74

15-75

15-76

15-77

15-78

15-79

15-80

15-81

15-82

15-83

15-84

15-85

15-86

15-87

15-88

15-89

15-90

15-91

15-92

15-93

15-94

15-95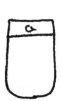

15-96

15-97

15-98

15-99

15-100
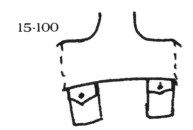

15-101

15-102

15-103
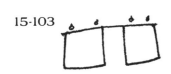

15-104
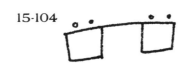

15-105

15-106

15-107
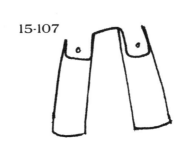

15-108
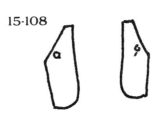

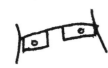

15-109

15-110

15-111

15-112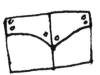

15-113

15-114

15-115

15-116

15-117

15-118

15-119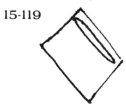

15-120

15-121

15-122

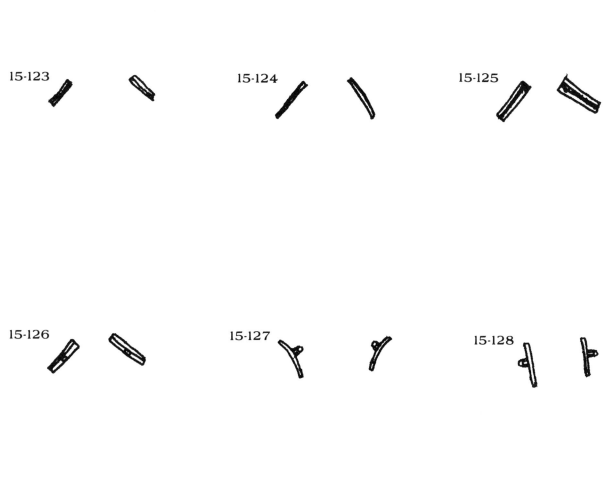

15-123 15-124 15-125

15-126 15-127 15-128

15-129 15-130 15-131

15-132 15-133 15-134

15-135

15-136

15-137

15-138

WELT POCKET STYLING

15-139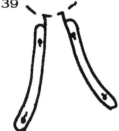

15-140

15-141

15-142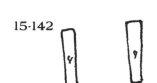

15-143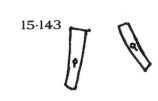

15-144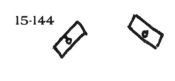

15-145

15-146

15-147

15-148   15-149   15-150   15-151

15-152

15-153

15-154

15-155

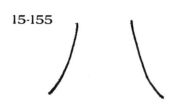

15-156

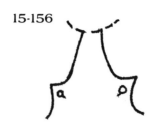

15-157

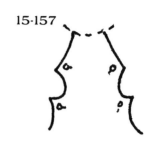

15-158

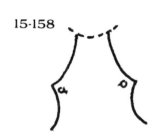

15-159

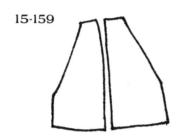

15-160

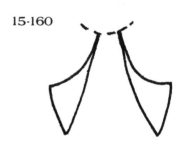

15-161

15-162

15-163

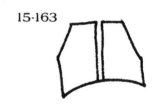

15-164

15-165

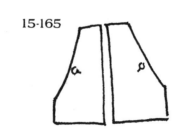

15-166

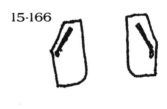

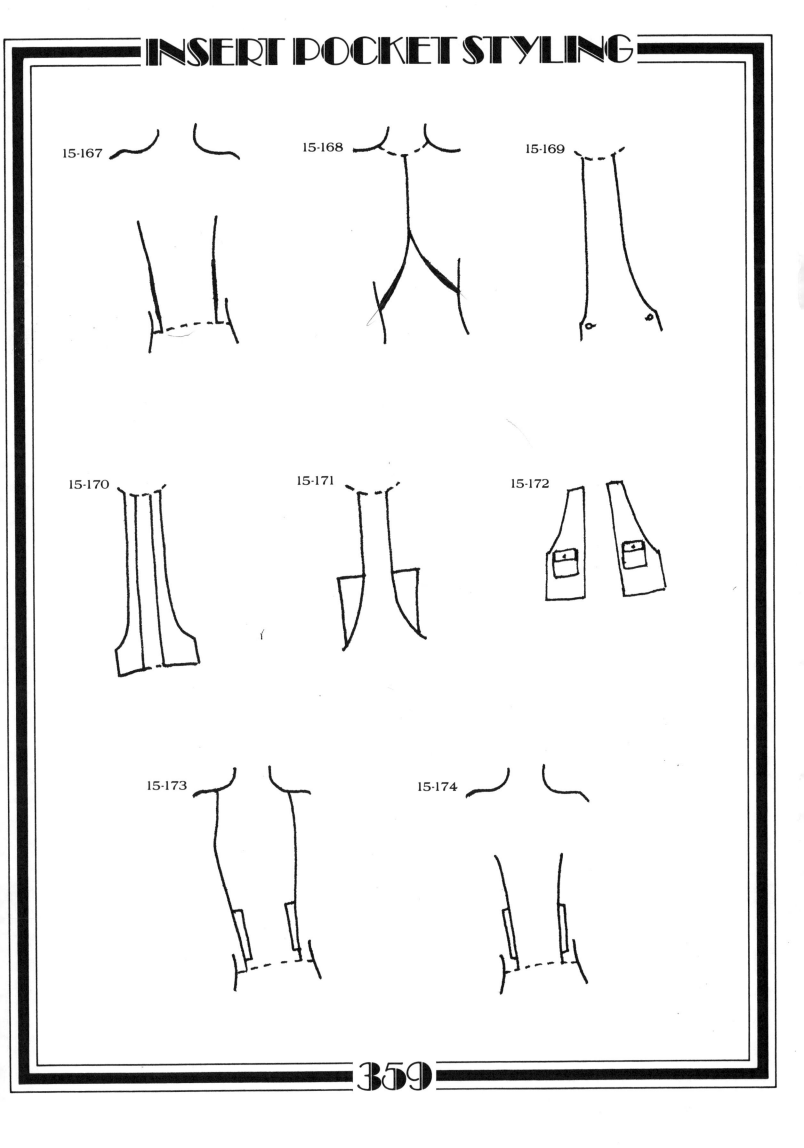

15-167

15-168

15-169

15-170

15-171

15-172

15-173

15-174

15-175 15-176 15-177

15-178 15-179 15-180

15-181  15-182 15-183

15-184 15-185 15-186

15-187

15-188

15-189

15-190

15-191

15-192

15-193

15-194

15-195

15-196

15-197

15-198

15-199

15-200

15-201

15-202

15-203

15-204

15-205

15-206

15-207

15-208

15-209

15-210

15-211

15-212

15-213

15-214

15-215

15-216

15-217

15-218

15-219

15-220

15-221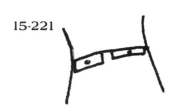

15-222

15-223

15-224

15-225

15-226

15-227

15-228

15-229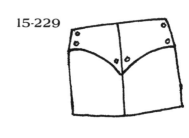

15-230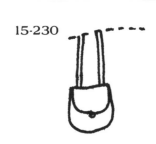

15-231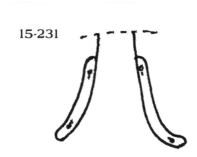

15-232

15-233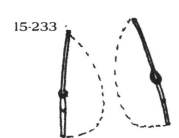

15-234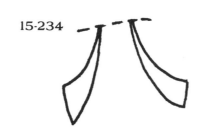

15-235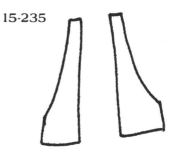

15-236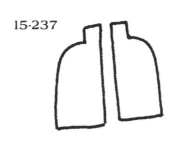

15-237

15-238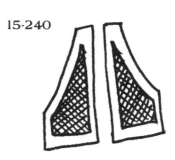

15-239

15-240

15-241

15-242

15-243

15-244

15-245

15-246

15-247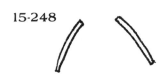

15-248

15-249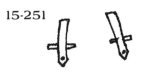

15-250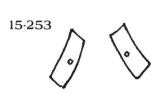

15-251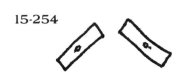

15-252

15-253

15-254

15-255

15-256

15-257

15-258

15-259

15-260

15-261

15-262

15-263

15-264

15-265

15-266

15-267

15-268

15-269

15-270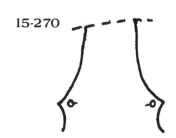

15-271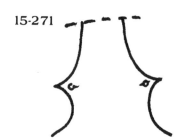

15-272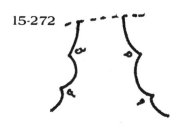

15-273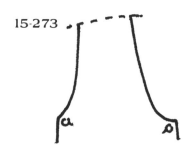

15-274

15-275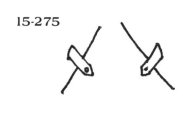

15-276

15-277

15-278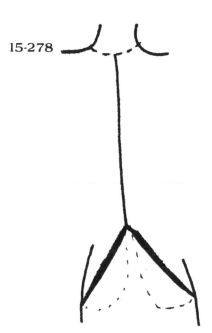

15-279

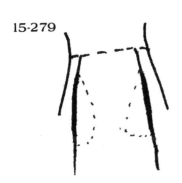

15-280

15-281

15-282